Eliza Ruhamah Scidmore

Jinrikisha days in Japan

Eliza Ruhamah Scidmore

Jinrikisha days in Japan

ISBN/EAN: 9783742829160

Manufactured in Europe, USA, Canada, Australia, Japa

Cover: Foto ©ninafisch / pixelio.de

Manufactured and distributed by brebook publishing software
(www.brebook.com)

Eliza Ruhamah Scidmore

Jinrikisha days in Japan

MOUSMI

Jinrikisha Days in Japan

BY

ELIZA RUHAMAH SCIDMORE

"Waga kuni no Yamato shima ne ni idzuru hi wa;
Morokoshi hito mo, awoga zarameya."

"In the ancient Yamato island, my native land, the sun rises;
Must not even the Western foreigner reverence?"
Ancient Japanese Poem.

"I cannot cease from praising these Japanese. They
are truly the delight of my heart."
St. Francis Xavier.

ILLUSTRATED

NEW YORK
HARPER & BROTHERS, FRANKLIN SQUARE

PREFACE

THE aim of this small book is to present, in outline sketches only, something of the Japan of to-day, as it appeared to a tourist who was a foreign resident as well. No one person can see it all, nor comprehend it, as the *jinrikisha* speeds through city streets and country roads, nor do any two people enjoy just the same experiences or draw the same conclusions as to this remarkable people.

The scientists, scholars, and specialists who have written so fully of Japan, have necessarily omitted many of those less important phases of life which yet leave the pleasantest impressions on less serious minds. The books of ten or twenty years ago hardly describe the country that a visitor now finds, and in another decade the present aspect will have greatly changed. Bewildered by its novelty and strangeness, too many tourists come and go with little knowledge of the Japan of the Japanese, and, beholding only the modernized seaports and the capital, miss the unique and distinctively national sights and experiences that lie close at hand.

This unassuming chronicle is the outcome of two

visits, covering nearly three years' stay in the Island Empire, a period during which a continued residence was maintained, by turns, in each of the larger ports, while many weeks were spent in Kioto, Nara, and Nikko. Its object will be attained if it helps the tourist to enjoy more satisfactorily his stay in Japan, or if it gives the stay-at-home reader a greater interest in those fascinating people and their lovely home. Unfortunately, it is impossible in acknowledging the kindness of the many Japanese friends and acquaintances who secured to me so many unusual enjoyments and experiences, to begin to give the long list of their names. Each foreign visitor must feel himself indebted to the whole race for being Japanese, and therefore the most interesting population in the world, and his obligation is to the whole people, as much as to particular individuals.

To Mr. John Brisben Walker, of *The Cosmopolitan*, thanks are extended for permission to reprint the chapter entitled "The Japanese Theatre," which first appeared in the pages of that magazine.

E. R. S.

CONTENTS

Contents

ILLUSTRATIONS

JINRIKISHA DAYS IN JAPAN

CHAPTER I

THE NORTH PACIFIC AND YOKOHAMA

ALL the Orient is a surprise to the Occidental. Everything is strange, with a certain unreality that makes one doubt half his sensations. To appreciate Japan one should come to it from the main-land of Asia. From Suez to Nagasaki the Asiatic sits dumb and contented in his dirt, rags, ignorance, and wretchedness. After the muddy rivers, dreary flats, and brown hills of China, after the desolate shores of Korea, with their unlovely and unwashed peoples, Japan is a dream of Paradise, beautiful from the first green island off the coast to the last picturesque hill-top. The houses seem toys, their inhabitants dolls, whose manner of life is clean, pretty, artistic, and distinctive.

There is a greater difference between the people of these idyllic islands and of the two countries to westward, than between the physical characteristics of the three kingdoms; and one recognizes the Japanese as the fine flower of the Orient, the most polite, refined, and æsthetic of races, happy, light-hearted, friendly, and attractive.

The bold and irregular coast is rich in color, the perennial green of the hill-side is deep and soft, and the perfect cone of Fujiyama against the sky completes the landscape, grown so familiar on fan, lantern, box, and

plate. Every-day life looks too theatrical, too full of
artistic and decorative effects, to be actual and serious,
and streets and shops seem set with deliberately studied
scenes and carefully posed groups. Half consciously
the spectator waits for the bell to ring and the curtain
to drop.

The voyage across the North Pacific is lonely and
monotonous. Between San Francisco and Yokohama
hardly a passing sail is seen. When the Pacific Mail
Steamship Company established the China line their
steamers sailed on prescribed routes, and outward and
homeward-bound ships met regularly in mid-ocean.
Now, when not obliged to touch at Honolulu, the cap-
tains choose their route for each voyage, either sailing
straight across from San Francisco, in 37° 47′, to Yokohama, in 35° 26′ N., or, following one of the great circles farther north, thus lessen time and distance. On
these northern meridians the weather is always cold,
threatening, or stormy, and the sea rough; but the stead-
iness of the winds favors this course, and persuades the
ship's officers to encounter wet decks, torn sails, destructive seas, and the grumbling of passengers. Dwellers in hot climates suffer by the sudden transition to
polar waters, and all voyagers dislike it. Fortunately,
icebergs cannot float down the shallow reaches of Behr-
ing Strait, but fierce winds blow through the gaps and
passes in the Aleutian Islands.

Canadian Pacific steamers, starting on the 49th parallel, often pass near the shores of Attu, the last little
fragment of earth swinging at the end of the great Aleutian chain. The shelter which those capable navigators,
Mrs. Lecks and Mrs. Aleshine, had the luck to find in
their memorable journey, mariners declare to be Midway Island, a circular dot of land in the great waste,
with a long, narrow, outlying sand-bar, where schooners
have been wrecked, and castaways rescued after months

of imprisonment. The steamer's course from San Francisco to Yokohama varies from 4500 to 4800 miles, and the journey takes from twelve to sixteen days. From Vancouver to Yokohama it is seventy hours shorter.

When the ship's course turns perceptibly southward the mild weather of the Japan Stream is felt. In winter the first sign of land is a distant silver dot on the horizon, which in summer turns to blue or violet, and gradually enlarges into the tapering cone of Fuji, sloping upward in faultless lines from the water's edge. One may approach land many times and never see Fuji, and during my first six months in Japan the matchless mountain refused to show herself from any point of view. Cape King, terminating the long peninsula that shelters Yeddo Bay, shows first a line of purple cliffs, and then a front of terraced hills, green with rice and wheat, or golden with grain or stubble. Fleets of square-sailed fishing-boats drift by, their crews, in the loose, flapping gowns and universal blue cotton head towels of the Japanese coolies, easily working the broad oar at the stern. At night Cape King's welcome beacon is succeeded by Kanonsaki's lantern across the Bay, Sagami's bright light, then the myriad flashes of the Yokosuka navy-yard, and last the red ball of the light-ship, marking the edge of the shoal a mile outside the Bund, or sea-wall, of Yokohama. When this craft runs up its signal-flag a United States man-of-war, if there be one in port, fires two guns, as a signal that the American mail has arrived.

Daylight reveals a succession of terraced hills, cleft by narrow green valleys and narrower ravines ; little villages, their clusters of thatched roofs shaded by pine, palm, or bamboo ; fishing-boats always in the foreground, and sometimes Fuji clear-cut against the sky, its base lost now and then behind the overlapping hills. In summer Fuji's purple cone shows only ribbon stripes of white near its apex. For the rest of the year it is a silvery, shining vision, rivalled only by Mount Rainier, which, pale with eternal snows, rises from the dense forests of Puget Sound to glass itself in those green waters.

Yokohama disappoints the traveller, after the splendid panorama of the Bay. The Bund, or sea-road, with its club-houses, hotels, and residences fronting the water, is not Oriental enough to be very picturesque. It is too European to be Japanese, and too Japanese to be European. The water front, which suffers by comparison with the massive stone buildings of Chinese ports, is, however, a creditable contrast to our untidy American docks and quays, notwithstanding the low-tiled roofs, blank fences, and hedges. The water life is vivid and spectacular. The fleet of black merchant steamers and white men-of-war, the ugly pink and red canal-steamers, and the crowding brigs and barks, are far outnumbered by the fleet of sampans that instantly surround the arriving mail. Steam-launches, serving as mail-wagon and hotel omnibus, snort, puff, and whistle at the gang-ways before the buoy is reached; and voluble boatmen keep up a steady *bzz, bzz, whizz, whizz*, to the strokes of their crooked, wobbling oars as they scull in and out. Four or five thousand people live on the shipping in the harbor, and in ferrying this population to and fro and purveying to it the boatmen make their livelihood. Strict police regulations keep them safe and peaceable, and the harbor impositions of other countries are unknown. On many of these sampans the whole family abides, the women cooking over a handful of charcoal in a small box or bowl, the children playing in corners not occupied by passengers or freight. On gala days, when the shipping is decorated, the harbor is a beautiful sight; or when the salutes of the foreign fleets assembled at Yokohama are returned by the guns of the fort on Kanagawa Heights, and the air tingles with excitement. Only three

of the large mail steamers, with a lone man-of-war or a sporadic sailing - ship, ever fly the Stars and Stripes among a forest of masts fluttering with the flags of all nations. The American navy is conspicuous by its absence, unless a venerable wooden side-wheeler represents the might of the world's most boastful country. A fleet of otter schooners flies the American flag, and enjoys seal-hunting in the Northern Ocean without disturbing international relations.

A mole and protected harbor with stone docks is being built with the money only lately returned to Japan by the United States, after being shamefully withheld for a quarter of a century, as our share of the Shimonoseki Indemnity Fund. The present basin lies so open to the prevailing south-east winds that loading and unloading is often delayed for days, and landing by launches or sampans is a wet process. The Bay is so shallow that a stiff wind quickly sends its waves breaking over the sea-wall, to subside again in a few hours into a mirror-like calm. The harbor has had its great typhoons, but does not lie in the centre of those dreaded circular storms that whirl up from the China seas. Deflected to eastward, the typhoon sends its syphoon, or wet end, to fill the air with vapor and drizzle, and a smothering, mildewy, exhausting atmosphere. A film of mist covers everything, wall - paper loosens, glued things fall apart, and humanity wilts.

Yokohama has its divisions —the Settlement, the Bluff, and Japanese Town — each of which is a considerable place by itself. The Settlement, or region originally set apart by the Japanese in 1858 for foreign merchants, was made by filling in a swampy valley opening to the Bay. This Settlement, at first separated from the Tokaido and the Japanese town of Kanagawa, has become the centre of a surrounding Japanese population of over eighty thousand. It is built up continuously to Kanagawa Bridge, two miles farther north, on the edge of a bold bluff, where the Tokaido—the East Sea Road—leading up from Kioto, reaches the Bay. In diplomatic papers Kanagawa is still recognized as the name of the great port on Yeddo Bay, although the consulates, banks, hotels, clubs, and business streets are miles away.

At the *hatoba*, or landing-place, the traveller is confronted by the *jinrikisha*, that big, two-wheeled baby-carriage of the country, which, invented by an American, has been adopted all over the East. The jinrikisha (or *kuruma*, as the linguist and the upper class more politely call it) ranges in price from seventeen to forty dollars, twenty being the average cost of those on the public stands. Some thrifty coolies own their vehicles, but the greater number either rent them from, or work for, companies, and each jinrikisha pays a small annual tax to the Government. An unwritten rule of the road compels these carriages to follow one another in regulated single file. The oldest or most honored person rides at the head of the line, and only a boor would attempt to change the order of arrangement. Spinning down the Bund, at the rate of ten cents a single trip to hotel or station, ten cents an hour, or seventy-five cents a day, one finds the jinrikisha to be a comfortable, flying arm-chair—a little private, portable throne. The coolie wears a loose coat and waistcoat, and tights of dark-blue cotton, with straw sandals on his bare feet, and an inverted washbowl of straw covered with cotton on his head. When it rains he is converted into a prickly porcupine by his straw rain-coat, or he dons a queer apron and cloak of oiled paper, and, pulling up the hood of the little carriage, ties a second apron of oiled paper across the knees of his fare. At night the shafts are ornamented with a paper lantern bearing his name and his license number; and these glowworm lights, flitting through the streets and country roads in the darkness, seem only another expression of the Japanese love of the picturesque. In the country, after dark, they call warnings of ruts, holes, breaks in the road, or coming crossways; and their cries, running from one to another down the line, are not unmusical. To this smiling, polite, and amiable little pony one says *Hayaku!* for "hurry," *Abunayo!* for "take care," *Sukoshimate!* for "stop a little," and *Soro!* for "slowly." The last command is often needed when the coolie, leaning back at an acute angle to the shaft, dashes downhill at a rapid gait. Jinrikisha coolies are said even to have asked extra pay for walking slowly through the fascinating streets of open shops. If you experiment with the jinrikisha on a level road, you find that it is only the first pull that is hard; once started, the little carriage seems to run by itself. The gait of the man in the shafts, and his height, determine the comfort of the ride. A tall coolie holds the shafts too high, and tilts one at an uncomfortable angle; a very short man makes the best runner, and, with big toe curling upward, will trot along as regularly as a horse. As one looks down upon the bobbing creature below a hat and two feet seem to constitute the whole motor.

The *waraji*, or sandals, worn by these coolies are woven of rice straw, and cost less than half a cent a pair. In the good old days they were much cheaper. Every village and farm house make them, and every shop sells them. In their manufacture the big toe is a great assistance, as this highly trained member catches and holds the strings while the hands weave. On country roads wrecks of old waraji lie scattered where the wearer stepped out of them and ran on, while ruts and mudholes are filled with them. For long tramps the foreigner finds the waraji and the *tabi*, or digitated stocking, much better than his own clumsy boots, and he ties them on as overshoes when he has rocky paths to climb. Coolies often dispense with waraji and wear heavy tabi, with a strip of the almost indestructible *hechima* fibre for the soles. The hechima is the gourd which furnishes the vegetable washrag, or looffa sponge of commerce. The snow-white cotton tabis of the better classes are made an important part of their costume.

Those coolies who pull and push heavily loaded carts or drays keep up a hoarse chant, which corresponds to the chorus of sailors when hauling ropes. "*Hilda.' Hoida.*" they seem to be crying, as they brace their feet for a hard pull, and the very sound of it exhausts the listener. In the old days people were nearly deafened with these street choruses, but their use is another of the hereditary customs that is fast dying out. In mountain districts one's chair-bearers wheeze out "*Hi rikisha! Ho rikisha.*" or "*Ito sha.' Ito sha.*" as they climb the steepest paths, and they cannot keep step nor work vigorously without their chant.

CHAPTER II

YOKOHAMA

THE Settlement is bounded by the creek, from whose opposite side many steep hill-roads wind up to the Bluff, where most of the foreigners have their houses. These bluff-roads pass between the hedges surrounding trim villas with their beautifully set gardens, the irregular numbering of whose gates soon catches the stranger's eye. The first one built being number one, the others were numbered in the order of their erection, so that high and low numerals are often side by side. To coolies, servants, peddlers, and purveyors, foreign residents are best known by their street-door numeration, and "Number four Gentleman" and "Number five Lady"

are recurrent and adequate descriptions. So well used
are the subjects of it to this convict system of identifica-
tion that they recognize their friends by their *alias* as
readily as the natives do.

Upon the Bluff stand a public hall, United States and
British marine hospitals, a French and a German hospital, several missionary establishments, and the houses
of the large American missionary community. At the extreme west end a colony of Japanese florists has planted
toy-gardens filled with vegetable miracles; burlesques
and fantasies of horticulture; dwarf-trees, a hundred
years old, that could be put in the pocket; huge single
flowers, and marvellous masses of smaller blossoms;
cherry-trees that bear no cherries; plum-trees that bloom
in midwinter, but have neither leaves nor fruit; and roses
— that favorite flower which the foreigner brought with
him—flowering in Californian profusion. A large business is done in the exportation of Japanese plants and
bulbs, encased in a thick coating of mud, which makes
an air-tight case to protect them during the sea-voyage.
Ingenious fern pieces are preserved in the same way.
These grotesque things are produced by wrapping in
moist earth the long, woody roots of a fine-leafed variety
of fern. They are made to imitate dragons, junks, temples, boats, lanterns, pagodas, bells, balls, circles, and
every familiar object. When bought they look dead. If
hung for a few days in the warm sun, and occasionally
dipped in water, they change into feathery, green objects
that grow more and more beautiful, and are far more
artistic than our one conventional hanging-basket. The
dwarf-trees do not stand transportation well, as they
either die or begin to grow rapidly.

The Japanese are the foremost landscape gardeners
in the world, as we Occidentals, who are still in that
barbaric period where carpet gardening seems beautiful
and desirable, shall in time discover. Their genius has

equal play in an area of a yard or a thousand feet, and a Japanese gardener will doubtless come to be considered as necessary a part of a great American establishment as a French maid or an English coachman. From generations of nature-loving and flower-worshipping ancestors these gentle followers of Adam's profession have inherited an intimacy with growing things, and a power over them that we cannot even understand. Their very farming is artistic gardening, and their gardening half necromancy.

On high ground, beyond the Bluff proper, stretches the race-course, where spring and fall there are running races by short-legged, shock-headed ponies, brought from the Hokkaido, the northern island, or from China. Gentlemen jockeys frequently ride their own horses in flat races, hurdle-races, or steeple-chases. The banks close, a general holiday reigns throughout the town, and often the Emperor comes down from Tokio. This race-course affords one of the best views of Fuji, and from it curves the road made in early days for the sole use of foreigners to keep them off the Tokaido, where they had more than once come in conflict with trains of travelling nobles. This road leads down to the water's edge, and, following the shore of Mississippi Bay, where Commodore Perry's ships anchored in 1858, strikes across a rice valley and climbs to the Bluff again.

The farm-houses it passes are so picturesque that one cannot believe them to have a utilitarian purpose. They seem more like stage pictures about to be rolled away than like actual dwellings. The new thatches are brightly yellow, and the old thatches are toned and mellowed, set with weeds, and dotted with little gray-green bunches of "hen and chickens," while along the ridge-poles is a bed of growing lilies. There is an old wife's tale to the effect that the women's face-powder was formerly made of lily-root, and that a ruler who wished to stamp out such vanities, decreed that the plant should not be grown on the face of the earth, whereupon the people promptly dug it up from their gardens and planted it in boxes on the roof.

The Japanese section of Yokohama is naturally less Japanese than places more remote from foreign influence, but the stranger discovers much that is odd, unique, and Oriental. That delight of the shopper. Honchodori, with its fine curio and silk shops, is almost without a shop-window, the entire front of the cheaper shops being open to the streets. But the old lacquer and bronzes, ivory, porcelains, enamels, silver, and silks of Chojiro, Matsuishiya, Musashiya, Shieno, Shobey, and Kinuya are concealed by high wooden screens and walls. The silk shops are filled with goods distracting to the foreign buyer, among which are the wadded silk wrappers, made and sold by the hundreds, which, being the contrivance of some ingenious missionary, were long known as missionary coats.

Benten Dori, the bargain-hunter's Paradise, is a delightful quarter of a mile of open-fronted shops. In the silk shops, crapes woven in every variety of cockle and wrinkle and rippling surface, as thin as gauze, or as thick and heavy as brocade, painted in endless, exquisite designs, are brought you by the basketful. Each length is rolled on a stick, and finally wrapped in a bit of the coarse yellow cotton cloth that envelopes every choice thing in Japan, though for what reason, no native or foreigner, dealer or connoisseur can tell.

Nozawaya has a godown or fire-proof storehouse full of cotton crapes, those charmingly artistic fabrics that the Western world has just begun to appreciate. The pock-marked and agile proprietor will keep his small boys running for half an hour to bring in basketfuls of cotton crape rolls, each roll measuring a little over eleven yards, which will make one straight, narrow *kimono* with a pair of big sleeves. These goods are woven in the usual thirteen-inch Japanese width, although occasionally made wider for the foreign market. A Japanese kimono is a simple thing, and one may put on the finished garment an hour after choosing the cloth to make it. The cut never varies, and it is still sewn with basters' stitches, although the use of foreign flat-irons obviates the necessity of ripping the kimono apart to wash and iron it. The Japanese flat-iron is a copper bowl filled with burning charcoal, which, with its long handle, is really a small warming-pan. Besides this contrivance. there is a flat arrow point of iron with a shorter handle, which does smaller and quite as ineffectual service.

To an American, nothing is simpler than Japanese money. The *yen* corresponds to our dollar, and is made up of one hundred *sen*, while ten *rin* make one sen. The yen is about equal in value to the Mexican dollar, and is roughly reckoned at seventy-five cents United States money. One says dollars or yens indiscriminately, always meaning the Mexican. which is the current coin of the East. The old copper coins. the rin and the oval *tempo*, each with a hole in the middle, are disappearing from circulation, and at the Osaka mint they are melted and made into round sens. Old gold and silver coins may be bought in the curio shops. If they have not little oblong silver *bu*. or a long oval gold *ko ban*, the silversmith will offer to make some, which will answer every purpose!

When you ask for your bill, a merchant takes up his frame of sliding buttons—the *soroban*. or abacus—and plays a clattering measure before he can tell its amount. The soroban is infallible, though slow, and in the head of the educated Japanese, crowded with thousands of arbitrary characters and words, there is no room for mental arithmetic. You buy two toys at ten cents apiece. Clatter, clatter goes the soroban. and the calculator asks you for twenty cents. Depending entirely on the soroban, they seem unable to reckon the smallest sums without it, and any peddler who forgets to bring his frame may be puzzled. The dealer in old embroideries will twist and work his face, scratch his head, and move his fingers in the air upon an imaginary soroban over the simplest addition, division, and subtraction. At the bank, the *shroff* has a soroban a yard long; and merchants say that in book-keeping the soroban is invaluable, as by its use whole columns of figures can be added and proved in less time than by our mental methods.

By an iron bridge, the broad street at the top of Benten Dori crosses one of the many canals extending from the creek in every direction, and forming a net-work of water passages from Mississippi Bay to Kanagawa. Beyond the bridge is Isezakicho, a half mile of theatres, side-shows, merry-go-rounds, catchpenny games, candy shops, restaurants, second-hand clothes bazaars, labyrinths of curio, toy, china, and wooden-ware shops. Hundreds of perambulating restaurateurs trundle their little kitchens along, or swing them on a pole over their shoulders. Dealers in ice-cream, so called, abound, who will shave you a glass of ice, sprinkle it with sugar, and furnish a minute teaspoon with which to eat it. There are men who sell *soba*, a native vermicelli, eaten with pungent *soy;* and men who, for a penny, heat a big gridiron, and give a small boy a cup of batter and a cup of soy, with which he may cook and eat his own griddle cakes. There the people, the middle and lower classes, present themselves for study and admiration, and the spectator never wearies of the outside dramas and panoramas to be seen in this merry fair.

Pretty as she is on a pictured fan, the living Japanese woman is far more satisfying to the æsthetic soul as she patters along on her wooden clogs or straw sandals. The very poorest, in her single cheap cotton gown, or kimono, is as picturesque as her richer sister in silk and crape. With heads elaborately dressed, and folds of gay crape, or a glittering hair-pin thrust in the smooth loops of blue-black hair, they seem always in gala array ; and, rain or shine, never protect those elaborate coiffures with anything less ornamental than a paper umbrella, except in winter, when the *zukin*, a yard of dark crape lined with a contrasting color, is thrown over the head, concealing the whole face save the eyes. A single hair-pin of tortoise-shell, sometimes tipped with coral or gold, is all that respectable women of any class wear at one time. The heavily hair-pinned women on cheap fans are not members of good society, and only children and dancing-girls are seen in the fantastic flowers and trifles sold at a hundred shops and booths in this and every street.

The little children are the most characteristically Japanese of all Japanese sights. Babies are carried about tied to the mothers' back, or to that of their small sisters. They sleep with their heads rolling helplessly round, watch all that goes on with their black beads of eyes, and never cry. Their shaven crowns and gay little kimonos, their wise, serene countenances, make them look like cabinet curios. As soon as she can walk, the Japanese girl has her doll tied on her back, until she learns to carry it steadily and carefully : after that the baby brother or sister succeeds the doll, and flocks of these comical little people, with lesser people on their backs, wander late at night in the streets with their parents. and their funny double set of eyes shine in every audience along Isezakicho.

These out-of-door attractions are constantly changing. Native inventions and adaptations of foreign ideas continually appear. "Pigs in clover" and pot-hook puzzles followed only a few weeks behind their New York season, and street fakirs offer perpetual novelties. Of jugglers the line is endless, their performances filling inter-

ludes at theatres, coming between the courses of great dinners, and supplying entertainment to any garden party or flower fête in the homes of rich hosts. More cunning than these gorgeously clad jugglers is an old man, who roams the vicinity of Yokohama, wearing poor cotton garments, and carrying two baskets of properties by a pole across his shoulders. On a street corner, a lawn, a piazza, or a ship's deck, he sets up his baskets for a table, and performs amazing feats with the audience entirely encircling him. A hatful of coppers sufficiently rewards him, and he swallows fire, spits out eggs, needles, lanterns, and yards of paper-ribbon, which he twirls into a bowl, converts into actual soba, and eats, and by a magic sentence changes the remaining vermicelli into the lance-like leaves of the iris plant. This magician has a shrewd, foxy old face, whose grimaces, as well as his pantomime, his capers, and poses, are tricks in themselves. His chuckling, rippling stream of talk keeps his Japanese auditors convulsed. Sword walkers and knife swallowers are plenty as blackberries, and the phonograph is conspicuous in Isezakicho's tents and booths. The sceptic and investigator wastes his time in the effort to penetrate the Japanese jugglers' mysteries. Once, at a dinner given by Governor Tateno at Osaka, the foreign guest of honor determined to be cheated by no optical delusions. He hardly winked, so close was his scrutiny, and the juggler played directly to him. An immense porcelain vase having been brought in and set in the middle of the room, the juggler, crawling up, let himself down into it slowly. For half an hour the sceptic did not raise his eyes from the vase, that he had first proved to be sound and empty, and to stand on no trap-door. After this prolonged watch the rest of the company assailed him with laughter and jeers, and pointed to his side, where the old juggler had been seated for some minutes fanning himself.

CHAPTER III

YOKOHAMA—CONTINUED

In the Settlement, back of the main street, the Chinese have an ill-smelling corner to themselves. Their greasy walls and dirty floors affront the dainty doll dwellings across the creek, and the airy little box of a teahouse, whose lanterns swing at the top of the perpendicular bluff behind them. Vermilion paper, baggy clothes, pigtails, harsh voices, and vile odors reign in this Chinatown. The names on the signs are curiosities in themselves, and Cock Eye, tailor, Ah Nie and Wong Fai, ladies' tailors, are the Poole, Worth, and Felix of the foreign community. Only one Japanese has a great reputation as dress-maker, but the whole guild is moderately successful, and prices are so low that the British and French houses of Yokohama cannot compete with them.

There is a large joss-house near the Chinese consulate, and at their midsummer, autumn, and New-year's festivals the Celestials hold a carnival of lanterns, fire-crackers, incense, paper-flowers, varnished pigs, and cakes. The Japanese do not love these canny neighbors, and half the strictures of the passport laws are designed to limit their hold on the business of the country. The Chinese are the stronger and more aggressive people, the hard - headed financiers of the East, handling all the money that circulates this side of India. In every bank Chinese shroffs, or experts, test the coins and make the actual payments over the counters. The money-changers are Chinese, and every business house has its Chinese *compradore* or superintendent, through whom all contracts and payments are made. The Chinaman has the methodical, systematic brain, and no convulsion of nature or commerce makes him lose his head, as the charmingly erratic, artistic, and polite Japanese does. In many foreign households in Japan a Chinese butler, or head boy, rules the establishment; but while his silent, unvarying, clock-like service leaves nothing undone, the attendance of the bright-faced, amiable, and exuberant little natives with their smiles, their matchless courtesy, and their graceful and everlasting bowing is far more agreeable.

Homura temple, whose stone embankments and soaring roof rise just across the creek, is generally the first Buddhist sanctuary seen by the tourist coming from American shores. Every month it has its *matsuri*, or festival, but sparrows are always twittering in the eaves, children playing about the steps, and devout ones tossing their coppers in on the mats, clapping their hands and pressing their palms together while they pray. One of the most impressive scenes ever witnessed there was the funeral of its high-priest, when more than a hundred *bonzes*, or priests, came from neighboring temples to assist in the long ceremonies, and sat rigid in their precious brocade vestments, chanting the ritual and the sacred verse. The son, who succeeded to the father's office by inheritance, had prepared for the rites by days of fasting, and, pale, hollow-eyed, but ecstatic, burned incense, chanted, and in the white robes of a mourner bore the mortuary tablets from the temple to the tomb. Homura's commercial hum was silenced when the train of priests in glittering robes, shaded by enormous red umbrellas, wound down the long terrace steps and out between the rows of tiny shops to the distant graveyard. Yet after it the crowd closed in, barter and sale went on, jinrikishas whirled up and down, and pattering women and toddling children fell into their places in the tableaux which turn Homura's chief street into one endless panorama of Japanese lower-class life.

Half-way up one of the steep roads, climbing from Homura to the Bluff, is the famous silk store of Tenabe Gengoro, with its dependent tea-house of Segiyama, best known of all tea-houses in Japan, and rendezvous for the wardroom officers of the fleets of all nations, since Tenabe's uncle gave official welcome to Commodore Perry. When a war-ship is in port, the airy little lantern-hung houses continuously send out the music of the *koto* and the *samisen*, the banjo, bones, and zither, choruses of song and laughter, and the measured hand-clapping that proclaims good cheer in Japan. Tenabe herself has now lost the perfect bloom and beauty of her younger days, but with her low, silver-sweet voice and fascinating manner, she remains the most charming woman in all Japan. In these days Tenabe presides over the silk store only, leaving her sisters to manage the fortunes of the tea-house. Tenabe speaks English, French, and Russian; never forgets a face, a name, or an incident; and if you enter, after an absence of many years, she will surely recognize you, serve you sweets and thimble-cups of pale yellow tea, and say *dozo, dozo,* "please, please," with grace incomparable and in accents unapproachable.

Both living and travelling are delightfully easy in Japan, and no hardships are encountered in the ports or on the great routes of travel. Yokohama has excellent hotels; the home of the foreign resident may be Queen Anne, or Colonial, if he like, and the markets abound in meats, fish, game, fruits, and vegetables at very low prices. Imported supplies are dear because of the cost of transportation. Besides the fruits of our climates, there are the *biwa,* or loquat, and the delicious *kaké,* or Japanese persimmon. Natural ice is brought from Hakodate; artificial ice is made in all the ports, the

Japanese being as fond of iced drinks as Americans. Three daily English newspapers, weekly mails to London and New York, three great cable routes, electric lights, breweries, gas, and water-works add utilitarian comfort to ideal picturesqueness. The summers are hot, but instead of our eccentric variations of temperature, the mercury stands at 80°, 85°, and 90° from July to September. With the fresh monsoon blowing steadily, that heat is endurable, however, and the nights are comfortable. June and September are the two *nyubai*, or rainy seasons, when everything is damp, clammy, sticky, and miserable. In May, heavy clothing is put away in sealed receptacles, even gloves being placed in air-tight glass or tin, to preserve them from the ruinous mildew. While earthquakes are frequent, Japan enjoys the same immunity from thunder-storms as our Pacific Coast.

There is no servant problem, and house-keeping is a delight. Both Chinese and Japanese, though unfamiliar with western ways, can be trained to surpass the best European domestics. Service so swift, noiseless, and perfect is elsewhere unknown. Indeed, cooks as well as butlers are adjusted to so grand a scale of living that their employers are served with almost too much formality and elaboration. The art of foreign cookery has been handed down from those exiled *chefs* who came out with the first envoys, to insure them the one attainable solace of existence before the days of cables and regular steamships. There is a native cuisine of great excellence, and each legation or club chef has pupils, who pay for the privilege of studying under him, while the ordinary kitchener of the treaty ports is a more skilful functionary than the professional cook of American cities. Such cooks do their own marketing, furnish without complaint elaborate menus three times a day, serve a dinner party every night, and out of their monthly pay, ranging from ten to twenty Mexican dollars, supply their own board and lodging. The brotherhood of cooks help each other in emergencies, and if suddenly called upon to feed twice the expected number of guests, any one of them will work miracles. He runs to one fellow-craftsman to borrow an extra fish, to another to beg an entrée, a salad, or a sweet, and helps himself to table ware as well. A bachelor host is often amazed at the fine linen, the array of silver, and the many courses set before him on the shortest notice, and learns afterwards that everything was gathered in from neighboring establishments. Elsewhere he may meet his own monogram or crest at the table. Bachelors keep house and entertain with less trouble and more comfort than anywhere else in the world. To these sybarites, the "boy," with his rustling kimono, is more than a second self, and the soft-voiced *amahs*, or maids, are the delight of woman's existence. The musical language contributes not a little to the charm of these people, and the chattering servants seem often to be speaking Italian.

After the Restoration many *samurai*, or warriors, were obliged to adopt household service. One of these at my hotel had the face of a Roman senator, with a Roman dignity of manner quite out of keeping with his broom and dust-pan, or livery of dark-blue tights, smooth vest, and short blouse worn by all his class in Yokohama. When a card for an imperial garden party arrived, I asked Tatsu, my imperial Roman, to read it for me. He took it, bowed low, sucked in his breath many times, and, muttering the lines to himself, thus translated them: "Mikado want to see Missy, Tuesday, three o'clock." When a curio-dealer left a piece of porcelain, Tatsu, always critical of purchases, went about his duties slowly, waiting for the favorable moment to give me, in his broken English, a dissertation on the old wares, their marks and qualities, and his opinion of that particular specimen of blue and white. He knew embroideries, understood pictures, and was a living dictionary of Japanese phrase and fable. A pair of Korean shoes procured me a lecture on the ancient relations between Japan and Korea, and an epitome of their contemporary history.

Social life in these foreign ports presents a delightful fusion of English, continental, and Oriental customs. The infallible Briton, representing the largest foreign contingency, has transferred his household order unchanged from the home island, yielding as little as possible to the exigencies of climate and environment. The etiquette and hours of society are those of England, and most of the American residents are more English in these matters than the English. John Bull takes his beef and beer with him to the tropics or the poles indifferently, and in his presence Jonathan abjures his pie, and outlaws the words "guess," "cracker," "trunk," "baggage," "car," and "canned." His East Indian experiences of a century have taught the Briton the best system of living and care-taking in hot or malarial countries, and he thrives in Japan.

In the small foreign communities at Yokohama, Kobé, and Nagasaki the contents of the mail-bags, social events, and the perfection of physical comfort comprise the interests of most of the residents. The friction of a large community, with its daily excitements and affairs, the delights of western art, music, and the drama, are absent, and society naturally narrows into cliques, sets, rivalries, and small aims. If most residents did not affect indifference to things Japanese, life would be much more interesting. As it is, the old settler listens with an air of superiority, amusement, and fatigue to the enthusiasm of the new-comer. Not every foreign resident is familiar with the art of Japan, nor with its history, religion, or political conditions. If the missionaries, of whom hundreds reside in Yokohama and Tokio, mingled more with the foreign residents, each class would benefit ; but the two sets seldom touch, the missionaries keep to themselves, and the lives of the other extra-territorial people continually shock and offend them. Each set holds extreme, unfair, and prejudiced views of the other, and affords the natives arguments against both.

Socially, Tokio and Yokohama are one community, and the eighteen miles of railroad between the two do not hinder the exchange of visits or acceptance of invitations. When the Ministers of State give balls in Tokio, special midnight trains carry the Yokohama guests home, as they do when the clubs or the naval officers entertain at the seaport town. With the coming and going of the fleets of all nations great activity and variety pervades the social life. In the increasing swarm of tourists some prince, duke, or celebrity is ever arriving, visitors of lesser note are countless, and the European dwellers in all Asiatic ports east of Singapore make Japan their pleasure-ground, summer resort, and sanitarium. That order of tourist known as the "globe-trotter," is not a welcome apparition to the permanent foreign resident. His generous and refined hospitality has been so often abused, and its recipients so often show a half-contemptuous condescension to their remote and uncomprehended hosts, that letters of introduction are looked upon with dread. Now that it has become common for parents to send dissipated young sons around the "Horn" and out to Japan on sailing vessels, that they may reform on the voyage, a new-comer must prove himself an invalid, if he would not be avoided after he confesses having come by brig or bark. Balls, with the music of naval bands, and decorations of bamboo and bunting, are as beautiful as balls can be ; picnics and country excursions enliven the whole year; and there are perennial dinners and dances on board the men-of-war.

Those East-Indian contrivances, the *chit* and the *chit-*book, furnish a partial check on native servants. The average resident carries little ready money, but writes a memorandum of whatever he buys, and hands it to the seller instead of cash. These chits are presented monthly; but the system tempts people to sign more chits than they can pay. This kind of account-keeping is more general in Chinese ports, where one may well object to receive the leaden-looking Mexicans and ragged and dirty notes of the local banks. When one sends a note to an acquaintance he enters it in his chit-book, where the person addressed adds his initials as a receipt, or even writes his answer. The whole social machinery is regulated by the chit-book, which may be a source of discord when its incautious entries and answers lie open to any Paul Pry.

Summer does not greatly disturb the life of society. Tennis, riding, boating, and bathing are in form, while balls and small dances occur even in July and August. At many places in the mountains and along the coast one may find a cooler air, with good hotels and tea-houses. Some families rent country temples near Yokohama for summer occupation, and enjoy something between the habitual Japanese life and Adirondack camping. The sacred emblems and temple accessories are put in the central shrine room, screens are drawn, and the sanctuary becomes a spacious house, open to the air on all sides, and capable of being divided into as many separate rooms as the family may require. Often the priests set the images and altar-pieces on a high shelf concealed by a curtain, and give up the whole place to the heretical tenants. In one instance the broad altar-shelf became a recessed sideboard, whereon the gilded Buddhas and Kwannons were succeeded by bottles, decanters, and glasses. At another temple it was stipulated that the tenants should give up the room in front of the altar on a certain anniversary day, to allow the worshippers to come and pray.

CHAPTER IV

THE ENVIRONS OF YOKOHAMA

THE environs of Yokohama are more interesting and beautiful than those of any other foreign settlement, affording an inexhaustible variety of tramps, rides, drives, railroad excursions, and sampan trips.

At Kanagawa proper the Tokaido comes to the bay's edge, which it follows for some distance through double rows of houses and splendid old shade-trees. Back of Kanagawa's bluff lie the old and half-deserted Bukenji temples, crowded on rare fête days with worshippers, merrymakers, and keepers of booths, and at quieter times serving as favorite picnic grounds for foreigners.

On the Tokaido, just beyond Kanagawa, is the grave of Richardson, who was killed by the train of the Prince of Satsuma, September 14, 1862. Although foreigners had been warned to keep off the Tokaido on that day, the foolhardy Briton and his friends deliberately rode into the daimio's train, an affront for which they were attacked by his retainers and severely wounded, Richardson himself being left for dead on the road-side, while the rest escaped. When the train had passed by, a young girl ran out from one of the houses and covered the body with a piece of matting, moving it in the night to her house, and keeping it concealed until his friends claimed it. A memorial stone, inscribed with Japanese characters, marks the spot where Richardson fell. Since that time the kindly black-eyed Susan's tea-house has been the favorite resort for foreigners on their afternoor. rides and drives. Susan is a tall woman, with round eyes, aquiline nose, and a Roman countenance—quite fit for a heroine. Riders call at her tea-house for tea, rice, and eels, prawns, clams, pea-nuts, sponge-cake, or beer, and insist upon seeing her. This Richardson affair cost the Japanese the bombardment of Kagoshima, and an indemnity of £125,000; but Susan did not share in the division of that sum.

According to one version Susan's strand is the spot where Taro of Urashima, the Rip Van Winkle of Japan, left his boat and nets, and, mounting a tortoise, rode away to the home of the sea-king, returning by the same tortoise to the same spot. On its sands he opened the box the sea-king had given him, and found himself veiled in a thin smoke, out of which he stepped an old, old man, whose parents had been dead a hundred years. The fishermen listened to his strange tale, and carried him to their daimio, and on fans, boxes, plates, vases, and *fukusas* Taro sits relating his wonderful tale to this day.

Ten miles inland from Bukenji's temples is the little village of Kawawa, whose headman has a famous collection of chrysanthemums, the goal of many autumnal pilgrimages. This Kawawa collection has enjoyed its fame for many years, the owner devoting himself to it heart and soul, and knowing no cooling of ardor nor change of fancy. His great thatched house in a courtyard is reached through a black gate-way at the top of a little hill, and the group of buildings within his black walls gives the place quite a feudal air. Facing the front of the house are rows of mat sheds, covering the precious flowers that stand in files as evenly as soldiers, the tops soft masses of great frowsy, curly-petalled, wide-spreading blooms, shading to every tint of lilac, pink, rose, russet, brown, gold, orange, pale yellow, and snow white. It was there that we ate a salad made of yellow chrysanthemum petals, most æsthetic of dishes. The trays of golden

leaves in the kitchen of the house indicated that the
master enjoyed this ambrosial feast habitually, and perhaps dropped the yellow shreds in his *saké* cup to pro-
long his life and avert calamities, as they are warranted

AT KAWAWA

to do.   Beyond Kawawa lies a rich silk district, and all
the region is marked by thrift and comfort, signs of the
prosperity that attends silk-raising communities.

From Negishi, where Yokohama's creek debouches

into Mississippi Bay, one looks across to Sugita, a fishing village with an ancient temple set in the midst of plum-trees and cherry-trees that make it a place of fêtes in February and April, when those two great flower festivals of the empire, the blossoming of the plum and the cherry, are observed. From the bluff above Sugita, at the end of the watery cresent, is a superb view of the Bay and its countless sharp, green headlands. Wherever the view is fine some Japanese family has encamped in a *tateba*, the least little mat shed of a house, furnished with a charcoal brazier, half a dozen tea-pots and cups, and a few low benches covered with the all-pervading red blanket. Their national passion for landscape and scenery draws the Japanese to places having fine prospects, and a thrifty woman, with her family of children, turns many a penny by means of her comfortable seat and good cheer for the wayfarer. Japan is the picnicker's own country, whether he be native or foreign. Everywhere, climbing the mountain-tops, or crouching in the valleys, hidden in the innermost folds of the hills, or perched on the narrowest and remotest ledges overhanging the water, one finds the tea-house, or its summer companion, the tateba, with its open sides and simmering kettle. Everywhere hot water, tea, rice, fruits, eggs, cups, plates, glasses, and corkscrews may be had. These things become so much a matter of course after a time, that the tourist must banish himself to China, to value, as they deserve, the clean Japanese tea-house, and the view-commanding tateba with its simple comforts.

Sugita's plum-trees bud in January, and blossom as mild days and warm suns encourage, so that the last week of February finds the dead-looking branches clothed with clouds of starry white flowers. The blossoming plum-tree is often seen when snow is on the ground, and the hawthorn pattern of old porcelains is only a conventional representation of pale blooms fallen on the seamed ice of ponds or garden lakelets. The plum is the poet's tree, and symbolic of long life, the snowy blossoms upon the gnarled, mossy, and unresponsive branches showing that a vital current still animates it, and the heart lives. At New-years a dwarf-plum is the ornament of every home, and to give one is to wish your friend length of days. *Ume*, the plum blossom, has a fresh, delicate, elusive, and peculiar fragrance, which in the warm sun and open air is almost intoxicating, but in a closed room becomes heavy and cloying. The blossoming of the plum-tree is the first harbinger of spring, and to Sugita regularly every year go the Empress Dowager, many princes, and great officials to see those billows of bloom that lie under the Bluff, and the pink and crimson clouds of trees before the old temple.

During the rest of the year little heed is paid to Sugita's existence, and the small fishing village in the curve of the Bay, with its green wall of bluffs, is as quiet as in the days when Commodore Perry's fleet anchored off it and Treaty Point acquired its name. With the blossoms Sugita puts on its holiday air, tea-houses open, tateba spring from the earth, and scores of low, red-blanketed benches are scattered through the grove, signals of tea and good cheer, equivalent to the iron tables and chairs of Parisian boulevards. Strings of sampans float in to shore, lines of jinrikishas file over the hills, zealous pilgrims come on foot, and horsemen trot down the long, hard beach. The tiny hamlet often has a thousand visitors in a day, and the pretty little *nesans*, or tea-house maids, patter busily about with their trays of tea and solid food, welcoming and speeding the guests, and looking —quaint, odd, and charming maidens that they are— like so many *tableaux vivants* with their scant kimonos, voluminous sleeves, ornate coiffures, and pigeon-toes.

Notwithstanding the crowds, everything is decorous, quiet, and orderly, and no more refined pleasure exists than this Japanese beatitude of sitting lost in revery and rapturous contemplation of a blossoming tree, or inditing a verse to *ume no hana*, and fastening the bit of paper to the branches. In this Utopia the spring poem is never rejected, nor made the subject of cruel jokes. The winds fan it gently, it hangs conspicuous, it is read by him who runs, but it is not immortal, and the first heavy rain leaves it a wet and withered wreck, soon to fall to the ground and disappear.

Just outside the temple-door is a plum-tree whose age is lost in legend. Its bent and crooked limbs and propped-up branches sustain a thick-massed pyramid of pale rose-pink. The outer boughs droop like a weeping-willow, and their flowers seem to be slipping down them like rosy rain-drops. Poets and peers, dreamers and plodders, coolies, fishermen, and the unspiritual foreigner, all admire this lovely tree, and its wide arms flutter with poems in its praise. All around the thatched roof of the old temple stand plum-trees covered with fragant blossoms—snow white, palest yellow, rose, or deep carnation-red. The sheltering hill back of the temple is crowded with gravestones, tombs, tablets, and mossy Buddhas, sitting calm and impassive in tangles of grasses and vines under the shadow of ancient trees. A wide-spreading pine on the crest of the hill is a famous landmark, whence one looks down on the flower-wreathed village, the golden bow of the beach curving from headland to headland, and the blue bay flashing with hundreds of square white sails. It is a place for poesy and day-dreams, but the foreign visitor dedicates it to luncheon, table-talk, and material satisfactions, and, perhaps, the warm sun and air, and the mild fragrance of the plum-blossoms aid and abet the insatiable picnic appetite.

All this part of Japan is old, and rich in temples, shrines, and picturesque villages, with a net-work of narrow roads and shady by-paths leading through perpetual scenes of sylvan beauty. Thatched roofs, whose ridge poles are beds of lilies, shaded by glorified green plumes of bamboo-trees, tall, red-barked cryptomerias, crooked pines, and gnarled camphor-trees, everywhere charm the eye. Little red temples, approached through a line of picturesque *torii*—that skeleton gate-way that makes a part of every Japanese view or picture—red shrines no larger than marten boxes; stone Buddhas, sitting cross-legged, chipped, broken-nosed, headless, and moss-grown; odd stone tablets and lanterns crowd the hedges and banks of the road-side, snuggle at the edges of groves, or stand in the corners of rice fields.

Fair as the spring days are, when the universal green mantle of the earth is adorned with airy drifts of plum and cherry-blossoms, the warm, mellow sunshine, glorious tints and clear bright air of autumn are even fairer. One may forget and forgive the Japanese summer for the sake of the weeks that follow, an Indian summer which often lasts without break for four months after the equinoctial storm. Except that Fujiyama gleams whiter and whiter, there is no suggestion of winter's terrors, and only a pleasant crispness in the bracing and intoxicating air. When the maple leaves begin to turn, and a second rose-blossoming surpasses that of June in color, prodigality, and fragrance, autumnal Japan is the typical earthly Paradise. Every valley is a floor of golden rice stubble, every hill-side a tangle of gorgeous foliage. The persimmon-trees hang full of big golden kaké, sea and sky wear their intensest blue, and Fujiyama's loveliness shines out against the western sky. In among the yellowing stubble move blue-clad farmers with white mushroom hats. Before the farm-houses men and women swing their flails, beating the grain spread out on straw matting. The rice straw, whether bunched in pretty sheaves, tied across poles, like a New-year's fringe, or stacked in collars around the tree-trunks, is always decorative. Meditative oxen, drawing a primitive plough made of a pointed stick, loosen the soil for the new planting, and tiny green wheat-shoots, first of the three regular crops of the year, wait for the warm winter sun that opens the plum-blossoms.

Above and beyond Sugita is Minë, a temple on a mountain-top, with a background of dense pine forest, a foreground of bamboos, and an old priest, whose successful use of the *moxa* brings sufferers from long distances for treatment. A bridle-path follows for several miles the knife-edge of a ridge commanding noble views of sea and shore, of the blue Hakone range, its great sentinel Oyama, and Fuji beyond. The high ridge of Minë is the backbone of a great promontory running out into the sea, the Bay of Yeddo on one side and Odawara Bay on the other. Square sails of unnumbered fishing-boats fleck the blue horizon, and the view seaward is unbroken. Over an old race-course and archery-range of feudal days the path leads, till at a sudden turn it strikes into a pine forest, where the horses' hoofs fall noiseless on thick carpets of dry pine-needles, and the cave-like twilight, coolness, and stillness seem as solemn as in that wood where Virgil and Dante walked, before they visited the circles of the other world.

A steep plunge down a slippery, clayey trail takes the rider from the melancholy darkness to a solitary forest clearing, with low temple buildings on one side. Here, massed against feathery fronds of giant bamboos, blaze boughs of fine-leafed maples, all vivid crimson to the tips. While the priests bring saké tubs, and the *amado*, or outside shutters of their house, to make a table, and improvise benches with various temple and domestic properties, visitors may wander through the forest to open spaces, whence all the coasts of the two bays and every valley of the province lie visible, and a column of smoke proclaims the living volcano on Oshima's island, far down the coast.

Groups of cheery pilgrims come chattering down from the forest, untie their sandals, wash their feet, and disappear within the temple ; where the old priest writes sacred characters on their bared backs to indicate where his attendant shall place the lumps of sticky moxa dough. Another attendant goes down the line of victims and touches a light to these cones, which burn with a slow, red glow, and hiss and smoke upon the flesh for agonizing seconds. The priest reads pious books and casts up accounts, while the patients endure without a groan tortures compared with which the searing with the white-hot irons of Parisian moxa treatment is comfortable. The Minë priest has some secret of composition for his moxa dough which has kept it in favor for many years, and almost the only revenue of the temple is derived from this source. Rheumatism, lumbago, and paralysis yield to the moxa treatment, and the Japanese resort to it for all their aches and ills, the coolies' backs and legs being often finely patterned with its scars.

The prospect from Minë's promontory is rivalled by that at Kanozau, directly across the Bay, one of the highest points on the long tongue of separating land. Here are splendid old temples, almost unvisited by foreigners, but the glory of the place is the view of the ninety-nine valleys, of Yeddo Bay, the ocean, and the ever - dominant Fujiyama. Every Japanese knows the famous landscapes of his country, and the mention of these ninety-nine valleys and the thousand pine - clad islands of Matsuyama brings a light to his eyes.

At Yokosuka, fifteen miles below Yokohama, are the Government arsenal, navy - yard, and dry docks, with their fleets of war-ships that put to shame the American squadron in Asiatic waters. The Japanese Government has both constructed and bought a navy ; some vessels coming from Glasgow yards, and others having been built at these docks.

Uraga, reached from Yokosuka by a winding, Cornice-like road along the coast, is doubly notable as being the port off which Commodore Perry's ships first anchored, and the place where *midzu ame*, or millet honey, is made. The whole picturesque, clean little town is given up to the production of the amber sweet, and there are certain families whose midzu ame has not varied in excellence for more than three hundred years. The rice, or millet. is soaked, steamed. mixed with warm water and barley malt. and left to stand a few hours, when a clear yellow liquid is drawn off and boiled down to a thick syrup or paste, or cooked until it can be moulded into hard balls. Unaffected by weather, it is the best of Japanese sweets, and in its semiliquid stage is twisted out on chopsticks at all seasons of the year. The older and browner the midzu ame is, the better. It may be called the apotheosis of butter-scotch, a glorified Oriental taffy, constantly urged upon one for one's own good, and conceded by foreign physicians in Japan to be of great value for dyspeptics and consumptives. Though prepared all over the empire, this curative sweet is the specialty of Uraga; and the secrets and formulas held in the old families make for Uraga midzu ame. as compared with other productions, a reputation akin to that of the Grande Chartreuse, or Schloss Johannisberger, among other cordials or wines. Street artists mould midzu ame paste, and blow it with a pipe into myriad fantastic shapes for their small patrons: while at the greatest banquets. and even on the Emperor's table. it appears in the fanciful flowers that decorate every feast.

CHAPTER V

KAMAKURA AND ENOSHIMA

THE contemporary Yankee might anticipate the sage reflections of the future New Zealander on London Bridge were there left enough ruins of the once great city of Kamakura to sit upon ; but the military capital of the Middle Ages has melted away into rice fields and millet patches. One must wrestle seriously with the polysyllabic guide-book stories of the shoguns, regents, and heroes who made the glory of Kamakura, and attracted to it a population of five hundred thousand, to repeople these lonely tracts with the splendid military pageants of which they were the scene.

The plain of Kamakura is a semicircle, bounded by hills and facing the open Pacific, the surf pounding on its long yellow beach between two noble promontories. The Dai Butsu, the great bronze image of Buddha, which has kept Kamakura from sinking entirely into obscurity during the centuries of its decay, stands in a tiny valley a half-mile back from the shore. The Light of Asia is seated on the lotus flower, his head bent forward in meditation, his thumbs joined, and his face wearing an expression of the most benignant calm. This is one of the few great show-pieces in Japan that is badly placed and lacks a proper approach. Seen. like the temple gate-ways and pagodas of Nikko, at the end of a long avenue of trees, or on some height silhouetted against the sky, Dai Butsu (Great Buddha) would be far more imposing. Within the image is a temple forty-nine feet in height; and through an atmosphere thick with incense may be read the chalked names of ambitious tourists, who have evaded the priests and left their signatures on the irregular bronze walls. An alloy of tin and a little gold is mingled with the copper, and on the joined thumbs and hands, over which visitors climb to sit for their photographs, the bronze is polished enough to show its fine dark tint. The rest of the statue is dull and weather-stained, its rich incrustation disclosing the seams where the huge sections were welded together.

A pretty landscape-garden, banks of blossoming plum-trees, and the usual leper at the gate-way furnish the accustomed temple accessories, and Buddha broods and meditates serene in his quiet sanctuary. The photographic skill of the priest brings a good revenue to the temple, and a fund is being slowly raised for building a huge pavilion above the great deity, like that which stood there three hundred years ago. During his six centuries of holy contemplation at Kamakura, Dai Butsu has endured many disasters. Earthquakes have made him nod and sway on the lotus pedestal, and tidal waves have twice swept over and destroyed the sheltering temple, the great weight and thickness of the bronze keeping the statue itself unharmed.

Kamakura is historic ground, and each shrine has its legends. The great temple of Hachiman, the God of War, remains but as a fragment of its former self, the buildings standing at the head of a high stone-embanked terrace, from which a broad avenue of trees runs straight to the sea, a mile and a half away. Here are the tomb of Yoritomo and the cave tombs of his faithful Satsuma and Chosen Daimios; and the priests guard sacredly the sword of Yoritomo, that of Hachiman himself, the helmet of Iyeyasu, and the bow of Iyemitsu.

In the spring. Kamakura is a delightful resort, on whose dazzling beach climate and weather are altogether different from those of Yokohama or Tokio. In summer-time, the steady south wind, or monsoon, blows straight from the ocean, and the pine grove between the hotel and shore is musical all day long with the pensive sough of its branches. In winter it is open and sunny, and the hot sea-water baths, the charming walks and sails, the old temples and odd little villages, attract hosts of visitors.

On bright spring mornings men, women, and children gather sea-weed and spread it to dry on the sand, after which it is converted into food as delicate as our Iceland moss. Both farmers and fishermen glean this salty harvest, and after a storm, whole families collect the flotsam and jetsam of kelp and sea-fronds. Barelegged fisher-maidens, with blue cotton kerchiefs tied over their heads, and baskets on their backs. roam along the shore; children dash in and out of the frothing waves. and babies roll contentedly in the sand ; men and boys wade knee-deep in the water, and are drenched by the breakers all day long, with the mercury below 50°, in spite of the warm, bright sun. Women separate the heaps of sea-weed. and at intervals regale their dripping lords with cups of hot tea, bowls of rice, and shredded fish. It is all so gay and beautiful, every one is so merry and happy, that Kamakura life seems made up of rejoicing and abundance, with no darker side.

The poor in Japan are very poor, getting comparative comfort out of smaller means than any other civilized people in the world. A few cotton garments serve for all seasons alike. The cold winds of winter nip their bare limbs and pierce their few thicknesses of cloth, and the fierce heat of summer torments them ; but they endure these extremes with stoical good-nature, and enjoy their lovely spring and autumn the more. A thatched roof, a straw mat. and a few cotton wadded *futons*. or comforters, afford the Japanese laborer shelter. furniture, and bedding, while rice, millet, fish, and sea-weed constitute his food. With three crops a year growing in his fields, the poor farmer supports his family on a patch of land forty feet square ; and with three hundred and sixty varieties of food fish swimming in Japanese waters, the fisherman need not starve. Perfect cleanliness of person and surroundings is as much an accompaniment of poverty as of riches.

Beyond Kamakura's golden bow lies another beach— the strand of Katase, at the end of which rises Enoshima, the Mont St. Michel of the Japanese coast. Enoshima is an island at high tide, rising precipitously from the sea on all sides save to the landward, where the precipice front is cleft with a deep wooded ravine, that runs out into the long tongue of sand connecting with the shore at low tide.

Like every other island of legendary fame, Enoshima rose from the sea in a single night. Its tutelary genius is the goddess Benten, one of the seven household deities of good-fortune. She is worshipped in temples and shrines all over the woody summit of the island, and in a deep cave opening from the sea. Shady paths, moss-grown terraces, and staircases abound, and little tea-houses and tateba offer seats, cheering cups of tea, and enchanting views. The near shores, the limitless waters of the Pacific, and the grand sweep of Odawara Bay afford the finest setting for Fujiyama anywhere to be enjoyed.

Enoshima's crest is a very Forest of Arden, an enchanted place of lovely shade. The sloping ravine which gives access to it holds only the one street, or foot-path, lined with tea-houses and shell-shops, all a-flutter with pilgrim flags and banners. The shells are cut into whistles, spoons, toys, ornaments, and hair-pins; and tiny pink ones of a certain variety form the petals of most perfect cherry blossoms, which are fastened to natural branches and twigs.

The fish dinners of Enoshima are famous, and the Japanese, who have the genius of cookery, provide more delicious fish dishes than can be named. At the many tateba set up in temple yards or balanced on the edges of precipices, conch-shells, filled with a black stew like terrapin, simmer over charcoal fires. This concoction has a tempting smell, and the pilgrims, who pick at the inky morsels with their chopsticks, seem to enjoy it; but in the estimation of the foreigner it adds one more to the list of glutinous, insipid preparations with which the Japanese cuisine abounds. The great marine curiosity of Enoshima is the giant crab, with its body as large as a turtle, and claws measuring ten, and even twelve, feet from tip to tip. These crustaceans are said to promenade the beach at night, and glare with phosphorescent eyes. Another interesting Japanese crab, the *Doryppe Japonica*, comes more often from the Inland Sea. A man's face is distinctly marked on the back of the shell, and, as the legend avers, these creatures incarnate the souls of the faithful samurai, who, following the fortunes of the Tairo clan, were driven into the sea by the victorious Minamoto. At certain anniversary seasons, well known to true believers, the spirits of these dead warriors come up from the sea by thousands and meet together on a moonlit beach.

In time Enoshima will be the great summer resort of the cities north of it, the Nahant or Marblehead of the far East, though a thousand times more picturesque than they. When typhoons rage or storms sweep in from the ocean, billows ring the island round with foam, spray dashes up to the drooping foliage on the summit, the air is full of the wild breath and wilder roar of the breakers, while the very ground seems to tremble. The underground shrine of Benten is then closed to worshippers, and looking down the sheer two hundred feet of rock, one sees only the whirl and rage of waters that hide the entrance. When these storms rage, visitors are sometimes imprisoned for days upon the island. At low tide and in ordinary seas Benten's shrine is easily entered by a ledge of rocks, the hard thing being the climb up the long stone stair-ways to the top of the island again. Guides are numerous, and an old man or a small boy generally attaches himself to a company of strangers, and is so friendly, polite, and amiable, that, after escorting it unbidden round the island, he generally wins his cause, and is bidden to *maru maru* (go sight-seeing) as escort and interpreter.

CHAPTER VI

TOKIO

THE first view of Tokio, like the first view of Yokohama, disappoints the traveller. The Ginza, or main business street, starting from the bridge opposite the station, goes straight to Nihombashi, the northern end of the Tokaido, and the recognized centre of the city, from which all distances are measured. Most of the roadway is lined with conventional houses of foreign pattern, with their curb-stones and shade-trees, while the tooting tram-car and the rattling *basha*, or light omnibus, emphasize the incongruities of the scene. This is not the Yeddo of one's dreams, nor yet is it an Occidental city. Its stucco walls, wooden columns, glaring shop-windows, and general air of tawdry imitation fairly depress one. In so large a city there are many corners, however, which the march of improvement has not reached, odd, unexpected, and Japanese enough to atone for the rest.

Through the heart of Tokio winds a broad spiral moat, encircling the palace in its innermost ring, and reaching, by canal branches, to the river on its outer lines. In feudal days the Shogun's castle occupied the inner ring, and within the outer rings were the *yashikis*, or spread-out houses, of his daimios. Each gate-way and angle of the moat was defended by towers, and the whole region was an impregnable camp. Every daimio in the empire had his yashiki in Tokio, where he was obliged to spend six months of each year, and in case of war to send his family as pledges of his loyalty to the Shogun. The Tokaido and the other great highways of the empire were always alive with the trains of these nobles, and from this migratory habit was developed the passion for travel and excursion that animates every class of the Japanese people. When the Emperor came up from Kioto and made Tokio his capital, the Shogun's palace became his home, and all the Shogun's property reverted to the crown, the yashikis of the daimios being confiscated for government use. In the old days the barrack buildings surrounding the great rectangle of the yashiki were the outer walls, protected by a small moat, and furnished with ponderous, gable-roofed gate-ways, drawbridges, sally-ports, and projecting windows for outlooks. These barracks accommodated the samurai, or soldiers, attached to each daimio, and within their lines were the parade ground and archery range, the residence of the noble family, and the homes of the artisans in his employ. With the new occupation many yashiki buildings were razed to the ground, and imposing edifices in foreign style erected for government offices. A few of the old yashiki remain as barracks, and their white walls, resting on black foundations, suggest the monotonous street views of feudal days. Other yashiki have fallen to baser uses, and sign-boards swing from their walls.

Modern sanitary science has plucked up the miles of

lotus beds that hid the triple moats in midsummer. From the bridges the lounger used to overlook acres of pink and white blossoms rising above the solid floors of bluish-green leaves ; but the Philistines could not uproot the moats, which remain the one perfect feudal relic of Japanese Yeddo. The many-angled gate-ways, the massive stone walls, and escarpments, all moss and lichen-grown, and sloping from the water with an inward curve, are noble monuments of the past. Every wall and embankment is crowned with crooked, twisted, creeping, century-old pines, that fling their gaunt arms wildly out, or seem to grope along the stones. Here and there on the innermost rings of the moat still rise picturesque, many-gabled towers, with white walls and black roofs, survivors from that earlier day when they guarded the *shiro*, or citadel, and home of the Shogun.

The army is always in evidence in Tokio, and the little soldiers in winter dress of dark-blue cloth, or summer suits of white duck, swarm in the neighborhood of the moats. In their splendid uniforms, the dazzling officers, rising well in the saddle, trot by on showy horses. On pleasant mornings, shining companies of cavalry file down the line of the inner moat and through the deep bays of the now dismantled Cherry-Tree gate to the Hibiya parade-ground, where they charge and manœuvre. When it rains, the files of mounted men look like so many cowled monks, with the peaked hoods of their great coats drawn over their heads, and they charge, gallop, and countermarch through mud and drizzle, as if in a real campaign. Taking the best of the German, French, Italian, and British military systems, with instructors of all these nationalities, the Japanese army stands well among modern fighting forces. There is a military genius in the people, and the spirit of the old samurai has leavened the nation, making the natty soldiers of to-day worthy the traditions of the past.

A large foreign colony is resident in Tokio, the diplomatic corps, the great numbers of missionaries, and those employed by the Government in the university, schools, and departments constituting a large community. The missionary settlement now holds the Tsukiji district near the railway station; that piece of made ground along the shore first ceded for the exclusive occupation of foreigners. Besides being malarial, Tsukiji was formerly the rag-pickers' district, and its selection was not complimentary to the great powers, all of whose legations have now left it. To reside outside of Tsukiji is permitted to non-officials only when in Japanese employ. Rich art collectors, scientists, and enthusiasts, who choose to live in Tokio, must be claimed as employés or teachers by some kindly Japanese friend, who becomes responsible for the stranger's conduct. These limitations pertain to the treaty regulations, which permit no foreigners to go more than twenty-five miles beyond a treaty port without a passport, which may be obtained through a legation. and which names the places to be visited. The police register the arrival of all strangers, and keep a record of their movements. The United States Legation issues as a passport only a page of thick mulberry paper covered with the essential writings in Japanese characters. The British Legation encloses a similar passport in a small pamphlet of instructions, wherein the holder is minutely admonished as to his behavior, warned not to quarrel, not to deface monuments, not to destroy shrubs or trees, nor break windows. At Kobé, any American citizen may, if he likes, procure a passport for Kioto from the *Kencho*, or governor's office, without applying to his consul. Travellers of all other nationalities must proceed through their consuls, and this recognition of the freedom and independence of the American citizen is a tribute to the individual sovereignty of his nation, concerning which a Japanese poet writes:

> "What are those strangely-clad beings
> Who move quickly from one spot of interest to another
> Like butterflies flitting from flower to flower?
>   These are Americans.
> They are as restless as the ocean,
> In one day they will learn more of a city
> Than an inhabitant will in a year.
>   Are they not extraordinary persons?"

All the legations are now on the high ground in the western part of the city near the castle moats. All legation buildings are owned and kept up by their respective governments, except that of the United States, which still uses rented property, although the Japanese Government has offered the land as a gift, if the United States will erect a permanent edifice.

The English possess a whole colony of buildings in the midst of a large walled park, affording offices and residences for all the staff. Germany, Russia, France, and the Netherlands own handsome houses with grounds. The Chinese legation occupies part of an old yashiki, inside whose bright vermilion and pea-green gate-way the Chinese gate-keepers lounge, and over which the triangular yellow dragon flag flies.

The show places of Tokio are the many government museums at Uyéno Park, the many mortuary temples of the Tokugawa Shoguns at Shiba and Uyéno, the popular temple of Asakusa, and the Shinto temple at the Kudan, with its race-course and view of the city; but the Kanda, the Kameido, the Hachiman temples, many by-streets and queer corners, the out-door fairs, the peddlers, and shops give the explorer a better understanding of the life of the people than do the great monuments. Here and there he comes upon queer old nameless temples with ancient trees, stones, lanterns, tanks, and urns that recall a forgotten day of religious influence, when they possessed priests, revenues, and costly altars.

An army of jinrikisha coolies waits for passengers at the station, and among them is that Japanese Mercury, the winged-heeled Sanjiro, he of the shaven crown and gun-hammer topknot of samurai days. His biography includes a tour of Europe as the servant of a Japanese official. On returning to Tokio he took up the shafts of his *kuruma* again, and is the fountain-head of local news and gossip. He knows what stranger arrived yesterday, who gave dinner parties, in which tea-house the "man-of-war gentlemen" had a *geisha* dinner, where your friends paid visits, even what they bought, and for whom court or legation carriages were sent. He tells you whose house you are passing, what great man is in view, where the next matsuri will be, when the cherry blossoms will unfold, and what plays are coming out at the Shintomiza. Sanjiro is cyclopædic at the theatre, and as a temple guide he exhales ecclesiastical lore. To take a passenger on a round of official calls, to and from state balls or a palace garden party, he finds bliss unalloyed, and his explanations pluck out the heart of the mystery of Tokio. "Mikado's mamma," prattles Sanjiro in his baby-English, as he trots past the green hedge and quiet gate of the Empress Dowager's palace, and "*Tenno San*," he murmurs, in awed tones, as the lancers and outriders of the Emperor appear.

First, he carries the tourist to Shiba, the old monastery grounds that are now a public park. Under the shadow of century-old pines and cryptomeria stand the mortuary temples of the later Shoguns, superb edifices ablaze with red and gold lacquer, and set with panels of carved wood, splendid in color and gilding, the gold trefoil of the Tokugawas shining on every ridge-pole and gable. These temples and tombs are lesser copies of the magnificent shrines at Nikko, and but for those originals would be unique. On a rainy day, the green shadow and gloom, the cawing of the ravens that live in the old pine-trees, and their slow flight, are solemn as death itself: and the solitude of the dripping avenues and court-yards, broken only by the droning priests at prayer, and the musical vibrations of some bell or sweet-voiced gong, invite a gentle melancholy. On such a day, the priests, interrupted in their statuesque repose, or their pensive occupation of sipping tea and whiffing tiny pipes in silent groups around a brazier, display to visitors the altars and ceilings and jewelled walls with painstaking minuteness, glad of one ripple of excitement and one legitimate fee. Led by a lean, one-toothed priest, you follow, stocking-footed, over lacquer floors to behold gold and bronze, lacquer and inlaying, carving and color, golden images sitting in golden shadows, enshrined among golden lotus flowers, and sacred emblems. In one temple the clear, soft tones of the bronze gong, a bowl eighteen inches in diameter and a little less in depth, vibrate on the air for three full minutes before they die away.

Up mossy stair-ways, between massive embankments, and through a shady grove, the priest's clogs scrape noisily to the hexagonal temple, where the ashes of Hidetada, the Ni Dai Shogun, Iyeyasu's son, lie in a great gold lacquer cylinder, the finest existing specimen of the lacquer of that great art age. The quiet of Shiba, the solemn background of giant trees, the deep shadows and green twilight of the groves, the hundreds of stone lanterns, the ponds of sacred lotus, the succession of dragon-guarded gate-ways, and carved and gorgeously-colored walls, crowd the memory with lovely pictures. Near a hill-top pagoda commanding views of the Bay and of Fuji, stands the tateba of a cheerful family, who bring the visitor a telescope and cups of cherry-blossom tea.

A colony of florists show gardens full of wonderful plants and dwarf-trees, and then Sanjiro minces, " I think more better we go see more temples ;" and we go, spin-ning past the giant Shiba gate and up the road to Atago

Yama, a tiny temple on the edge of a precipitous hill-top, approached by men's stairs, an air-line flight of broad steps, and women's stairs, curving by broken flights of easier slope. A leper, with scaly, white skin and hideous ulcers, extends his miserable hand for alms, and picturesque, white-clad pilgrims, with staff and bell, go up and down those breathless flights. The tateba, with their rows of lanterns, where the nesans offer tea of salted cherry blossoms, that unfold again into perfect flowers in the bottom of the cup, overhang the precipice wall, and look down upon the Shiba quarter as upon a relief map.

A breathless rush of two miles or more straight across the city, past flying shops, beside the tooting tram-way and over bridges, and Sanjiro runs into Uyéno Park, with its wide avenues, enormous trees, and half-hidden temple roofs. The ground slopes away steeply at the left, and at the foot of the hill lies a lotus lake of many acres that is a pool of blossoms in midsummer. A temple and a tiny tea-house are on an island in the centre, and around the lake the race-course is overarched with cherry-trees. Great torii mark the paths and stairs leading from the shore to the temples above.

At Uyéno are more tombs and more sanctuaries, avenues of lanterns, bells, and drinking-fountains, and a black, bullet-marked gate-way, where the Yeddo troops made their last stand before the Restoration. Near this gate-way is the sturdy young tree planted by General Grant. Far back in the park stand the mortuary temples, splendid monuments of Tokugawa riches and power, though the most splendid, here as at Shiba, have been destroyed by fire.

When the Tokio Fine Arts Club holds one of its loan exhibitions in its Uyéno Park house, Sanjiro is inexorable, deposits his fare at the door-way, shows the way to the ticket-office, and insists upon his seeing the best work of the great artists.   The noble club-men contribute specimens from their collections of lacquer, porcelain, ivories, bronzes, and *kakemonos*.   Behind glass doors hang kakemonos by the great artists, and Japanese visitors gaze with reverence on the masterpieces of the Kano and Tosa schools.   The great art treasures of the empire are sequestrated in private houses and godowns, and to acquire familiarity with them, to undertake an art education in semiannual instalments by grace of the Fine Arts Club, is a discouraging endeavor.   It would be more hopeful to seek the Boston Museum of Fine Arts, the British Museum, or Mr. Walters's Baltimore galleries, which contain an epitome of all Japanese art.   At the Tokio Club, however, works of Sosen and Hokusai, the two masters of the last century, are often exhibited. Sosen painted inimitable monkeys, and connoisseurs of to-day award him the tardy fame which his contemporaries failed to give.   As a rule, foreigners prefer Hokusai to all other masters, and they search old book-shops in the hope of stumbling upon one of the innumerable books illustrated and sometimes engraved by this prolific genius.   His genius never lacked recognition, and a century ago all feudal Yeddo went wild over his New-year's cards, each one a characteristic and unique bit of landscape, caricature, or fantasy.   His fourteen volumes of *Mangwa*, or rough sketches, and his One Hundred Views of Fuji are most celebrated ; but wonderfully clever are his jokes, his giants, dwarfs, demons, goblins, and ghosts ; and when he died, at the age of ninety, he sighed that he could not live long enough to paint something which he should himself esteem.   After the visit to the club Sanjiro takes his patron to the tomb of Hokusai, in a near-by temple yard, and shows the brushes hung up by despairing and prayerful artists, who would follow his immortal methods.

East of Uyéno stands the great Asakusa temple, shrine

of one of the most famous of the thirty-three famous Kwannons of the empire, the great place of worship for the masses, and the centre of a Vanity Fair unequalled elsewhere. Every street leading to the temple grounds is a bazaar and merry fair, and theatres, side shows, booths, and tents, and all the devices to entrap the idle and the pleasure-seeking, beset the pilgrim on his way to the sanctuary. In florists' gardens are shown marvels of floriculture, in their ponds swim gold-fish with wonderfully fluted tails, and in tall bamboo cages perch Tosa chickens with tail feathers ten and twelve feet long. Menageries draw the wondering rustics, and they pay their coppers for the privilege of toiling up a wood, canvas, and pasteboard Fujiyama to view the vast plain of the city lying all around it, and on timbered slopes enjoy tobogganing in midsummer. Penetrating to the real gate-way, it is found guarded by giant Nio, whose gratings are spotted with the paper prayers that the worshipful have chewed into balls and reverently thrown there. If the paper wad sticks to the grating, it is a favorable omen, and the believer may then turn the venerable old prayer-wheel, and farther on put his shoulder to the bar, and by one full turn of the revolving library of Buddhist scriptures endow himself with all its intellectual treasure.

The soaring roof of the great temple is fitly shadowed by camphor-trees and cryptomeria that look their centuries of age, and up the broad flagging there passes the ceaseless train of believers. One buys corn and feeds the hundreds of pigeons, messengers of the gods, who live secure and petted by all the crowds in the great enclosure, or pays his penny to secure the release of a captive swallow, that flies back every night to its owner. At the foot of the steps the pilgrim begins to pray, and, ascending, mumbles his way to the altar. The colossal money-box, which is said to gather in over a thousand dollars on great holidays, rings and echoes well to the fall of the smallest coin. The sides of the temple are open to the air, and the visitor may retain shoes and clogs, so that the clatter of these wooden soles, the pilgrims' clapping and mumbling, mingle in one distracting roar.

Tame pigeons fly in and out through the open walls, and children chase each other across the floor; but behind the grating candles burn, bells tinkle, priests chant, and rows of absorbed worshippers clap, toss their coppers, and pray, oblivious of all their surroundings.

CHAPTER VII

TOKIO—CONTINUED

THERE are no such holiday-makers as the Japanese. The whole twelvemonth is fête - time, and the old year held three hundred and sixty-five festivals and anniversaries. All the great days of the Chinese calendar are observed, and the death-day of past sovereigns, instead of the birthday; while each religion, each sect, each temple, and each neighborhood has its own fête or matsuri, religious in its origin. Every night different temple grounds and different streets glow with lanterns and torches, an out-door fair is in full progress, and happy, laughing, chattering men, women, and children enjoy it all. The evening flower-fairs are as characteristic and picturesque as anything in Japan. The smoke of blazing flambeaux, the smell of the women's camellia seed hair-oil, and the mingled odors from booths and portable restaurants, are not enticing on a hot night, but at least they offend in an "artless Japanese way."

The booths along the whole length of the Ginza offer

innumerable odd notions, queer toys, pretty hair-pins, curios, and indescribable trifles, every night in the year. The Japanese hair-pin, by-the-bye, is a dangerous vanity, the babies often twisting themselves into the range of its point, and the mothers impaling them on it in shaking them up higher on their backs and tightening the bands that hold them. The comic and ingenious toys, embodying the simplest principles of mechanics, and by the aid of a little running water, or the heat of a candle, performing wonderful feats, are such trifles of bamboo, thin pine, paper, or straw, as American children would destroy at a touch. Yet the more truly civilized Japanese little people play with them for weeks; and they toddle home with minute wicker cages of *semi*, or cicada, on one finger, content to hang them up and listen peaceably to the strident captives' chirping mi-mi-mi all day long.

The first week of March is gala time for the small girls of Japan, when their *Hina Matsuri*, or Feast of Dolls, is celebrated. Then do toy shops and doll shops double in number and take on dazzling features, while children in gay holiday clothes animate the streets. Little girls with hair elaborately dressed, tied with gold cords and bright crape, and gowns and girdles of the brightest colors, look like walking dolls themselves. The tiniest toddler is a quaint and comical figure in the same long gown and long sleeves as its mother, the gay-patterned kimono, the bright inner garments showing their edges here and there, and *obis* shot with gold threads, making them irresistible. Nothing could be gentler or sweeter than these Japanese children, and no place a more charming play-ground for them. In the houses of the rich the Dolls' Festival is second only to the New Year in its importance. The family don their richest clothing, and keep open house for the week. The choicest pictures and art treasures are displayed, and with these the hina or images that have been preserved from grand-

THE SEMI'S CAGE

mothers' and great-grandmothers' time, handed down and added to with the arrival of each baby daughter. These dolls, representing the Emperor, Empress, nobles, and ladies of the old Kioto court, are sometimes numbered by dozens, and are dressed in correct and expensive clothing. During the holiday the dolls are ranged in a row on a shelf like an altar or dais, and food and gifts are placed before them. The tiny lacquer tables, with their rice-bowls, teapots, cups, plates, and trays, are miniature and exquisite likenesses of the family furnishings. Each doll has at least its own table and dishes, and often a full set of tableware, with which to entertain other dolls, and amazing prices have been paid for sets of gold and carved red lacquer dishes, or these Lilliputian sets in wonderful metal-work. After the festival is over, the host of dolls and their belongings are put away until the next March, and when the beautiful images emerge from the storehouses after their long hiding they are as enchanting as if new. Nothing better illustrates inherent Japanese ideas of life and enjoyment, and gentleness of manners, than this bringing out of all the dolls for one long fête week in the year, and the handing them down from generation to generation.

On the fifth day of the fifth month comes the boys' holiday. The outward sign is a tall pole surmounted with a ball of open basket-work, from which hang the most natural-looking fish made of cloth or paper. Such a pole is set before every house in which a boy has been born during the year, or where there are young boys, and some patriarchal households display a group of poles and a school of carp flying in the air. These *nobori*, as the paper carp are called, are of course symbolic, the carp being one of the strongest fish, stemming currents, mounting water-falls, and attaining a great age. Many of these nobori are four or five feet in length, and a hoop holding the mouth open lets them fill and float with as life-like a motion as if they were flapping their fins in their own element. In-doors, images and toys are set out in state array—miniature warriors and wrestlers, spears, banners, and pennants, and all the decorative paraphernalia that once enriched a warrior's train. In all classes children's parties and picnics prevail. The schools are given up to out-door exercises, and every sunny morning processions of youngsters file by, with banners and colored caps to distinguish them, and go to some park or parade-ground for exercises, drills, and athletic games.

Besides the public schools maintained by Government, there are scores of private schools and mission schools. With its higher institutions reaching up to the Imperial University, with its special schools of law, medicine, engineering, science, and the arts, Tokio offers the best education to the youth of Japan. The public-school system is the equal of that of the United States, and the Government employs foreign teachers in even the remotest provincial schools. At a kindergarten the aristocratic pupils, with a repose of manner inherited from generations of courtly and dignified ancestors, trot in, in their little long-sleeved kimonos, like a Mikado opera company seen through the wrong end of an opera-glass, sit down demurely around low tables, and fold their hands like so many old men and women of the kingdom of Lilliput. There is no tittering, no embarrassment, nor self-consciousness ; and these grave and serious mites will take the blocks from the teachers with a reverent bow and present them to other children with another formal salute, quite as their grandfathers might have done at court.. In some of the girls' schools the old Japanese methods are followed, and they are taught the traditional etiquette and the *cha no yu*, to embroider, to write poems, to arrange flowers, and to play the samisen. The koto, once almost obsolete, is restored to favor, and girls delight to touch this sweet-toned, horizontal harp.

The great summer festival is the opening of the river. This is the beginning of the nightly water fêtes on the Sumidagawa, and in the innumerable tea-houses that line its banks. This fête, appointed for the last week of June, is often postponed to the more settled season of July. Flat-bottomed house-boats, with open sides, awnings hung round with lanterns, and sturdy boatmen at either end of the craft, go up the river by hundreds and thousands at sunset, gliding out from the creeks and canals that everywhere intersect the city. The glittering fleet gathers in the broad stretch of stream lying between the Asakusa bashi and the Ryogoku bashi, and these two bridges are black with spectators. The rows of teahouses lining both shores spread red blankets over the balcony railings, and hang row upon row of lanterns along balustrades and eaves. With their rooms thrown wide open to the water, they themselves look like great lanterns. Every room of every house has its dinner party, the tea-house of the Thousand Mats being engaged months before hand, and every *maiko* and geisha bespoken. Boats command double prices, and nearly every boat has its family group; little children in holiday dress, their elders in fresh silk, crape, gauze, or cotton kimonos, sitting on the red floor-cloth, each with a tray of dolls' dishes, filled with the morsels of dainty things that make up a Japanese feast, and saké bottles circulating freely. The lines of lanterns shed a rose-colored light over all; and at one end a pretty maiko goes through her graceful poses, the company keeping time with her in rhythmical hand-clappings. Peddlers of fruit, candies, fireworks, and saké; performing jugglers, acrobats, and story-tellers; floating restaurants, theatres, side-shows, and boatloads of musicians row in and out among the rest. Talk, laughter, and the wailing notes of samisens fill the air with a hum that swells to cheers and roars as the swift rockets fill the air with balls, fountains, sheaves, sprays, jets, and trails of light; or fiery dragons, wriggling monsters, rainbows, and waterfalls shine out on the dark night sky. Although saké flows everywhere, there is no drunkenness or disorder to degrade these gentle, cheerful merry-makers.

Fires are among the thrilling but picturesque experiences of city life, confined chiefly to the winter months. The annual losses of Japan through conflagrations are very great, and Tokio has been destroyed many times. The flimsy little straw-matted, wooden houses are always ready to blaze ; and if a lamp explodes. a brazier upsets. or a spark flies. the whole place is in flames. which leap from roof to roof until the quarter is kindled. Each time a burned district is rebuilt the streets are widened. a measure which preserves property but ruins picturesqueness. for the broad thoroughfares. lined with low, unpainted buildings, make the modern Japanese city monotonous and uninteresting.

The diminutive Japanese dwellings, of toy-like construction, rest on corner posts set on large rocks, and made stable by their heavy roofs of mud and tiles. Fires are stemmed only by tearing down all buildings in the path of the flames, which is done as easily as a house of cards is overturned. A rope, fastened to one of the upright corner posts. brings the structure down with a crash, while the heavy roof covers it like an extinguisher. The ordinary city house or shop may have twelve feet of frontage. and even a second story seldom raises the roof more than fifteen feet from the ground. To hear of a thousand houses being burned in a night is appalling, but a thousand of these Lilliputian dwellings and their microscopic landscape gardens would not cover more area than two or three blocks of a foreign city.

Each section or ward has a high tower or ladder, with a long bell. and from this lookout the watchman gives the alarm or the near policeman sounds the fire-bell. Pandemonium follows, for a more excitable being than the Japanese does not exist, and the fire-bell's clang is suggestive of many sad and terrible experiences. Besides the municipal fire brigade with their ladders and handpumps. each ward maintains private watchmen and firemen. These watchmen roam their beats from dusk to daylight, jingling the loose iron rings on the tops of their long staffs. Throughout the night the watchman's clinking rings are heard at half-hour intervals or oftener. The policemen, on the contrary, go about quietly, lurking in shadow to pounce upon malefactors; and foreigners, mistaking the fire-guardian for the constable, have pointed many jokes at his noisy progress.

When the alarm-bell clangs, friends rush to help friends in saving their effects, and thieves make the most of the opportunity. Blocks away from the fire agitated people gather up mats, screens, bedding, clothing, and cooking utensils, and hurry from the neighborhood. Then does the simplicity of Japanese life justify itself. No cumbrous furniture is rolled out, to be broken in the transit; no tables, chairs, or clumsy beds are ruined in the saving. One small hand-cart holds the roll of wadded comforters and gowns that compose the bedding of the family, their clothing, and their few other effects. The sliding paper-screens are slipped from their grooves, the thick straw-mats are taken from the floor, and the household departs, leaving but the roof, corner posts, and rough floor behind them. Processions of these refugees stream away from the burning quarter, and the heart of the spectator goes out to the poor people, who, with so little, live so cheerfully and suffer so bravely.

The emblems or rallying banners always carried by native fire-companies astonish foreign eyes. Glorified drum-majors' sticks, gigantic clubs, spades, hearts, diamonds, balls, crescents, stars, or puzzles, are borne aloft by the color-bearer of the detachment, who stands in the midst of smoke, sparks, and the thickest of the hurlyburly, to show where his company is at work. Thrilling tales are told of these Casabiancas remaining on roofs or among flames until engulfed in the blazing ruins.

Sometimes carpenters begin to build new habitations on the still smoking ground, stepping gingerly among hot stones and tiles. The amazing quickness with which Japanese houses rise from their ashes defies comparison. In twelve hours after a conflagration the little shop-keepers will resume business at the old stand. Fire insurance is not suited to this country of wood and straw dwellings ; but thatched roofs are giving way to tiles in the cities, and brick is more and more used for walls. Stone is too expensive, and, in this earthquake country, open to greater objections than brick. The stone walls sometimes seen are a sham, the stones being thin slabs nailed on the wooden framework of a house, like tiles or shingles, to rattle down in a harmless shower when the earth heaves and rocks. Steam fire-engines are unknown, and hand-grenades are inevitably forgotten in the excitement of a conflagration.

Earthquakes, though frequent, are fortunately not severe, and no alarming catastrophe has been suffered since the convulsions of 1854 and 1855, which the malcontents attributed to the wrath of the gods at the spectacle of foreign barbarians entering the country. The old myth, that the earth — meaning the islands of Japan — rests upon the back of a huge fish, whose writhings cause these disturbances, places the head of the leviathan beneath Yezo, its tail under the southern island, and its vital and active body below Yokohama and Tokio. Now the Government has a seismologist on its university staff, and each tremor or palpitation is accurately recorded, the average number reaching four hundred annually. Kobé and Kioto seldom experience even the slightest motion, but in the vicinity of the capital one becomes fairly accustomed to the unpleasant visitation. A slight disturbance sets lamps and chandeliers vibrating ; with a heavier rock all bric-à-brac not wired fast to cabinets, mantels, or tables, slides to the floor ; and a harder shock loosens tiles, wrenches timbers, and sends brick chimneys, not boxed in wood or sheet-iron, crashing through the roofs. A small house rattles as if the earthquake fish had come out of the sea and seized it as a terrier does a rat. Pebbles grate in garden paths, tall evergreens snap their tops like switches, bells ring, clocks stop, and people rush frantically to open spaces or streets.

The Japanese seldom drink water, although they splash, dabble, or soak in it half the time; yet men who are working in moats or lotus-ponds, grubbing out the old roots or stalks, and dripping wet to their waists and shoulders, will quit work on rainy days. In Yokohama harbor, coolies who load and unload lighters, and are in and out of water continually, often refuse to work when a shower begins; but a wet day brings a new aspect to the streets, and fair weather has no monopoly of picturesqueness. The unoccupied women with babies tied on their backs, an apparently large leisure class, are always gadding about the town with the aimless unconcern of hens, taking no account of the weather, and enjoying the open air regardless of the barometer. Children are equally indifferent, and jinrikisha coolies, although they draw the hoods and tie their passengers in snug and dry with oil-paper or rubber aprons, trot along cheerfully, with their too scanty cotton garments more abbreviated than ever. They substitute for an umbrella a huge flat straw plate of a hat, and instead of putting on galoches, they take off even their straw sandals and run barefooted, tying up the big toe with a bit of rag or wisp of straw, apparently by way of decoration. Those pedestrians who wish to be stately and dry-shod thrust their bare feet into a half-slipper arrangement of wood and oil-paper, perched on two wooden rests three inches high, adding this cubit to their stature.

When the rain-drops patter the shops are a delight, and the great silk bazaars of Echigoya and Dai Maru, the Louvre and Bon Marché of Tokio, are as entertaining as a theatre. Both occupy corners on great thoroughfares, and have waving curtains of black cloth, with crest and name in white, as the only wall or screen from the street. The one vast open room of the first story is revealed at a glance. The floor proper of this great apartment, raised a foot and a half from the stone walk surrounding it, is covered with the usual straw-mats, the uniform glistening surface extending more than sixty feet either way. Here and there salesmen and accountants, the book-keepers being also cashiers, sit at low desks, where they keep their sorobans, money, and curious ledgers. There are no shelves nor counters, and in groups on the mats sit women with beautifully-dressed hair, and men in sober silk garments, inspecting the heaps of rainbow fabrics strewn about them. Small boys bring out arm-loads and baskets of silks from the godowns, for no stock is ever in sight until the purchaser asks for it. It is etiquette for these small boys to hail and cheer the arriving and departing customer, and they drone out some nasal chorus. We once lifted the street curtain at Dai Maru's on a rainy day to find the whole matted area deserted of customers. Immediately the battalion of small boys sprang to their feet, and, deafening us with a chanted canticle, hurried to the corner where a steaming bronze urn, various tea-caddies, and a shelved box full of tea-sets provide patrons with cups of amber-tinted nectar. For an hour these myrmidons ran to and fro, baskets were carried back and forth, and gold brocades supplied sunlight and rainbows for a gloomy day. All these precious brocades come in lengths of four and a half yards for the broad obis or sashes that are one secret of her looks in the toilet of a Japanese woman. Those woven of silk alone are as thick as leather and soft as crape, and the massed gold threads, while glistening like plates of chased metal, give stiffness but not hardness to the fabrics. When the woof threads are left

in thick, shaggy loops on the under side, not cut away
in any economical fashion, these are *yesso nishikis*, the
choicest of all Japanese stuffs, and valued from sixty to
one hundred and twenty dollars for the single obi length.

The Nakadori is a half-mile-long street of curio and
second-hand shops, which just before the New Year contain their best bargains, and no one can hold to the safety of his jinrikisha through that straight and narrow path,
beset by every temptation of old porcelains, lacquer, and
embroideries. Peddlers will gather from these shops and
carry packs twice their own size, to spread their contents out in the room of a customer. Their wares are so
tempting and cheap that the beholder cannot resist them,
after a reformation of prices, and that peddler who comes
twice has marked his victim for his own. On certain
days of the week a rag fair is held on the Yanagiwara.
Vendors in rows half a mile long sit under the willow-
trees on the canal bank, with neat piles of old clothing,
scraps of cloth, and ornaments for sale. Between Shiba
and the railway station is a rag alley, a Petticoat Lane of
old clothing, but most of it is foreign and unpicturesque,
even in the flying glimpses to be caught from a jinrikisha.

In curio-hunting the experienced buyer invariably re-
plies *takai*, "too much," to whatever price the dealer
names. If intent on the bargain he may add *takusan
takai*, "altogether too much." *Osoroshi takai*, or *toho-
moni takai*, "inexpressibly, unspeakably dear," sometimes serves to abate the price by reason of the dealer's
amazement at hearing those classic and grandiloquent
words brought down to common usage.

Once I visited the most charming of old-clothes shops,
one where theatrical wardrobes were kept; but Sanjiro
could not, or would not remember it, and I never returned. The shopmen were sober and serious automata,
whose countenances were stolid and imperturbable, and
one might as well have bargained with the high-priest

for the veil of the temple, as have offered them less than they asked. They sat, smoked, and cast indifferent glances at us while baskets of gorgeous raiment were borne in, and affected to look up the prices in a book of records. After baiting me long enough, and bringing me to raise my offer, the trio of partners would suddenly clap their hands, say something in concert, and deliver me the article. It was all as precisely ordered and acted as a set scene on the stage, and I longed in vain to assist at other acts in the unique drama.

CHAPTER VIII

TOKIO FLOWER FESTIVALS

WITH all its foreign sophistications, flower worship has not died out in the Japanese capital. The calendar is divided into the time of the camellia, the plum, the cherry, the wistaria, the lotus, the chrysanthemum, and the maple. Orange blossoms and tea blossoms alone are omitted among the special flower festivals, and the Japanese as naturally refer to the time of the cherry blooming or of maple-leaves, as we to spring or autumn. They infuse into these festivals a sentiment and feeling, a spirit and gayety, inherited from generations of flower-loving ancestors, who made their æsthetic pilgrimages year after year to see the acres of wonderful flowers in the different suburbs of each city. By the old calendar, the first unfolding of the plum-trees, the true awakening of the seasons, marked the new year. In the change from the Chinese method of reckoning to the Gregorian, the Japanese January fell to a churlish mood of nature, when only late chrysanthemums, camellias, and in-door dwarf-trees can bloom. But every door-way is then arched with evergreens and flowers; pine and bamboo, bound with braided straw ropes. are set before the house; tassels of rice straw are festooned across the eaves, and lanterns hang in rows. The emblematic rice-cake, prawn, orange, and fern-leaf are fastened above the lintel, the handsomest screen is brought forward, and more emblems and a large bowl for cards are set out at the entrance. This is the season when all debts are paid, while general visiting and feasting occupy three days. Everybody says to everybody else, *Shinen ome deto*, "I wish you a happy New-year;" or, *Man zai raku*, "Good-luck for ten thousand years." · Everybody sends his friend a present — a basket of fruit, or a dumpling of red beans or rice dough, wrapped in ceremonial paper. The streets of Tokio, crowded with merrymakers and lighted at night by thousands of lanterns and torches. hold out-of-door fairs without number. and from palace to hovel run sounds of rejoicing; yet this joyous homage to the spirit of life is paid in mid-winter, when snow-flakes may shroud the blooming camellia-trees, though the clear, bright Indian-summer weather often lasts until after the new year. Winter, a long calamity elsewhere in the same latitude. is only the disagreeable incident of a few weeks in Central Japan. A fortnight. a month, of melting snows. cold rains. and dull skies, and lo! the branches of the withered, old black plum-trees are starred with fragrant white flowers. For a few days a hazy calm hushes the air, sounds are veiled, light is softened, and spring has really come, no matter how many sullen relapses it may suffer before the glorious April cloud-burst of cherry blossoms decks the empire in wreaths of white and pink, and fills the people with joy. And this linked sweetness long drawn out. this gentle season of delight, lasts from the bursting of the plum blossoms in February to the end of the nyubai, or rainy season of June.

AT A FLOWER SHOW

Beyond Kameido's wistaria-bordered lake are ancient plum groves, whose trees—old, gnarled, twisted, black, and lichen-covered, propped with poles and stone posts—writhe and twist over the ground in contortions which explain their name — the *Gwariobai*, or the couchant dragon-trees. This Ume Yashiki was once the villa of a Shogun's favorite. Its buildings, fences, and hedges are gray with age, its stone tablets, moss-grown and something in the hoary antiquity of the place subdues one's pulses. The long cry of a hidden boatman in the creek beyond the high camellia hedge is the only sound that breaks the silence. People sit on the red-covered benches, women in soft-toned crapes walk under the strange skeleton shadows like moving figures of a dream, and children flash among the black trunks brilliant in their gay garb. Often one sees visionary old men sitting lost in reverie, and murmuring to themselves of *ume no hana* the, plum blossom. They sip tea, they rap out the ashes from tiny pipes, and slipping a writing-case from the girdle, unroll a scroll of paper and indite an ode or sonnet. Then, with radiant face and cheerful muttering, the ancient poet will slip his toes into his clogs and tie the little slip to the branches of the most charming tree. The well-bred spectators do not push upon the fluttering scroll, as my impetuous fellow-countrymen would do, but with a decent dignity read and criticise the praises of the blossoms and the solemn stillness of the old yashiki.

The veriest Gradgrind could not be indifferent to the poetic charm of the Japanese spring-time, wherein the setting of the buds, their swelling, and the gradual unfolding of *sakura*, the cherry blossoms, are matters of great public concern, the native newspapers daily printing advance despatches from the trees. Even more beautiful than the plum-tree festival is the Tokio celebration of the blossoming of the cherry, and gayer than the brilliant throngs are the marvellous trees. From the wild, indigenous dwarf seedling of the mountains have been developed countless varieties, culminating in that which bears the pink-tinged double blossoms as large as a hundred-leafed rose, covering every branch and twig with thick rosettes. A faint fragrance arises from these sheets of bloom, but the strange glare of pinkish light from their fair canopy dazzles and dizzies the beholder. The cherry-blossom Sunday of Uyéno Park is a holiday of the upper middle class. One week later, the double avenue of blossoming trees, lining the Mukojima for a mile along the river bank, invites the lower classes to a very different celebration from that of the decorous, well-dressed throng driving, walking, picnicking, and tea drinking under the famous trees. No warning to keep off the grass forbids their wandering at will over the great park, every foot of whose ground is historic, whose trees are ancient, whose avenues are broad and winding, and whose woods are as dark as the forest primeval. Temple bells softly boom, ravens croak, and happy voices fill the air.

Not the Bois, the Cascine, or the Thier Garten can vie with Uyéno on this blossom Sunday. Down every path and avenue are vistas of flowery trees, lofty and wide-spreading as vast oaks and elms, and through their snowy branches shine thousands of other snowy branches, or countless solitary trees gleaming against green backgrounds. The wide lotus lake below Uyéno reflects the white wonder that encircles the race-course, and the temple roofs on the tiny islands are smothered in pink branches. Under the great grove of cherry-trees teahouse benches are set close, and there the people lunch and dine and sup; and though saké flows freely, the most confirmed drinker is only a little redder, a little happier, a little more loquacious than the rest. Czars and kaisers may well envy this Oriental ruler, whose subjects gather by thousands, not to throw bombs and

A UYÉNO TEA-HOUSE

riot for bread or the division of property, but to fall in love with cherry-trees, and write poems in their praise. At the cherry-blossom season especially his inborn passion for flowers and landscapes shows itself in prince, poet, peasant, merchant, and coolie. Tattered beggars gaze entranced at the fairy trees, and princes and ministers of state go to visit the famous groves. Bulletins announce, quite as a matter of course, that Prince Sanjo or Count Ito has gone to Nara or Kioto, a three days' journey, to see the blossoming trees; which is as if Bismarck or Gladstone should interrupt his cares of state to undertake a pilgrimage to a distant rose show.

Later in the season the carefully tended trees in the palace grounds put forth their blossoms, and sovereign and courtiers hang poems on their branches, while the spring garden party gathers the whole court circle under the aisles of bloom in the palace grounds of Hama Rikiu. Every citizen who has a garden gives an out-door fête, and flower-bordered cards invite guests to see the native sakura, or the *cerisiers* of the diplomatic set.

The celebration of the Mukojima, an avenue along the east bank of the Sumidagawa, lined for more than two miles with double rows of cherry-trees, belongs to the lower ten thousand. On Sunday, which is officially a day of rest, the water is dotted with hundreds of boats, and solemn little policemen keep the holiday-makers moving along the shore. Friends recognize each other in the crowd by some distinctive article of clothing. One procession of jinrikishas will land a group with heads tied up in gayly-figured towels all alike, or bits of figured cotton folded as collars around the necks of their kimonos. Boat-loads of men, partly disguised by their queer head-dresses, are sculled and poled along the banks, shouting and singing, clapping and strumming the samisen, with an entire abandon that is the wonder and envy of the Anglo-Saxon. Every reveller has his saké gourd, or tiny tub slung over his shoulder, which he empties and refills, as long as his money and consciousness last. Every man offers friend, neighbor, and stranger a cup of the cheering spirit. One booth in three is a saké stand, and pyramids of straw-covered saké tubs stand before every tea-house. This saké, or rice brandy, tastes and looks like the weakest sherry, although it scents the air with alcoholic fumes. Made everywhere in Japan, the saké distilled from the rice of the broad Osaka plain is most esteemed by connoisseurs for a peculiarly delicate flavor. As it is the one liquor that does not improve with age, the newest is the best, and is kept in wooden tubs closed with spigots, and drawn off into open-mouthed porcelain bottles, which are set in hot water if warm saké is desired. The Japanese drink it from little shallow porcelain or lacquer cups that hold barely a tablespoonful, but by repetition they imbibe pints. Its first effect is to loosen the tongue and limber the joints; its second to turn the whole body a flaming red.

Mukojima's carnival rivals the saturnalia of the ancients. This spring revel affords another resemblance between this æsthetic people and the old Romans, and one half expects to find a flower-crowned statue of Bacchus in some lovely little landscape garden beside the Mukojima. Men dance like satyrs, cup and gourd in hand, or, extending a hand, make orations to the crowd—natural actors, orators, and pantomimists every one of them. But, with all this intoxication, only glee and affection manifest themselves. No fighting, no rowdyism, no rough words accompany the spring saturnalia; and the laughter is so infectious, the antics and figures so comical, that even sober people seem to have tasted of the insane cup. At night lanterns swing from all the rows of tea-houses, booths, and fairy branches, and interminable Japanese dinners are eaten, with beautiful maiko and geisha posing and gliding, twanging the samisen and

IN A FLORIST'S GARDEN

tsuzumi drums, their kimonos embroidered with cherry blossoms, hair-pins, and coronals of blossoms set in the butterfly loops of blue-black hair. Then the rain comes, the petals fall, and those snow storms not from the skies whiten the ground.

For a week in June, jinrikishas spin up this leafy tunnel to the iris fêtes at Hori Kiri, where in ponds and trenches grow acres of such fleur-de-lis as no Bourbon ever knew. Compared with the cherry-blossom carnival, this festival is a quiet and decorous garden party, where summer-houses, hills, lakes, armies of royal flowers, and groups of visitors seem to be consciously arranging themselves for decorative effects.

After the season opens, flower festivals crowd one another, and the miracles of Japanese floriculture presently exhaust the capacity of wonder. One of the most superb of their productions is the *botan*, or tree peony, whose fringed and silken flowers, as large as dinner-plates, show all delicate rose and lilac shades, a red that is almost black, and cream, pale yellow, straw color, and salmon hues of marvellous beauty. At the Ikegami temples, the Nichiren priests display with pride their botan, now three hundred years old, whose solid trunk and wrinkled bark uphold a multitude of stately blossoms. Azaleas, fire-red, snow-white, salmon-pink, and lilac, crowd every garden, and the mountains and wild river-banks are all ablaze with them in May.

Then, also, the wistaria, the *fuji*, is in bloom, and at the Kameido temple makes an eighth wonder of the world. Every householder has his wistaria trellis, generally reaching out as a canopy over some inlet, or, as at Kameido, forming the roofs of the open-air tea-houses edging the lake. The mat of leaves and blossoms overhead casts thick, cool shadows, and the long, pendent purple and white flowers are reflected in the water. Blossoms two and even three feet long are common, and only a great swaying tassel four feet in length draws a "*Naruhodo.*" (wonderful) from the connoisseurs. Whole families come to spend the day on the borders of the little lake, sipping amber tea, tossing *mochi* to the lazy goldfish, or sitting in picturesque groups on the low platforms under the canopies of flowers fluttering with poems and lanterns. The temple is ancient, and the grounds are full of tiny shrines, stone lanterns, tablets, and images, and dwarfed and curiously trained pine trees, with a high, hump-backed little bridge, over which, in the old days, only priests and grandees might walk. Golden carp, venerable old fellows, three or four feet in length, show an orange nose now and then above the surface of the pond. The people call these pets by clapping their hands, and the golden gourmands swim from one horn of plenty, filled with mochi, or rice-cakes, with which they are fed, to another. At Kasukabe, on the Oshukaido, north-east of Tokio, is the most famous wistaria in the empire. The vine is five hundred years old, with pendent blossoms over fifty inches long, and trellises covering a space of four thousand feet, and thither poets and pilgrims reverently go.

In August occurs the one great lotus show now seen in Tokio, when the lake below Uyéno Park shows acres of bluish-green plates of leaves starred with pink and white blossoms, and the enchanted beholder looks down from the bridges and tea-houses of the little islands straight into the heart of the great flowers. The castle moats no longer show their acres of lotus, and the mimic salutes no longer ring around the citadel, as when those myriad blossoms of Buddha opened with a gentle noise under the first warm rays of the sun. There is a lovely lotus-pond back of the Shiba pagoda, just seen as the jinrikisha whirls along the shady avenue skirting it, but the lotus of the moats was the summer glory of Tokio. The flower was not alone to blame for malarial exha-

WISTARIA-VINE AT KASUKABE

lations, as the contest still rages between the two sides of the city, as to whether the vapors from the moats, or those from the exposed mud flats and made ground of the Tsukiji section, are most pernicious.

The festival of the *kiku*, or chrysanthemum, in autumn, decks the whole empire with red, white, and yellow flowers. The sixteen-petalled chrysanthemum is the imperial or government crest; and the Emperor's birthday, the third of November, coming in the height of the season, is made a gala-day in every province, and the occasion of gorgeous flower shows. The Western mind is filled with envy to discover that the wide - spreading, spicy flowers selling here for a few coppers each, cost as many dollars under new names across the water. Dango-zaka, dismissed with a line in the guide-book, is more picturesquely Japanese in autumn than any other suburb of Tokio. A community of florists tend, prune, dwarf, and cultivate their chrysanthemum plants in obscurity until the blossoming time makes Dango-zaka a gay fair. The unique productions of their gardens are set pieces of flowers on a gigantic scale. Under matted sheds, which are so many temporary stages without footlights, groups with life-sized figures are arranged, whose faces and hands are of wax or composition, but whose clothes, the accessories, and scenery are made of living flowers, trained so closely over a framework that the mechanism is not even suspected. The plants forming the flower-pieces are taken up with all their roots, wrapped in straw and cloths, propped up inside the skeleton framework, and watered every day. The flowers, drawn to the outside and woven into place, produce a solid surface of color, and are shaded with the most natural effects. The tableaux represent scenes from history and legend, and from the latest plays, or even illustrate the last emotional crime of the day. Here are seen whole mountainsides of flowers, with water - falls of white blossoms

IN DANGO-ZAKA STREET

spreading into floral streams; and chrysanthemum women leading chrysanthemum horses, ridden by chrysanthemum men across chrysanthemum bridges. Gigantic flowers. microscopic flowers. plants of a single blossom, and single plants of two hundred blossoms, have bamboo tents to themselves. Touters invite one to enter. proprietors chant the story of their pictures, and the side-show, the juggler. the fakir, and the peddler make the bannered and lanterned lanes a gay and innocent Babel. All classes visit Dango-zaka,

THE FLORAL KWANNON

and wander together up and down its one steep street,
and in and out of the maze of gardens, paying a copper
or two at each gate-way. Giants and saintly images forty
and fifty feet high are enshrined in mat pavilions as lofty
as temples, and to these marvellous chrysanthemum creatures the phonograph has lately added its wonders. The
coolie, who draws the visitor's jinrikisha, is as voluble

SLAYING THE DEMON

over the flowers as any of his patrons, and quite as discriminating an admirer. Instead of stopping to rest after his long pull to that hilly suburb, he follows his passenger, pointing out beauties and marvels, approving and exclaiming with contagious enthusiasm.

In November, with the brilliant maple-leaves, the floral year ends. The coquette sends her lover a leaf or branch of maple to signify that, like it, her love has changed. Both the tea-plant and camellia are in bloom, but there is no rejoicing in their honor, and flower-worshippers count the weeks until the plum shall bloom again.

CHAPTER IX

JAPANESE HOSPITALITIES

AMONG Japanese virtues stands hospitality, but, until the adoption of foreign dress and customs by the court nobles, no Japanese allowed his wife to receive general visitors, or entertain mixed companies. The Japanese is, consequently, a born club-man, and makes the clubhouse a home. The Rokumeikwan, or Tokio Nobles' Club, is the most distinguished of these corporations. Its president is an imperial prince, and its members are diplomats, nobles, officials, rich citizens, and resident foreigners. The exquisite houses and gardens of the smaller, purely Japanese clubs, are perfect specimens of native architecture, decoration, and landscape gardening. By an arrangement of sliding screens, the houses themselves may afford one large room or be divided into many small ones, besides the tiny boxes in which are celebrated the rites of cha no yu, or ceremonial tea.

Their elaborate dinners, lasting for hours, with jugglers, dancers, and musicians between the courses, are very costly. Rich men display a Russian prodigality in entertaining, which was even greater in feudal times. A day or two after arriving in Japan it was my good-fortune to be a guest at one of these unique entertainments, given at the Koyokwan, or Maple Leaf Club-house, on the hill-side above the Shiba temples. We arrived at three o'clock, and were met at the door by a group of pretty nesans, or maids of the house, who, taking off our hats and shoes, led us, stocking-footed, down a shining corridor and up-stairs to a long, low room, usually divided into three by screens of dull gold paper. One whole side of this beautiful apartment was open to the garden beyond a railed balcony of polished cedar, and the view, across the maple-trees and dense groves of Shiba, to the waters of the Bay was enchanting. The decorations of the club-house repeat the maples that fill the grounds. The wall screens are painted with delicate branches, the *ramma*, or panels above the screens, are carved with them, and in the outer wall and balcony-rail are leaf-shaped openings. The dresses of the pretty nesans, the crape cushions on the floor, the porcelain and lacquer dishes, the saké bottles and their carved stands, the fans and bon-bons, all display the maple-leaf. In the *tokonoma*, or raised recess where the flower-vase and kakemono, or scroll picture, are displayed, and that small dais upon which the Emperor would sit if he ever came to the house, hung a shadowy painting, with a single flower in a bronze vase.

Before each guest were set the *tabako bon*, a tray holding a tiny *hibachi* with live coals lying in a cone of ashes, and a section of bamboo stem for an ash-receiver. Then came the tea and sweetmeats, inevitable prelude to all good cheer. Next the nesans set in front of each guest an *ozen*, or table, not four inches in height, on which stood a covered lacquered bowl containing the first course, a tiny cup of soy, or piquant bean sauce, in which to dip morsels of food, and a long envelope containing a pair of white pine chopsticks. The master of

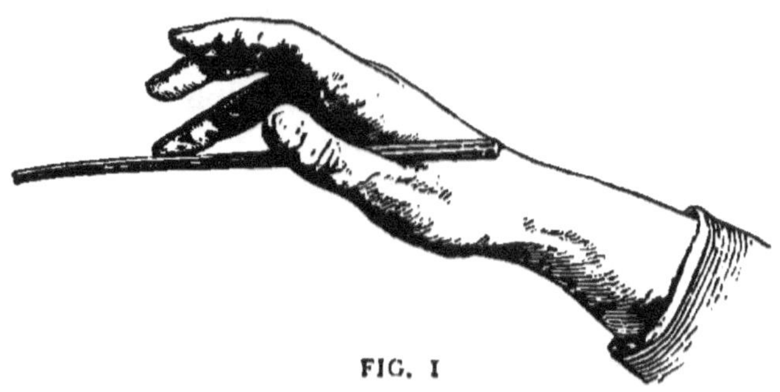

FIG. 1

the feast broke apart his chopsticks, which were whittled in one piece and split apart for only half their length, to show that they were unused, and began a nimble play with them. In his fingers they were enchanted wands, and did his bidding promptly; in ours they wobbled, made ×'s in the air, and deposited morsels in our laps

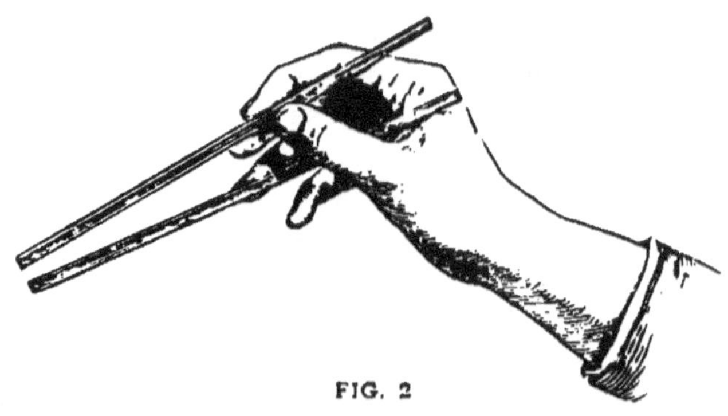

FIG. 2

and upon the mats alternately. The nesans giggled, and the host almost forgot his Japanese decorum, but the company patiently taught us how to brace one chopstick firmly in the angle of the thumb and against the third finger. That stick is immovable, and the other, held like a pen with the thumb and first and second fingers, plays upon it, holding and letting go with a sureness and lightness hardly attained with any other implements. The supreme test of one's skill is to lift and hold an egg, the round surface making a perfect balance and firm hold necessary, while too much force applied would cause disasters.

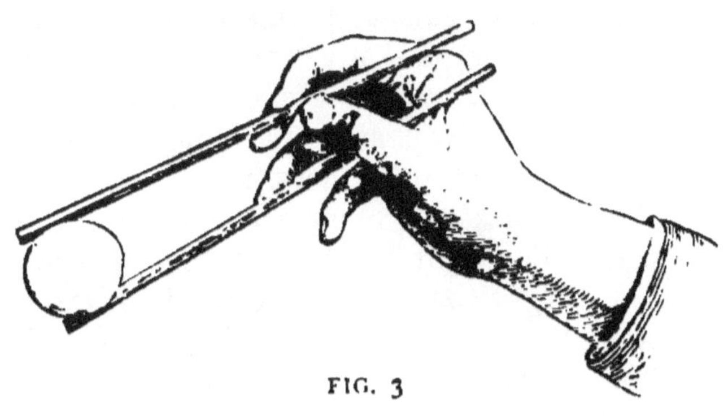

FIG. 3

Innumerable courses of dainty dishes followed, accompanied by cups of hot saké, which our host taught us to drink as healths, offered by each one of the company to the others in turn, rinsing, offering, filling, and raising the cup to the forehead in salutation, and emptying it in three prescribed sips. Custom even requires one to offer a health to the nesans, which they receive with a modest and charming grace.

Midway in the feast three charming girls in dark crape kimonos, strewn with bright maple-leaves, slipped the screens aside and knelt on the mats with the koto, samisen, and tsuzumi drum, on which they played a prelude of sad, slow airs. Then the gilded panels disclosed a troop of dazzling maiko in soft blue kimonos brocaded

with brilliant maple-leaves and broad obis of gold brocade, the loops of their blue - black hair thrust full of
golden flowers, and waving gold fans painted with gay
maples. To the melancholy accompaniment of the geisha,
they danced the song of the maple-leaf in measures that
were only a slow gliding and changing from one perfect
pose to another. Watching these radiant creatures in
their graceful movements, we were even deaf to the soft
booming of the temple bells at the sunset hour, and the
answering croak of the mighty ravens.

These maikó and geisha, professional dancers and
singers, are necessary to any entertainment, and are
trained to amuse and charm the guests with their ac-
complishments, their wit, and sparkling conversation;
lending that attraction, brightness, and charm to social
life, which wives and daughters are permitted to do in
the Occident. The maiko dances as soon as she is old
enough to be taught the figures and to chant the poems
which explain them; and when she begins to fade, she
dons the soberer attire of the geisha, and, sitting on the
mats, plays the accompaniments for her successors and
pupils. Until this modern era, the geisha were the most
highly educated of Japanese women, and many of them
made brilliant marriages.

Long before the beautiful band had finished their
poem and dance of the four seasons, twilight had fallen.
Andons, or saucers of oil, burning on high stands inside
square paper lantern frames, made Rembrandtesque effects. Everything was lost in shadow but the figures of
the maiko moving over the shining mats. One tiny girl
of thirteen, belonging to the house, slipped in and out
with a bronze box and snuffers, and, kneeling before the
andons, opened the paper doors to nip off bits of the
wicks. The child, a miniature beauty, was grace itself,
gentle and shy as a kitten, blushing and quaintly bowing
when addressed.

It was six hours after the entrance of the tabako bons before the guests rose to depart. All the troop of maidens escorted us to the door, and after endless bows and farewells, sat on the mats in matchless tableaux, their sweet *sayonaras* ringing after us as our jinrikishas whirled us down the dark avenues of Shiba.

Cha no yu might well be a religious rite, from the reverence with which it is regarded by the Japanese, and a knowledge of its forms is part of the education of a member of the highest classes. Masters teach its minute and tedious forms, and schools of cha no yu, like the sects of a great faith, divide and differ. The cha no yu ceremony is hedged round with the most awesome, elaborate, and exalted etiquette of any custom in polite Japanese life. Weddings or funerals are simple affairs by comparison. The cha no yu is a complication of all social usages, and was perfected in the sixteenth century, when it was given its vogue by the Shogun Hideyoshi. Before that it had been the diversion of imperial abbots, monarchs retired from business, and other idle and secluded occupants of the charming villas and monasteries around Kioto. Hideyoshi, the Taiko, saw in its precise forms, endless rules, minutiæ, and stilted conventionalities a means of keeping his daimios from conspiracies and quarrels when they came together. It was an age of buckram and behavior, when solemnity constituted the first rule of politeness. Tea drinking was no trivial incident, and time evidently had no value. The daimios soon invested the ceremony with so much luxury and extravagance that Hideyoshi issued sumptuary laws, and the greatest simplicity in accessories was enjoined. The bowls in which the tea was made had to be of the plainest earthen-ware, but the votaries evaded the edict by seeking out the oldest Chinese or Korean bowls, or those made by some celebrated potter. Tea - rooms were re-

stricted to a certain size—six feet square ; the entrance
became a mere trap not three feet high ; no servants
were permitted to assist the host, and only four guests
might take part in the six-hour or all-day-long ceremony.
The places of the guests on the mats, with relation to the
host, the door, and the tokonoma, or recess, were strictly
defined. Even the conversation was ordered, the objects
in the tokonoma were to be asked about at certain times,
and at certain other times the tea - bowl and its accompaniments were gravely discussed. Not to speak of them
at all would be as great an evidence of ill - breeding as
to refer to them at the wrong time.

The masters of cha no yu were revered above scholars
and poets. They became the friends and intimates of
Emperors and Shoguns, were enriched and ennobled, and
their descendants receive honors to this day. Of the
great schools and methods those of Senke, Yabunouchi,
and Musanokoji adhere most closely to the original
forms. Their first great difference is in the use of the
inward or the outward sweep of the hand in touching or
lifting the utensils. Upon this distinction the dilettanti
separated, and the variations of the many schools of to-
day arose from the original disagreement. To get some
insight into a curious phase of Japanese social life. I took
lessons in cha no yu of Matsuda, an eminent master of
the art, presiding over the ceremonial tea-rooms of the
Hoishigaoka club-house in Tokio.

There could be no more charming place in which to
study the etiquette of tea drinking. and the master was
one of those mellow, gentle. gracious men of old Japan.
who are the perfect flower of generations of culture and
refinement in that most æsthetic country of the world.
In the afternoon and evening the Hoishigaoka. on the
apex of Sanno hill, is the resort of the nobles. scholars,
and literary men, who compose its membership. but in
the morning hours, it is all dappled shadow and quiet.

THE NESANS AT THE HOISHIGAOKA

The master was much pleased at having four foreign pupils, and all the hill-side took an interest in our visits.
We followed the etiquette strictly, first taking off our
shoes—for one would as soon think of walking hob-
nailed across a piano-top, as of marring the polished
woods of Japanese corridors, or the fine, soft mats of
their rooms with heel-marks—and sitting on our heels,
as long as our unaccustomed and protesting muscles
and tendons permitted.

First, bringing in the basket of selected charcoal, with
its pretty twigs of charred azalea coated with lime, Mat-

suda replenished the fire in the square hearth in the floor, dusted the edges with an eagle's feather, and dropped incense on the coals. Then he placed the iron kettle, filled with fresh water from a porcelain jar, over the coals, and showed us how to fold the square of purple silk and wipe each article of the tea-service, how to scald the bowl, and to rinse the bamboo whisk. For cha no yu, tea-leaves are pounded to a fine powder, one, two, or three spoonfuls of this green flour being put in the bowl, as the guests may prefer a weak or a strong

MATSUDA, THE MASTER OF CHA NO YU

decoction. Boiling water is poured on the powder, and the mixture beaten to a froth with the bamboo whisk. This thick, green gruel, a real purée of tea, is drank as a loving-cup in the *usu cha* ceremony, each one taking three sips, wiping the edge of the bowl, and passing it to his neighbor. The measures and sips are so exact that the last one drains the bowl. Made from the finest leaves, this beverage is so strong that a prolonged course· of it would shatter any but Japanese nerves.

It is in the precise management of each implement, in each position of the fingers, in the deliberation and certainty of each movement, that the art of cha no yu lies, and its practice must be kept up throughout the lifetime of a devotee. Even with all the foreign fashions, the old ceremonial rites are as much in vogue with the upper classes as ever, and the youth of both sexes are carefully trained in their forms.

Much less pretentious and formal are the eel dinners with which Japanese hosts sometimes delight their foreign friends, as well as those of their own nationality. Even Sir Edwin Arnold has celebrated the delights of eels and rice at the Golden Koi, and there are other houses where the delicious dish may be enjoyed. When one enters such a tea-house, he is led to a tank of squirming fresh-water eels, and in all seriousness bidden to point out the object of his preference. Uncertain as the lottery seems, the cook, who stands by with a long knife in hand, quickly understands the choice made, and seizing the wriggling victim, carries it off to some sacrificial block in the kitchen. An eel dinner begins with eel-soup, and black eels and white eels succeed one another in as many relays as one may demand. The fish are cut in short sections, split and flattened, and broiled over charcoal fires. Black eels, so called, are a rich dark brown in reality, and the color is given them by dipping them in soy before broiling ; and white eels are the bits broiled without sauces. Laid across bowls of snowy rice, the eels make as pretty a dish as can be served one, and many foreigners besides the appreciative English poet have paid tribute to their excellence. An eel dinner in a river-bank tea-house, with a juggler or a few maiko to enliven the waits between the courses, is most delightful of Tokio feasts.

CHAPTER X

THE JAPANESE THEATRE

"SATURATED with the refinements of an old civilization," as Dr. Dresser says, and possessing all other arts in perfection, it is not surprising that the Japanese drama should be so well worthy of its people. The theatre has reached its present development slowly and with difficulty. Caste distinctions hindered its rise, actors ranking next the *eta*, or outcast class in feudal days, and the play-houses of such degraded beings lying under ban. Only the middle and lower classes patronized them, nobles never attending any public exhibitions, and all women being excluded.

In the golden age of the Tokugawas the drama began to win recognition ; theatres were built by the Shogun ; the marionette shows, the first departure from the No Kagura, gave way to living actors and realism succeeded. In the great social upheaval and rearrangement of classes following the Restoration. actors rose a little in social esteem and gained some rights of citizenship. But another quarter of a century will hardly rank the dramatic with the other arts and honor its interpreters. Noblemen now attend the theatre, but actors never receive an invitation to their clubs. A few years since, Tokio founded an association for the improvement of the theatre, and the development of the histrionic art of the country in its own distinctive way. Viscount Hijikata and Viscount Kawawa were elected president and vice-president of this Engei Kyokai, but little is known of its actual work.

Instead of farce or recitative prologue preceding the play, come one or two acts of classic pantomime or character dance, or an interlude of this kind in the middle of the drama. These classic pantomimes resemble the No Kagura simplified.

This No dance, or lyric drama, is the dramatic form current before the seventeenth century. Bordering on the religious, it suggests the Greek drama, and the passion and miracle plays of mediæval Europe. Originally, the No was the pantomime festival dance of the Shinto temples, fabled to have been first performed by Suzume before the cave of the Sun Goddess. The sacred dance is still a temple ceremonial, and the dances of the Shinto priestesses at Nikkō and Nara are famous. In time the No became the entertainment of honor in the yashikis of the great, and princes and nobles took part in the solemn measures when greater princes were their guests. To the slow and stately movements of the dancers, and their play with fan and bells, dialogue was added, and an exaggeration of detail and etiquette.

The No is wholly artificial, the movements of the actors being as stiff, stilted, and measured as the classic idiom in which the dialogue is spoken, and the ancient and obsolete ideographs which set forth the synopsis of the action. Confined to the yashikis and monasteries, the No was the entertainment of the upper classes, who alone could understand its involved and lofty diction and intricate symbolism. While the bare arguments of plays and dances are as familiar as fairy tales or folk-lore, only scholars of great attainments can read their actual lines, and the full translation of a No programme for the Duke of Edinburgh, on his visit to Japan, busied the interpreters of the British Legation for days, with the aid of all the old native poets and scholars in Tokio.

The No is a trilogy, occupying four or five hours of three successive days. The first set of scenes is to propitiate the gods; the second to terrify evil spirits and punish the wicked; and the third to glorify the good, beautiful, and pleasant. The *dramatis personæ* are gods, goddesses, demons, priests, warriors, and heroes of early legend and history, and much of the action is allegorical. By a long gallery at the left the actors approach the elevated pavilion or platform of the stage, which is without curtain or scenery, and almost without properties. The audience sits upon the matted area surrounding the three sides of the stage. Flute, drum, and pipes play continuously, and a row of men in old ceremonial dress sit statuesque at one side of the stage, chanting and wailing the explanatory chorus throughout the performance. In the great scenes the actors wear masks of thin lacquered or gilded wood, and valuable collections of such ancient dance masks are preserved in temples and yashikis. The costuming is superb, the old brocade and cloth-of-gold garments showing the court costumes of centuries ago, and the great families and monasteries hold their ancient No costumes as chiefest treasures.

The actors enter at a gait that out-struts the most exaggerated stage stride ever seen, the body held rigid as a statue, and the foot, never wholly lifted, sliding slowly along the polished floor. These buckram figures, moving with the solemnity of condemned men, utter their lines like automata, not a muscle nor an eyelash moving, nor a flicker of expression crossing the unmasked countenance. Their tones are unspeakably distressing, nasal, high-pitched, falsetto sounds, and many performers have ruined and lost their voices, and even burst blood-vessels, in the long-continued, unnatural strain of their recitatives. The children who take part equal the oldest members in their gravity and woodenness. In some delightful scenes the demons, with hideous masks and abundant wigs of long, red-silk hair, spread deliberate and conventional terror among the buckram grandees, and, stamping the stage wildly, leaping and whirling, relieve the long-drawn seriousness of the trilogy. It is only when the performers are without masks that the scene is recognized as intentionally a light and amusing farce, while the roars of the audience are elicited by stately, ponderous, and time-honored puns, and plays upon words that a foreigner cannot appreciate.

Fine representations of the No may be seen at the Koyokwan club-house in Tokio, and in the audiences one beholds all the bureaucracy, the court circles, and a gathering of aristocratic families not elsewhere to be encountered.

The existing theatre and the legitimate drama are not yet three centuries old, and the name *shibai*, meaning turf places, or grass plot, implies the same evolution from out-door representations that the occidental drama had. There is no Shakespeare, nor Corneille, nor, indeed, any famous dramatist, whose works survive from an earlier day, to align the stage with literature and make its history. Authorship is rarely connected with the plays, and authors' royalties are unknown. Many of the novels of Baku have been dramatized, but most often anonymously. Plays are usually written in the simpler *hirakana*, or running characters, in which light romances and books for women are written, and this fact alone shows the esteem in which dramatic literature is held. Incidents in history, lives of warriors, heroes, and saints furnish themes for the drama, and all the common legends and fairy tales are put upon the stage.

That great classic, the affecting history of the " Forty-seven Ronins," is always popular, and the crack-brained heroisms of the days of chivalry fire the Japanese heart notwithstanding its passion for the foreign and modern. The trials, tortures, and miracles of the early days of Buddhism, and the warlike histories of the great feudal houses, furnish tragedies and sensational and spectacular plays without end. There are, also, romantic melodramas, emotional dramas, and comedies of delicious humor and satire.

New plays, while rare, are not theatrical events, and first nights by no means indicate success or failure. The play is tried on the audience, changed, cut, and altered as actors, manager, scene-painter, carpenter, and patrons desire, without consideration of the author's rights or feelings.

I once asked a great star who had written his play.

" I do not understand," said the tragedian; and a bystander explained that the manager had cut reports of a theft, a murder, and a shipwreck from a newspaper, and, discussing them with the star, evolved the outlines of a connected play and decided on the principal scenes and effects. A hack writer was then called in, who, under dictation, shaped the plot and divided it into scenes. The managerial council elaborated it further, allotting the parts, and the star then composed his lines to suit himself. In rehearsal the play was rounded, the diction altered, and each actor directed to write out his own part, after which a full transcript was made for the prompter.

As to the authorship of the play of the " Forty-seven Ronins," he said: "That is our country's history. We all know the story of their lives and glorious deaths, and many novelists and poets have written of them."

" But who made it into a drama?"

"Oh, every theatre has its own way of representing

the different scenes, although the great facts are historical and cannot be misrepresented, now that the Tokugawa's ban against the play is removed. Danjiro plays it in one way, and other actors have their versions, but none of them play it the same at every engagement, nor repeat just the same acts on every day of an engagement."

With dramatic authorship so vague and uncertain, the origin or author of any play is far to seek. Revivals and rotations of the old favorites constitute a manager's idea of attractions, a new scene or two, a novel feature, and some local picture or allusion being enough to satisfy the most *blasé* patron. No accurate libretto nor printed book of the play can thus exist, but the illustrated programmes give a pictorial outline of it—a veritable impressionist sketch, noting its salient features, and leaving all details to time and imagination. There are no dramatic unities, no three-act or five-act limitations, and no hampering laws of verse and rhythm. An orchestra and half-concealed chorus explains, heralds, and lauds the action, a survival of the No gradually disappearing with other things before the demand for shorter hours and briefer plays.

Women do not appear on the Japanese stage, female parts being played by men, who often make these roles their specialty, cultivating and using their voices always in a thin, high falsetto. The make-up, the voices, gait, action, and manner of some of these actors are wonderful, and Genoske, the greatest impersonator of female characters, when dressed for the part of some noble heroine, is an ideal beauty of the delicate, aristocratic type. Outside the great theatres, in plays and side-show entertainments, that may be compared with our dime museums, a woman is occasionally found on the stage ; and, a few years ago, a Tokio manager amazed the town with the performances of a company made up entirely of women. In the interludes, where jugglers and acrobats entertain the audience, women are sometimes seen. and. in time, plays will be cast for both sexes, and female stars will shine. The infant prodigy is known to the Japanese stage. and in some wonderfully pretty and affecting scenes in the " Ronins " little children utter their lines and go through their parts with great naturalness.

The great theatre of Tokio is the Shintomiza, a long, gabled building. ornamented above the row of entrance doors by pictures of scenes from the play. The street is lined with tea-houses. or restaurants, for a play is not a hap-hazard two-hour after-dinner incident. A man goes for the day. carefully making up his theatre party beforehand, the plays generally beginning at eleven o'clock in the morning. and ending at eight or nine in the evening. After a short run the hours during which the great actors appear and the great stage effects are made become known. and the spectator may time his visit accordingly. It is bad form for a Japanese of position to go to the theatre door. pay for a box. and enter it. He must send a servant, at least a day beforehand. to one of the tea-houses near the theatre to engage its attentions for the day. and through its agency secure a box. The tea-house people are the ticket speculators in league with the box-office. At the proper hour, the party assemble at the tea-house. and give orders for the lunch, dinner, and frequent teas to be served during the day. The tea-house attendants conduct them to their box. and at each intermission come to see what is wanted. bringing in at the dinner-hour the large lacquer *chow* boxes with their courses of viands. that their patrons may dine comfortably where they sit. Everybody smokes. and each box has its little tabako bon, with its cone of glowing coals to light the tiny pipes. the rat-tat of the pipes. as the ashes are knocked out, often making a chorus to the action.

Theatre buildings are light and flimsy wooden structures, with straw-mats and matting everywhere. They
are all alike—a square auditorium with a sloping floor,
a single low gallery, and a stage the full width of the
house. The floor space is divided into so-called boxes
by low railings, that serve as bridges for the occupants
to pass in and out. Visitors always sit on the floor, each
box being six feet square and designed for four people.
The gallery has one row of boxes at either side, several
rows facing the stage, and behind them a pen, where the
multitude stand and listen, paying one or two coppers
for each act. This gallery of the gods is called the "deaf
seat," but the deaf hear well enough to be vociferous.
The theatre-goer takes a check for his shoes, and racks
hanging full of wooden clogs are the ornaments of the
foyer. Within the building are booths for the sale of
fruits, tea, sweets, tobacco, toys, hair-pins, photographs
of the stars, and other notions, so that a box-party need
not leave the house in pursuit of any creature comforts.
The ventilation is too good, and the light and open construction invites wintry draughts.

Charges are made in detail, and the following is one
bill presented for a party of seven at a Yokohama theatre. No charge was made for the two family servants,
who came and went at will.

Admission (seven persons)	$ 98
Box	1 60
Carpeting, chairs, etc.	50
Messenger hire	10
Tea and confectionery	30
Persimmons, figs, and grapes	30
Eels and rice, etc. (seven persons)	3 50
Tea-house	1 00
Presents to servants	30
	$8 58

Received payment,
Fukkuya.

There is always a drop-curtain, generally ornamented with a gigantic character or solitary symbol, and often nowadays covered with picturesque advertisements. Formerly, so much of the play was given by day that no footlights and few lamps were used. In those good old days a black-shrouded mute hovered about each actor after dark, holding out a candle at the end of a long stick to illuminate his features, that the audience might see the fine play of expression. With the adoption of kerosene the stage was sufficiently lighted, and the Shintomiza has a full row of footlights, while the use of electricity will soon be general. The black mutes act as "supers" throughout all plays where changes are made or properties manœuvred while the curtain is up.

The actors enter the stage by two long, raised walks through the auditorium, so that they seem to come from without. These raised walks, on a level with the stage and the heads of the spectators in the floor boxes, are called the *hana michi*, or flower-walks, and as a popular actor advances his way is strewn with flowers. The exits are sometimes by the hana michi and sometimes by the wings, according to the scene.

The miniature scale of things Japanese makes it possible to fill a real scene with life-like details. The stage is always large enough for three or four actual houses to be set as a front. The hana michi is sufficiently broad for jinrikishas, *kagos*, and pack-horses, and with the illumination of daylight the unreality of the picture vanishes, and the spectator seems to be looking from some tea-house balcony on an every-day street scene. Garden, forest, and landscape effects are made by using potted trees, and shrubs uprooted for transplanting. The ever-ready bamboo is at hand and the tall dragon-grass, and the scene-painters produce extraordinary illusions in the backgrounds and wings. Some of the finest stage pictures I have seen were in Japan, and its stage ghosts, demons, and goblins would be impossible elsewhere. In the play of "Honest Sebi" there was a murder scene in a bamboo grove in a rainy twilight that neither Henry Irving nor Jules Claretie could have surpassed; and in "The Vampire Cat of the Nabeshima," or "The Enchanted Cat of the Tokaido," a beautiful young woman changed, before the eyes of the audience, to a hideous monster, with a celerity more ghastly than that which transforms Dr. Jekyll into Mr. Hyde.

Japanese theatres use the revolving stage, which has been their original and unique possession for two centuries. A section of the stage flooring, twenty or thirty feet in diameter, revolves like a railway turn-table, on lignum-vitæ wheels, moved by coolies below stairs, who put their shoulders to projecting bars, as with the silk-press. The wings come to the edge of this circle, and at a signal a whole house whirls around and shows its other rooms or its garden. Sometimes the coolies turn too quickly, and the actors are rolled out of sight gesticulating and shouting. The scenery is painted on wings that draw aside, or on flies hoisted overhead. Curiously enough, the signal for opening the curtain is the same as that used at the Comédie Française—three blows on the floor with a big stick.

The Japanese theatre of to-day is given over to realism and the natural school, and Jefferson and Coquelin are not more quietly, easily, and entirely the characters they assume than Danjiro, their Japanese fellow-Thespian. The play is a transcript of actual life, and everything moves in an every-day way, though Japanese manners and customs often seem stilted, artificial, and unnatural to the brusque Occidental, with his direct and brutally practical etiquette. Pathos is always deep and long drawn out, and the last tear is extracted from the eyes of audiences quick to respond to emotional appeals. Tragedies are very tragic and murders very sanguinary.

Death is generally accomplished by edged tools, and the antics of the fencers, the wonderful endurance of the hacked victims, and the streams of red paint and red silk ravellings that ooze forth delight the audiences, who shout and shriek their " *Ya! Ya!*" and " *Yeh! Yeh!*" The swordsmen are often acrobats and jugglers in disguise, who enliven the extended slaughters with thrilling *tours de force*. *Seppuku* the honorable death, or *hara-kiri* as it is most commonly known, is always received with breathless interest and wild applause, and the self-disembowelling of the hero, with a long last oration, still seems to the Japanese something fine and heroic and the most complete revenge upon an insulting foe.

The detail and minuteness with which everything is explained, and the endless etiquette and circumlocution, are thoroughly Japanese. Little is left to the imagination in their dramatic art, and an ordinary play has more sub-plots and characters than one of Dickens's novels. With the rapid adoption of new customs, the theatre is becoming the only conserver of the old life and manners.

If the Japanese stage has its blood-and-thunder and its tank drama, it has also its millinery play. The costumes alone are often worth going to see, and the managers announce the appearance of historic brocades and armor worthy of museums. Danjiro owns and wears a sacred coat of mail that belonged to one of the Ronins, and his appearance in it is the signal for the maddest applause. Such treasures of costume and of armor are bequeathed from father to son, and from retiring star to favorite pupil. As tokens of high approval rich and noble patrons send to actors rare costumes, swords, pipes, and articles of personal use. Excited spectators even throw such tributes upon the stage. One approving foreigner, seeing the rain of hats, coats, obis, and tobacco-pouches, once tossed his hat down. Later the manager and the actor's valet returned the hat and asked for ten

SCENE FROM THE PLAY OF THE "FORTY-SEVEN RONINS."

dollars, as those seeming gifts from the audience were merely pledges or forfeits, to be afterwards redeemed by money under the star's regular schedule of prices. As protests availed nothing, and the whole house only roared in derision when he said that he had wished Danjiro to keep the battered derby as a souvenir, the enthusiast paid his forfeit.

The audience is as interesting a study as the players, each little square box being another stage, whereon the picturesque drama of Japanese life is enacted. Trays of tea and sweetmeats and single teapots are constantly supplied to the spectators by attendants, who tread the narrow partition rails between the boxes like acrobats. Whenever the curtain closes there is a swift scurrying of these Ganymedes to the boxes, while the children climb upon the partition rails and the hana michi, or run about the theatre, even romping upon the stage itself, and peeping under the curtain to see what the carpenters are hammering; all with perfect ease and unconsciousness.

Visiting the star in his dressing-room is a simple commercial transaction. The actors make a fixed charge for receiving such visits, deriving a regular income from this source. Danjiro's dressing-room is high up among the flies back of the Shintomiza stage, with a window looking down upon it, so that he needs no call-boy. He often shouts down to the stage himself, and has the action of the play delayed or hastened, according to his toilet or his humors. Nothing could be more scornful and indifferent than Danjiro's treatment of the high-priced visitors to his dressing-room. Fulsome flattery, if offered with the florid and elaborate Japanese forms, will mollify him, and the old fellow — eighth idolized Danjiro in succession — will finally offer tea, present a hair-pin to a lady, or write an autograph on a fan in his most captivating stage daimio manner. When making up for a part, the great actor sits on the mat before a large swinging mirror. Except for a character face little disguise is used, as daylight spoils its effect. Three or four meek valets wait upon this spoiled and whimsical old autocrat, and the whole theatre staff attends. The value of his wardrobe, kept in immense covered bamboo baskets, is very great, and its care a serious matter. Part of it was once stolen, and when the whole Tokio police force succeeded in restoring it Danjiro announced that he could never again wear what the touch of a thief had defiled.

Genoske, fourth of his name and line, and Sodanje, a cousin of Danjiro, equally prove the heredity of Japanese genius, and are favorites of the Tokio public. Young actors pay the great stars for the privilege of joining their companies, and studying their methods. Danjiro is said to receive three thousand dollars from the Shintomiza theatre for the year or season, which lasts from early fall until after the cherry blossoms. His connection with the Shintomiza is like that of a *societaire* with the Comédie Française. Yet he plays in other Tokio theatres, has filled engagements in other cities, and everywhere receives from perquisites, fees, and gifts more than the amount of his salary.

The Japanese artist is fully aware of the aid ingenious advertising may lend to genius. Drawing-room engagements do not yet contribute a part of the income of a great actor; but such a one was once brought to drink tea at a foreign house, and obligingly recited from his great roles, and through the interpreter, talked most interestingly to us of his art and stage business. In a few days the native newspapers, the vernacular press, as the British dailies term it, contained accounts of a great entertainment offered this favorite actor by some foreign residents, and the simple afternoon tea of six people was lost to view in the description of the elaborate banquet and attending crowd.

The Government exercises a certain censorship of the stage, as of the press, suppressing an obnoxious play, and arresting manager and company if necessary. No allusions to present political events are allowed, and the authorities permit the expression of no disturbing ideas. The Tokugawas exercised this censorship towards the play of the " Forty-seven Ronins," because its main argument and many of its scenes reflected too clearly the corrupt practises of the Shogun's court. Even its name was changed, and, until the Restoration, it was presented as the *Chiushingura* (Loyal League), and the scenes strayed far from historic fact. Since the new era, managers advertise their representations as most closely following the actual records, and every fresh contribution from historian or antiquarian is availed of.

CHAPTER XI

THE IMPERIAL FAMILY

EUROPEAN sovereigns and reigning families are parvenus compared to the ruler and the imperial house of Japan, which shows an unbroken line from the accession of Jimmu Tenno, the first Emperor in 660 B.C., down to the present son of Heaven, Mutsu Hito, one hundred and twenty-first Emperor of his line.

During the feudal period, the Emperors, virtually prisoners of their vassals, the Shoguns, lived and died within the yellow palace walls of Kioto, knowing nothing of their subjects, and unknown by them. After death, each was deified under a posthumous appellation, and there his history ceased. Too sacred a being to be spoken of by his personal name, at the mention of his title all Japanese make an unconscious reverence even now. When his patronymic was written, it was purposely left incomplete by the omission of one stroke of the writing-brush. In the spoken language, the ruler is the Shujo, the Heika, or the Tenno, while in the written language he is the Tenno, the Kotei, or the Mikado. The Empress is the Kogo in both the spoken and the written language, and the honorific *sama* follows all of these imperial appellations.

Mutsu Hito, the most significant figure in Japanese history, was born in the Kioto palace, November 3, 1852, and, taught and trained as imperial princes had been before him, succeeded to the throne after the death of his father, February 13, 1867. In the following autumn the Shogun sent in his formal resignation, gave back the supreme power to the rightful ruler, and retired to Osaka. In February, 1868, the Emperor, not yet sixteen years of age, received the foreign envoys in the Kioto palace with uncovered face; then, defeating the rebellious Shogun at Osaka, removed his capital to Yeddo, and chose the name Meiji (enlightenment), to designate the era of his reign.

As seen at the rare court functions, at military reviews, and races, the Emperor is easily the central figure. Taller than the average of his race, and possessing great dignity and majesty, his slow, military step and trailing sword effectually conceal the unequal gait rheumatism sometimes obliges. He wears a trimmed beard, and his features, more decided and strongly marked than is usual with the aristocratic type of Japanese countenance, wear a calm and composure as truly Oriental as imperial. In public he wears the uniform of generalissimo of the army, a heavily-frogged and braided one of dark-blue broadcloth in winter, and of white duck in summer, with a gold-mounted sword and many decorations. In recognition of the honors and orders conferred upon him by other royalties, the Emperor bestows the cordon and jewel of the princely Order of the Chrysanthemum. The

Order of the Rising Sun is given for merit and distinguished services, and its red button is worn by many foreigners as well as natives.

Of late, the Emperor has abandoned his attempts to learn English and German, and relies upon interpreters, but he reads translations of foreign literature with great interest. When he passes through the streets, he is received with silent reverence, an advance guard of police and a body-guard of lancers escorting him. While his own people never shout or cheer, he accepts very graciously the foreign custom, and bows an acknowledgment to the hurrahs that sometimes greet him at Yokohama. While the Emperor has been absorbed in the changing affairs of state during the two decades of his reign, he still seems, in comparison with European sovereigns, to dwell in absolute quiet and seclusion. Often, for weeks together, he remains within the palace grounds, where he has riding courts, archery, and rifle ranges, well-stocked fish-ponds, and every means of amusing himself. Disliking the sea, he has no yacht, a chartered mail-steamer or man-of-war carrying him to naval stations or new fortifications, when the railroad is impracticable. His mountain palaces and remote game preserves he never visits.

Immediately after establishing his court at Yeddo, the boy-Emperor returned to Kioto to wed Haruko, daughter of Ichijo Takada, a *kuge*, or court noble of the highest rank. The marriage was solemnized by some Shinto ceremony within the temple of the palace, a ceremony so sacred and private that no Japanese even conjectures its form.

The Empress Haruko, born May 29, 1850, was educated in the strictest conventions of old Japan, and taught only the Chinese classics, her own literature and poetic composition, the use of the koto, the forms of cha no yu, needle-work, and the arrangement of flowers

—a broad and most liberal education for a maiden even of high degree.

Upon her marriage, an extraord'nary life opened before the little Empress, demanding a very unusual activity and study, courage, adaptiveness, and comprehension. She is poetic as well as practical, and her poems are not only traced on imperial screens and kakemono in autograph characters, but several of them have been set to music as well.

Even now, her Majesty is more delicately pretty than her younger sisters, although for years an invalid. She is short in stature, slender, and small, with the long, oval face and refined features of the ideal aristocratic type of Japanese beauty. At her marriage, she shaved her eyebrows, painted two shadowy suggestions of them high up on her forehead, and blackened her teeth, in accordance with Japanese custom ; but after a few years, she ceased to disfigure herself in this way. It was an event. in 1873, when she gave her first audience to the envoys' wives. It cost the court chamberlains months of study to arrange for the appearance of the Emperor and Empress together, to reconcile the pretensions of their suites as to rank and precedence. and to harmonize the Occidental, chivalrous ideas of deference to women with the unflattering estimate of the Orient. When. on the day of the declaration of the new constitution (February 11, 1890), the Emperor and Empress rode side by side in the same state carriage through the streets of Tokio, and when, that night, he offered his arm to lead her to a twin arm-chair in the state dining-hall, a new era was begun in Japanese history.

The Empress has her secretaries and readers, and gives a part of each day to informal audiences. She visits her schools and hospitals, and makes liberal purchases at charity bazaars. She exercises in the saddle within the palace grounds, and drives in a brougham with half-drawn curtains, her men on the box wearing a dark-blue livery with red cords and facings, silver buttons, and cocked hats.

IN THE PALACE GARDENS

One of the two annual imperial garden-parties is given when the chrysanthemums are in bloom, and the other at the time of the cherry blossoms. The etiquette of these is quite simple, although an appearance at one is still equivalent to a presentation at court. A few days before the festivity each guest receives a large chrysanthemum-bordered card:

November —, ——.

By order of their Majesties, the Emperor and Empress, the Minister of State for the Household Department presents his compliments to ———, and asks their company at the "Chrysanthemum Party" at the garden of the Imperial Temporary Palace on the 8th inst., at 3 o'clock in the afternoon.

On an accompanying slip are these instructions:

Frock-coat required.
To alight at the "Kurumayose" after entering the palace gate.
This card to be shown to officers in attendance on arrival.
No party to be held if the day happens rainy.

The guests having assembled in the gardens at the hour indicated, the Kimigayo, or national anthem, announces the approach of the imperial personages. The Emperor, the Empress, and their suite, passing between the rows of guests and the flower-tents, lead the way to marquees on the lawn, where a collation is served, the Emperor addressing a few remarks to the ministers and envoys as he greets them. Sometimes special presentations are made to him and the Empress, and often the Empress summons an envoy's wife or a peeress to her, while she sits at table. After another tour of the flower-tents, the company, following the imperial lead, desert the gardens. Calls of ceremony must be made upon the wife of the premier within one week after these parties.

When the Empress and her ladies wore the old dress the garden-parties at the palace were wonderfully picturesque and distinctly Japanese. It was my good fortune to attend the chrysanthemum fête of 1885, when the Empress and her suite made their last appearance in the red *hakama* and loose brocade kimonos of the old regime. The day was warm, with the brilliant autumnal tints peculiar to Japan, clear and sunny. There were rows of chrysanthemum beds in the Asakasa gardens,

shielded from sun and wind by matted awnings, screens, and silk hangings, and all the myriad flowers were at one even and perfect period of unfolding. Under silk tents by themselves stood single plants bearing from two hundred to four hundred blossoms each, every blossom full and symmetrical.

The peeresses waiting in that sunny garden were most brilliant figures, rivalling the glow of the flowers in their splendid old brocade robes. At last came the Empress and the whole gorgeous train of her attendants, following the shore of the mirror-like lake, past camellia hedges to the esplanade of the upper garden of the great Asakasa park. As the Emperor was housed by illness, the Empress, for the first time, conducted a general court ceremony alone. Her costume consisted of the loose hakama, or divided skirt, of the heaviest scarlet silk, under a long loose kimono of dull heliotrope, brocaded with conventional wistarias and the imperial crests in white. No outer obi, or sash, was worn, and the neck was closed high with surplice folds of rainbow-tinted silks. Many under-kimonos of fine white and scarlet silk showed beneath the long, square sleeves of the heavy brocade kimono. The imperial hair was stiffened into a thin halo behind the face, falling thence to the waist, but tied here and there with bits of silky white rice-paper, like that of a Shinto priestess. Above her forehead shone a little golden ornament in the shape of the *ho-o*, or phœnix, and she carried a parasol and an old court fan of painted sticks of wood, wound with long cords of many-colored silks. The dignity and majesty of the little woman were most impressive. Every head bowed low, and when she had passed eyes were lifted to her reverently and admiringly. All the princesses and peeresses following her wore a similar costume, many of their brocade kimonos being stiffened with embroidery and gold thread, and making dazzling effects of color. When, in the brilliant sunset flush, the imperial train retraced its steps, its kaleidoscopic flashes of white and gold and color reflected in the still lake, and showing vividly as the ladies formed in a semicircle on the lawn, while the Empress withdrew to her apartments, there ended a series of pictures so beautiful that they seemed an illusion of the imagination.

Before the following April Paris fashions had set in with great rigor, and all the soft, pink reflections from the clouds of cherry blossoms in the Hama Rikiu palace garden could not give the groups of little women in dark, ugly, close-fitting gowns any likeness to the beautiful assemblages of other years. Gone were poetry and picturesqueness. Progress and Philistia were come. Except for the costumes of the Chinese and Korean legations, and that of the Chinese Minister's wife, with its cap-like ornaments of filigree and pearls, and tiny jewelled slippers, nothing Oriental or Asiatic in aspect remained to that court gathering.

The Empress ordained and defended this change of dress in a famous court circular, whose chief argument seemed to be that the alteration from the sitting and kneeling etiquette of the Orient to the standing etiquette of the Occident required western fashions for women as well as men. Every lover of the picturesque protested, but it was suspected that this manifesto was a shrewd political move of Count Ito's to convince the treaty powers that the Japanese do not differ from other civilized people. Should the sacrifice of the old life and the beautiful national dress help to secure for Japan a revision of the shameful and unjust treaties forced upon her from 1854 to 1858, and promote the political liberty and commercial prosperity of the country, the Empress's patriotic iconoclasm may be justified.

The sacredness of the imperial person long postponed her Majesty's change of fashion, as no ignoble dress-

maker could be allowed to touch her. Countess Ito, the
clever wife of the premier, and leader of foreign fashions
at court, was finally chosen as lay figure, to be fitted until a model could be made. The Empress now wears
European dress altogether, conduct little short of heroic
for one accustomed only to the loose, simple, and comfortable garments of her country. Her gowns are made
of Japanese fabrics, and a lace school under her patron-
age supplies her with flounces and trimmings. At in-
door state ceremonies, low bodices and court trains are
prescribed, and the Empress wears a tiara, *rivière*, and
innumerable ornaments of diamonds. The court ladies,
who formerly wore no ornaments but the single long
hair-pin and the gold balls and trifles on the obi cord,
have been seized by a truly American craze for diamonds,
and greatly covet the new Order with cordon and jewelled star lately established by the Empress.

In adopting the expensive foreign dress court ladies
ruthlessly sacrificed irreplaceable heirlooms of rich old
brocades and embroideries. For a long time their countenances and mien betrayed the discomfort of the new
dress, but they soon acquired ease with familiarity, and
no Japanese woman, in her first Parisian gown, was ever
such a burlesque and caricature as are the foreign visitors who essay the kimono, and, blind to the ridiculous,
are photographed with its folds and fulness all awry.
Only two foreign women have I ever seen who could
wear Japanese dress gracefully in the Japanese way, with
full regard to the meaning which each color, fold, pucker,
and cord implies.

Asahiko, the Empress Dowager, one of the Kujo family of kuges, and of Fujiwara descent, has her separate
palace and court, where old customs are followed. Born
in 1834, she lives by the traditional code, and the use of
a landau with liveried and cockaded men on the box is
almost her only concession to the new order. She never

appears at any of the state functions at the palace, though the ladies of her suite are sometimes seen in the impe-rial loges at a Koyokwan No performance, when given for the benefit of her pet charities.

The Empress Dowager has nominal charge of the im-perial nurseries in the Nakayama Yashiki, where the chil-dren of the Emperor and his inferior wives remain until their fourth or fifth years. These wives are all of kugé birth, and have establishments within the palace enclos-ure. They are an Oriental survival, of which little is said or definitely known, although they still have a fixed rank.

The Empress Haruko has no children, and Prince Haru, the Crown Prince, is the son of the Emperor and Madame Yanagiwara. One little imperial princess is liv-ing, but ten imperial children have died. Prince Haru was born September 6, 1879, proclaimed heir apparent August 31, 1887, and elected Crown Prince November 3, 1889, dispossessing as heir to the throne Prince Arisu-gawa Takehito, a young cousin, who had been adopted by the Emperor in the absence of any direct heirs. Prince Haru attends the Nobles' school, reciting in classes with other boys, and enjoying a more democratic life than any other crown prince of this era. He is quick, energetic, and ambitious, inclined to foreign ways, and is altogether the most emancipated and untram-melled little man in Tokio. When he is older Prince Haru will be sent around the world to see other coun-tries and courts, and it is prophesied that this energet-ic young man will make great changes in the already changed order of things. To Emperor, Empress, and Empress Dowager he is a marvel, but to him these au-gust personages are but ordinary mortals. Yet the princeling can be a stickler for etiquette, and boy com-panions venturing too far, or becoming too democratic, have been sharply brought to task by Jimmu Tenno's latest descendant.

CHAPTER XII

TOKIO PALACES AND COURT

THIRTY different places have been the capital and home of the Emperors of Japan, and Omi, Settsu, and Yamashiro were imperial provinces before the Tokugawa's city of Yeddo (bay's gate) became Tokio, the eastern capital and seat of imperial power. The Shogun's old castle, the Honmaru, or the Shiro, was the imperial palace until destroyed by fire in May, 1873. and its interior is said to have been far more splendid than the Nijo castle in Kioto. The yashiki of the Tokugawa daimio of Kiushiu, on the high ground of the Akasaka quarter, next sheltered the imperial household, though ill adapted to its changing and growing needs.

At the end of 1888 the Emperor took possession of the new imperial palace, which had been six years in building, and which stands upon the ruins of the Shogun's castle, protected by all the rings of moats. Two drawbridges and two ponderous old towered gate-ways defend the entrance to the front wing of the building, a long yellow brick edifice, with the conical towers and steep roof of a French chateau. The offices of the Imperial Household Department are assigned to this foreign wing, except for which the new structure is such a labyrinthine collection of temple-like buildings, as the old palace at Kioto. Built on sloping and uneven ground, there is a constant change of level in the innumerable roofs and floors. Before it was completed a tour of the palace occupied a full hour, and attendants and workmen were often lost in the maze. Combining Japanese and European architecture, decorations, furnishings, and ideas, the palace is a jumble of unsatisfactory incongruities, nobody being found to admire thatched roofs and electric lights, partition walls of sliding paper screens and steam-heating apparatus, a modern ball-room, and a No dance pavilion all side by side.

Each lofty state apartment is a building by itself, the outer galleries on the four sides being the corridors that touch other corridors at their angles. Plate-glass doors in maroon lacquer frames, with superb metal mountings, take the place of the usual paper *shoji*; but with the low eaves and the light entering from the level of the floor, the rooms need all their Edison lamps. Unfortunately, the best examples of national decorative art are not preserved in this national palace. Only the richly panelled ceilings are at all Japanese or worthy their place. The famous embroidered ceiling and embroidered wainscoting in the great drawing-room, and some *makimonos* in the private rooms, exhibit the best Kioto needle-work. This wonderful ceiling, costing ten thousand dollars, is panelled with yard-squares of gold-thread tapestry, upon which are embroidered crest-like circles of various flowers. The wainscoting is green damask wrought with fruits, and the walls of the drawing-room are hung with a neutral-tinted damask.

The beautiful Japanese woods and the marvellous Japanese carvers were set aside, that the steam factories of Hamburg might supply the cheap and ugly oak furniture of the banquet-hall. The state table, seating one hundred people, surrounds three sides of a square. The imperial arm - chairs are at the middle of the board, facing elaborate buffets, framing painted tapestry-panels of the most tawdry German design. The ball-room has a costly inlaid floor, and is decorated in white and gold. The throne-room has nothing Japanese but the crests in the panelled ceiling. A large gilded arm - chair stands on a red-carpeted dais, with canopy and curtains of red plush, the sacred sword and seal resting on lacquer tables beside it. At court functions the Empress stands on a dais below and to the right of the throne, with the imperial princes and princesses grouped about her. The members of the diplomatic corps are placed at the Emperor's left, the ministers and higher officials fill the space facing the throne, and the imperial guard line the gallery corridors that surround the throne-room.

In the private apartments of the Emperor and Empress moquette carpets, plush furniture, and easy-chairs confess foreign influence and etiquette. The old rules of the simplicity of a Shinto shrine in the sovereign's dwelling are observed in leaving all the wood-work unpainted, while wax-candles and open grates replace the electric bulbs and gilded radiators of the official parts of the palace. Some of the private rooms display exquisite panelled and coffered ceilings of pure white pine, or the beautiful gray bog-wood. Each suite has one room in pure Japanese style, and a tiny box for celebrating the rites of cha no yu with a favored four. The Emperor's sleeping-room is the same unlighted, unventilated dark closet which his ancestors used. This sleeping-room is E in the accompanying diagram, surrounded by rooms occupied at night by his attendants and guards.

Above this floor is a suite of studies, libraries, and secretaries' rooms, all finished in the same exquisite woods, that show their natural grain and color. There is a separate suite of rooms for the Emperor's toilet and wardrobe, a robing and disrobing room, and an exquisite Japanese bath - room with inlaid floor and walls. The sovereign uses the regular oval wooden tub of his people, which is filled from a well in the adjoining court by means of the primitive bucket and rope. The screens in these private rooms are undecorated, or at the most only flecked with gold-leaf. From time to time, by special command, artists will decorate these, and squares of colored paper put here and there upon them invite the autograph poems of the tea-drinking improvisators.

Somewhere in the recesses of the palace is a chapel or Shinto shrine, but the officials are very reticent concerning it. It is known that the mortuary tablets of the Emperor's ancestors are there, simple *ihai*, or pieces of pine wood, upon which are written the posthumous names of the deceased rulers. Official bulletins often announce that a newly appointed minister of the cabinet, or a diplomatic officer about departing for his post is " ordered to worship the cenotaphs in the imperial chapel," before an audience with the Emperor. Presumably, such devotions are a form equivalent to the oath of allegiance in other countries. Upon the anniversaries of the death of certain of his ancestors, on the days of the spring and autumn festival, when the first rice is sown and harvested, as well as before any great ceremonial, it is announced that the Emperor will worship in the imperial chapel. The aged Prince Kuni Asahiko is conductor of divine services to the imperial family; but everything about that simple, formal state religion is baffling and incomprehensible, and no one knows what form the Shinto services in the palace assume.

The Emperor used to give a Japanese banquet on the morning of his birthday to princes, ministers, and envoys. Chopsticks were used, and the imperial health was drunk from saké-cups of fine egg-shell porcelain, decorated with chrysanthemums and broken diaper patterns in gold, which the guests carried away with them as souvenirs. That celebration and the New-year breakfast are now state banquets, served in foreign fashion, with sovereign and consort seated at the head of the room. Indeed, the entire service of the palace and of the Emperor's table is European; silver, porcelain, and glass being marked with the imperial crest of the sixteen-petalled chrysanthemum, and the *kiri*

IMPERIAL SAKÉ-CUP

mon of the *Paulownia imperialis* appearing in the decorative design woven in the white silk napery and traced on the delicate porcelain service. The palace lackeys are uniformed in dress-coats with many cords and aiguillettes, striped vests, knee-breeches, white silk stockings, and buckled shoes. Their costume resembles that of the Vienna palace, colored sketches of which Prince Komatsu sent home during his winter stay on the Danube. The palace tiring-women wear the garb of Kioto days, purple hakama and russet silk kimonos, and are the most fascinating and almost the only Japanese spectacle in the imperial precincts. In all modifications the usages of the Berlin court have been followed, and no Prussian military martinet or court chamberlain could be more punctilious in matters of etiquette than the Japanese court officials.

Of the Empress Dowager's palace only its gate-way is known. The Hama Rikiu palace is a sea-shore villa, owing its beautiful garden to the Shoguns, but it is occupied only when the ministers of state give balls, or foreign guests of the Emperor are domiciled there, as was General Grant. An imperial garden-party is held in its confines each spring, and, with the Fukiage gardens adjoining the new palace, it is visited upon presentation of special cards of admission issued by the legations.

For the support of these palaces and the expenses of the imperial family the Imperial Household Department's expenditures were 3,000,000 yens in 1889.

Tokio court circles have, of course, their factions and cliques, their wars and triumphs, and the favor of the sovereign is the object of perpetual scheming and intriguing.

The peerage of Japan numbers ten princes, twenty-five marquises, eighty counts, three hundred and fifty-two viscounts, and ninety-eight barons. All the old kugé families are enrolled in this new peerage, and such daimios of the Shogun's court as gave aid and allegiance to the Emperor, or made honorable surrender in the conflict of 1868. Rank and title were conferred upon many of the samurai also, the leaders in the work of the Restoration, and the statesmen, who have advised and led in the wonderful progress of these last twenty years; but the old kugés have never brought themselves to accept the pardoned daimios and ennobled samurai of other days. It is the Oriental version of the relations between the Faubourg St. Germain, the aristocracy of the empire, and the bureaucracy of the present French republic.

The imperial princes of the blood, all nearly related to the Emperor, rank above the ten created princes, who head the list of the nobility. Five of these ten princely houses are the old Gosekke, the first five of the one hundred and fifty-five kugé families comprising the old Kioto court. With the Gosekke, which includes the Ichijo, Kujo, Takatsukasa, Nijo, and Konoye families, rank, since 1883, the houses of Sanjo, Iwakura, Shimadzu, Mori, and Tokugawa, sharing with them the privilege of offering the bride to the heir-apparent.

The Emperor visits personally at the houses of these

ten princes, and recently the Tokugawas entertained him with a fencing-match and a No dance in old style, the costumes and masks for which had been used at Tokugawa fêtes for centuries. In accordance with other old customs, a sword by a famous maker was presented to the guest of honor, and a commemorative poem offered in a gold lacquer box. Yet the head of the Tokugawa house is a grandson of the Shogun who first refused to treat with Commodore Perry, and son of Keiki, the arch rebel and last of the Shoguns, who for so long lived forgotten as a private citizen on a small estate near Shidzuoka, keeping alive no faction, awaking no interest—attaining, in fact, a political Nirvana.

Under new titles the old fiefs are lost sight of and old associations broken up. The marquises, counts, and barons of to-day are slender, dapper little men, wearing the smartest and most irreproachable London clothes, able to converse in one or two foreign languages on the subjects that interest cosmopolitans of their rank in other empires, and are with difficulty identified with their feudal titles. The Daimio of Kaga has become the Marquis Maeda, his sister married the Emperor's cousin, and the great yashiki of their ancestors has given way to the buildings of the Imperial University. The Daimio of Satsuma is now Prince Shimadzu. It is not easy to associate these modern men-about-town, who dance at state balls, who play billiards and read the files of foreign newspapers at the Rokumeikwan, who pay afternoon calls, attend teas, garden-parties, dinners, concerts, and races; who have taken up poker and tennis with equal ardor, and are victimized at charity fairs and bazaars, with their pompous, stately, two-sworded, brocade and buckram bound ancestors.

There are great beauties, favorites, and social leaders among the ladies of the court circle, and the change in their social position and personal importance is incred-

ible. Japanese matrons, who, a few years ago, led the
most quiet and secluded existence, now preside with
ease and grace over large establishments, built and
maintained like the official residences of London or
Berlin. Their struggles with the difficulties of a new
language, dress, and etiquette were heroic. Mothers
and daughters studied together with the same English
governess, and princesses and diplomats' wives, returning from abroad, gave new ideas to their friends at
home. Two Japanese ladies, now foremost at court,
are graduates of Vassar College, and many high officials
are happily married to foreign wives; American, English, and German women having assumed Japanese
names with their wedding vows. The court has its
reigning beauty in the wife of the grand master of ceremonies, the richest peer of his day, and representative
of that family which gave its name to the finest porcelain known to the ceramic art of the empire.

Tokio society delights in dancing, and every one at
court dances well. Leaders of fashion go through the
quadrille d'honneur, with which state balls open, and
follow the changes of the lancers with the exactness of
soldiers on drill, every step and movement as precise
and finished as the bending of the fingers in cha no yu.
The careless foreigner who attempts to dance an unfamiliar figure repents him of his folly. Japanese politeness is incomparable, but the sedateness, the precision,
and exactness of the other dancers in the set will re-
proach the blunderer until he feels himself a criminal.
The ball is the more usual form of state entertainments.
The prime-minister gives a ball on the night of the
Emperor's birthday, and the governor of Tokio gives a
ball each winter. From time to time the imperial princes
and the ministers of state offer similar entertainments,
and every legation has its ball-room. The members of
the diplomatic corps are as much in social unison with

the higher Japanese circles as it is possible to be with such subjects at any capital, and the round of tiffins, dinners, garden-parties, and small dances makes Tokio very gay during the greater part of the year.

The first formal visiting of the season begins in October, and by May social life is at an end until hot weather is over. Lent makes little break in the social chain. Great seriousness and exactness in social usage is inherent in this high-bred people. Visits of ceremony are scrupulously paid within the allotted time, and a newly-arrived official in Tokio finds no diminution of the card leaving and visiting which awaits him in any other capital. At the houses of the imperial princes cards are not left, the visitor inscribing his name in a book in the hall. After each state ball, a guest must call at once upon the princess, or minister's wife, who presided, and any remissness strikes his name from her list.

Garden-parties are the favorite expression of Tokio hospitality. All official residences in the city have fine grounds, and many ministers of state own suburban villas. A few of the legations are able to entertain in the same way, and many military officers make the garden of the old Mito yashiki, now the Arsenal grounds, the scene of their courtesies.

There is a stately court journal, which is the official bulletin, but Tokio has not yet set up a paper of society gossip and scandal for the rigorous censorship of the Japanese press to expunge; nor are there books of court memoirs. Yet what memoirs could be more interesting than those that might be written by the men and women who were born in feudal times, who have lived through the exciting days of the Restoration, and have watched the birth and growth of New Japan.

CHAPTER XIII

THE SUBURBS OF TOKIO

THE suburbs of Tokio are full of holiday resorts for the people and the beautiful villas of nobles. To the north-east. in Oji, are the Government chemical works and paper mills, where rough bits of mulberry-wood are turned into papers of a dozen kinds, the silkiest tissue-paper, smooth, creamy writing-paper, thick parchment, bristol-board. and the thin paper for artists and etchers. On a sheet of the heaviest parchment paper I once stood and was lifted from the floor, the fabric showing no mark of rent or strain, and it is wellnigh impossible to tear even a transparent Oji letter sheet. The Oji tea-house has a famous garden, and in autumn Oji's hill-sides blaze with colored maples, and then the holiday makers mark the place for their own.

Waseda, the northern suburb, contains an old temple, a vast, gloomy bamboo-grove, and the villa of Countess Okuma, to whose genius for landscape-gardening is also due the French Legation's paradise of a garden, in the heart of the city, that place having been Count Okuma's town residence before he sold it to the French Government. From Waseda's rice fields a greater marvel grew.

Meguro, south of Tokio, is a place of sentimental pilgrimage to the lovers of Gompachi and Komurasaki, the Abelard and Heloise of the East, around whose tomb the trees flutter with paper poems, and prayers. In the temple grounds are falling streams of water. beneath which, summer and winter, praying pilgrims stand. to be thus pumped on for their sins. Similar penitents may be seen at a little temple niched in the bluff of Mississippi Bay. Meguro has an annual azalea fête and a celebration of the maple-leaf, and its resident nobles, among whom is General Saigo, give feasts in honor of the season's blooms.

The Sengakuji temple, near Shinagawa, is a sacred spot and shrine of chivalry, the burial-place of the Forty-seven Ronins; and here come pious pilgrims to say a prayer and leave a stick of burning incense, and view the images and relics in the little temple.

Near Omori, half-way between Yokohama and Tokio, Professor Morse discovered the shell-heaps of prehistoric man. The neighborhood is made beautiful by old groves, old temples and shrines, tiny villages, picturesque farm-houses, and hedge-lined roads, while Ikegami's temples shine upon the hill that stands an evergreen island in the lake of greener rice fields or golden stubble. Here died Nichiren, founder of the Buddhist sect bearing his name. For six centuries these splendid temples have resounded with the chantings of his priesthood, who still expound his teachings to the letter. The Nichiren sect is the largest, richest, most influential, and aggressive in Japan. They are the Protestants and Presbyterians of the Buddhist religion; firm, hard, and unrelenting in their faith, rejecting all other creeds as false, and zealously proselyting. Nichiren was a great scholar, who, poring over Chinese and Sanscrit sutras, believed himself to have discovered the true and hidden meaning of the sacred books. His labors were colossal, and though exiled, imprisoned, tortured, and condemned to death, he lived to see his followers increasing to a great body of true believers, and himself established as high-priest over the temples of Ikegami. In the popular play " Nichiren," one has thrilling evidence of what the pious founder and his disciples endured.

On the twelfth and thirteenth of each October special services are held in memory of Nichiren, which thou-

sands of people attend. On the first day of this matsuri
the railway is crowded with passengers. Bonfires and
strings of lanterns mark the Omori station by night, and
by day the neighboring matsuri is announced by tall
bamboo poles, from which spring whorls of reeds covered
with huge paper flowers. These giant flower-stalks are
the conventional sign for festivities, and when a row of
them is planted by the road-side, or paraded up and
down with an accompaniment of gongs, the holiday spirit
responds at once. The quiet country road is blockaded
with hundreds of jinrikishas going to and returning from
Ikegami's terraced gate-ways. Men, women, and children, priests, beggars, and peddlers pack the highway.
The crowd is amazing—as though these thousands of
people had been suddenly conjured from the ground, or
grown from some magician's powder—for nothing could
be quieter than Omori lanes on all the other days of the
year.

Along the foot-paths of the fields women in tightly-
wrapped kimonos with big umbrellas over their beautifully-dressed heads; young girls with the scarlet petti-
coats and gay hair-pins indicative of maidenhood; little
girls and boys with smaller brothers and sisters strapped
on their backs, trudge along in single files, high above
the stubble patches, to the great matsuri. In farm-house
yards persimmon-trees hang full of mellow, golden fruit,
and the road is literally lined with these apples of the
Hesperides. Peddlers sit on their heels behind their
heaped persimmons and busily tie straw to the short
stems of the fruit, that the buyer may carry his purchase
like a bunch of giant golden grapes. Fries, stews, bakes,
and grills scent the air with savors, and all sorts of little
balls and cubes, pats and cakes, lumps and rolls of eat-
ables are set out along the country road. A queer sort
of sea-weed scales, stained bright red, is the chewing-
gum of the East, and finds a ready market.

On the days of the matsuri the village street is impassable, and the whole broad walk of the temple grounds leading from the pagoda is lined with booths, jugglers, acrobats, side-shows, and catch-penny tricksters. The "sand-man," with bags of different colored sands, makes beautiful pictures on a cleared space of ground, rattling and gabbling without cessation while he works. First he dredges the surface with a sieve full of clean white sand, and then sifts a little thin stream of black or red sand through his closed hand, painting warriors, maidens, dragons, flowers, and landscapes in the swiftest, easiest way. It is a fine example of the trained hand and eye, and of excellent free-hand drawing. A juggler tosses rings, balls, and knives in the air, and spins plates on top of a twenty-foot pole. His colleague balances a big bamboo on one shoulder, and a small boy climbs it and goes through wonderful feats on the cross-piece at the top. A ring of gaping admirers surrounds a master of the black art, who swallows a lighted pipe, drinks, whistles, produces the pipe for a puff or two, swallows it again, and complacently emits fanciful rings and wreaths of smoke. Hair-pins, rosaries, toys, and sweets are everywhere for sale.

A huge, towering, heavy-roofed red gate-way admits streams of people to the great court-yard, surrounded on three sides by temples large and small, where the priests chant and pound and the faithful pray, rubbing their rosaries and tossing in their coins. At one shrine greasy locks of hair tied to the lattices are votive offerings from those who have appealed to the deity within. There is a little temple to the North Star, where seamen and fisher-folk pray, and one to Daikoku, the god of riches and abundance, the latter a fat little man sitting on bags of rice, and always beset by applicants.

In the great temple pyramids of candles burn, incense rises, bells sound, and money rains into the big cash-box

at the head of the steps. The splendid interior is a
mass of lacquer, gilding, and color, the panelled ceiling
has an immense filigree brass baldaquin hanging like a
frosted canopy over the heads of the priests, and a superb altar, all images, lotus-leaves, lights, and gilded
doors, dazzles the eye. Under the baldaquin sits the
high-priest of the temple, who is a bishop of the largest
diocese in Japan, while at either side of him more than
two hundred celebrants face each other in rows. The
priestly heads are shaven, the smooth faces wear the ecstatic, exalted expression of devotees purified by vigil
and fasting, and over their white or yellow gauze kimonos are tied *kesas*, or cloaks of rich brocade. The
lesser hierarchy appear in subdued colors — gray, purple, russet—but the head priest is arrayed in gorgeous
scarlet and gold, and sits before a reading-desk, whose
books are covered with squares of similar brocade. He
leads the chanted service from a parchment roll spread
before him, at certain places touching a silver-toned
gong, when all the priests bow low and chant a response,
sitting for hours immovable upon the mats, intoning and
reading from the sacred books in concert. At intervals
each raps the low lacquer table before him and bends
low, while the big temple drum sounds, the high-priest
touches his gong, and slowly, behind the lights and incense clouds of the altar, the gilded doors of the shrine
swing open to disclose the precious image of sainted
Nichiren. On all sides stand the faithful, extending
their rosary-wrapped hands and muttering the Nichi-
rene's special form of prayer: "*Namu mio ho ren ge
kio*" (Glory to the salvation-bringing book, the blossom
of doctrine).

After seven hours of worship a last litany is uttered,
and the procession of priests files through the grounds
to the monastery, stopping to select from the two hundred and odd pairs of wooden clogs, waiting at the edge

of the temple mats, each his proper pair. The high-
priest walks near the middle of the line underneath an
immense red umbrella. He carries an elaborate red lacquer staff, not unlike a crozier, and even his clogs are
of red lacquered wood. The service in the temple suggests the forms of the Roman Church, and this Buddhist
cardinal, in his red robes and umbrella, is much like his
fellow-dignitary of the West.

To citizens of the United States Ikegami has a peculiar interest. When the American man-of-war *Oneida* was
run down and sunk with her officers and crew by the
P. and O. steamer *Bombay*, near the mouth of Yeddo
Bay, January 23, 1870, our Government made no effort
to raise the wreck or search it, and finally sold it to a
Japanese wrecking company for fifteen hundred dollars.
The wreckers found many bones of the lost men among
the ship's timbers, and when the work was entirely completed, with their voluntary contributions they erected a
tablet in the Ikegami grounds to the memory of the dead,
and celebrated there the impressive Buddhist *segaki*
(feast of hungry souls), in May, 1889. The great temple was in ceremonial array; seventy-five priests in
their richest robes assisted at the mass, and among
the congregation were the American admiral and his
officers, one hundred men from the fleet, and one sur-
vivor of the solitary boat's crew that escaped from the
Oneida.

The Scriptures were read, a service was chanted, the
Sutra repeated, incense burned, the symbolic lotus-leaves
cast before the altar, and after an address in English by
Mr. Amenomori explaining the segaki, the procession
of priests walked to the tablet in the grounds to chant
prayers and burn incense again.

No other country, no other religion, offers a parallel to
this experience; and Americans may well take to heart

the example of piety, charity, magnanimity, and liberality that this company of hard-working Japanese fishermen and wreckers have set them.

CHAPTER XIV

A TRIP TO NIKKO

THE Nikko mountains, one hundred miles north of Tokio, are the favorite summer resort of foreign residents and Tokio officials. The railway goes to Utsonomiya, and the remaining twenty-five miles of the journey are made in jinrikisha over the most beautiful highway, leading through an unbroken avenue of over-arching trees to the village of Hachi-ishi, or Nikko.

On the very hottest day of the hottest week of August we packed our *koris*, the telescope baskets which constitute the Japanese trunk, and fled to the hills. Smoke and dust poured in at the car windows, the roof crackled in the sun, the green groves and luxuriant fields that we whirled through quivered with heat, and a chorus of grasshoppers and scissors-grinders deafened us at every halt. At Utsonomiya it was a felicity to sit in the upper room of a tea-house and dip our faces and hold our hands in basins of cool spring-water, held for us by the sympathetic nesans. They looked perfectly cool, fresh, and unruffled in their clean blue-and-white cotton kimonos, for the Japanese, like the creoles, appear never to feel the heat of summer, and, indeed, to be wholly indifferent to any weather. The same placid Utsonomiya babies, whose little shaved heads bobbed around helplessly in the blaze of that midsummer sun, I have seen equally serene with their bare skulls reddening, uncovered, on the frostiest winter mornings.

Once out of the streets of this little provincial capital, the way to Nikko leads up a straight broad avenue, lined on both sides for twenty-seven miles with tall and ancient cryptomerias, whose branches meet in a Gothic arch overhead. The blue outlines of the Nikko mountains showed in the distance as we entered the grand avenue. The road is a fine piece of engineering, with its ascent so slow and even as to seem level; but at times the highway, with its superb walls of cryptomeria, is above the level of the fields. then even with them, and then below them, as it follows its appointed lines. Before the railway reached Utsonomiya, travellers from Tokio had a boat journey, and then a jinrikisha ride of seventy miles through the shaded avenue. This road was made two centuries ago, when the Shoguns chose Nikko as their burial place, and these venerable trees have shaded the magnificent funeral trains of the old warriors, and the splendid processions of their successors, who made pilgrimages to the tombs of Iyeyasu and Iyemitsu. In our day, alas, instead of mighty daimios and men-at-arms in coats of mail, or brocaded grandees in gilded palanquins, telegraph-poles, slim, ugly, and utilitarian, impertinently thrust themselves forward before the grand old tree-trunks, and the jinrikisha and the rattle-trap basha take their plebeian way.

The cryptomeria has the reddish bark and long, smooth bole of the California sequoia, and through the mat of leaves and branches, high overhead, the light filters down in a soft twilight that casts a spell over the place. After sunset the silence and stillness of the shaded avenue were solemn, and its coolness and the fragrance of moist earth most grateful. Two men ran tandem with each jinrikisha, and they went racing up the avenue for ten miles, halting only once for a sip of cold water before they stopped at the hamlet of Osawa. The villages, a row of low houses on either side of the way, make the only break in the long avenue. With its dividing screens drawn back, the Osawa tea-house was one long room, with only side walls and a roof, the front open to the street, and the back facing a garden where a stream dashed through a liliputian landscape, fell in a liliputian fall, and ran under liliputian bridges. At the street end was a square fireplace, sunk in the floor, with a big teakettle swinging by an iron chain from a beam of the roof, teapots sitting in the warm ashes, and bits of fowl and fish skewered on chopsticks and set up in the ashes to broil before the coals. The coolies, sitting around this kitchen, fortified their muscle and brawn with thimble cups of green tea, bowls of rice, and a few shreds of pickled fish. We, as their masters and superiors, were placed as far as possible from them, and picnicked at a table in the pretty garden. After the severe exertion of sitting still and letting the coolies draw us, we restored our wasting tissues by rich soup, meats, and all the stimulating food that might be thought more necessary to the laboring jinrikisha men.

When we started again, with all the tea-house staff singing sweet sayonaras, a glow in the east foretold the rising moon, and a huge stone torii at the end of the village loomed ghostly against the blackness of the forest. The glancing moonlight shot strange shadows across the path, and we went whirling through this lattice of light and darkness in stillness and solitude. The moon rose higher and was hidden in the leafy arch overhead, and before we realized that its faint light was fading, came flashes of lightning, the rumble of approaching thunder, and a sudden crash, as the flood of rain struck the tree-tops and poured through. The hoods of the jinrikishas were drawn up, the oil-papers fastened across us, and through pitch darkness the coolies raced along. Vivid flashes of lightning showed the thick, white sheet of rain, which gusts of wind blew into our faces, while insidious streams slipped down our shoulders and glided into our laps. Putting their heads down, the coolies beat their way against the rain for two more soaking miles to Imaichi, the last village on the road, only five miles from Nikko. The tea-house into which we turned for shelter was crowded with belated and storm-bound pilgrims coming down from the sacred places of Nikko and Chiuzenji. All Japanese are talkative, the lower in station the more loquacious, and the whole coolie company was chattering at once. As the place was too comfortless to stay in, we turned out again in the rain, and the coolies splashed away at a walk, through a darkness so dense as to be felt. At midnight our seven jinrikishas rattling into the hotel court, and fourteen coolies shouting to one another as they unharnessed and unpacked, roused the house and the whole neighborhood of Nikko. Awakened sleepers up-stairs looked out at us and banged the screens angrily, but no sounds can be deadened in a tea-house.

To the traveller the tea-house presents many phases of comfort, interest, and amusement altogether wanting in the conventional hotel, which is, unfortunately, becoming common on the great routes of travel. The dimensions of every house in the empire conform to certain unvarying rules. The verandas, or outer galleries of the house, are always exactly three feet wide. A foreigner, who insisted on a nine-feet-wide veranda, entailed upon his Nikko carpenter many days of painful thought, pipe-smoking, and conference with his fellows. These mechanics were utterly upset in their calculations. They sawed the boards and beams too long or too short, and finally produced a very bad, un-Japanese piece of work. The floors of these galleries are polished to a wonderful smoothness and surface. They are not varnished, nor oiled, nor waxed, but every morning rubbed with a cloth wrung out of hot bath-water which contains oily matter enough to give, in time, this peculiar lustre. Three years of daily rubbing with a hot cloth are required to give a satisfactory result, and every subsequent year adds to the richness of tone and polish, until old tea-houses and temples disclose floors of common pine looking like rose-wood, or six-century-old oak.

The area of every room is some multiple of three feet, because the soft *tatami*, or floor-mats, measure six feet in length by three in width. These are woven of common straw and rushes, faced with a closely-wrought mat of rice-straw. It is to save these tatami and the polished floors that shoes are left outside the house.

The thick screens, ornamented with sketches or poems, that separate one room from another, are the *fusuma;* the screens shutting off the veranda, pretty lattice frames covered with rice-paper that admit a peculiarly soft light to the rooms, are the *shoji*, and in their management is involved an elaborate etiquette. In opening or closing them, well-bred persons and trained servants kneel and use each thumb and finger with ordered precision, while it is possible to convey slight, contempt, and mortal insult in the manner of handling these sliding doors. The outer veranda is closed at night and in bad weather by *amados*, solid wooden screens or shutters, that rumble and bang their way back and forth in their grooves. These amados are without windows or air-holes, and the servants will not willingly leave a gap for ventilation. "But thieves may get in, or the *kappa!*" they cry, the kappa being a mythical animal always ready to fly away with them. In every room is placed an andon, or night-lamp. If one clap his hands at any hour of the twenty-four, he hears a chorus of answering *Hei! hei! hei's!* and the thump of the nesans bare feet, as they run to attend him. While he talks to them, they keep ducking and saying *Heh! heh!* which politely signifies that they are giving their whole attention.

The Japanese bed is the floor, with a wooden box under the neck for a pillow and a futon for a covering. To the foreigner the Japanese landlord allows five or six futons, or cotton-wadded comforters, and they make a tolerable mattress, although not springy, and rather apt to be damp and musty. The traveller carries his own sheets, woolen blankets, feather or air pillows, and flea-powder, the latter the most necessary provision of all. The straw mats and the futons swarm with fleas, and without a liberal powdering, or, better, an anointing with oil of pennyroyal, it is impossible to sleep. These sleeping arrangements are not really comfortable, and, after the fatigue of walking and mountain-climbing, stiffen the joints. By day the futons are placed in closets out of sight, or hung over the balconies to air, coming back damper than ever, if the servants forget to bring them in before sunset. The bedroom walls are the sliding paper screens; and if one's next neighbor be curious, he may slip the screen a little or poke a hole through the paper. A whisper or a pin-drop travels from room to room, and an Anglo-Saxon snorer would rock the whole structure.

At ordinary Japanese inns the charge for a day's accommodation ranges from forty cents to one dollar. A Japanese can get his lodgings and all his meals for about thirty cents, but foreigners are so clumsy, untidy, and destructive, and they demand so many unusual things, that they are charged the highest price, which includes lodging, bedding, and all the tea, rice, and hot water they may wish. All other things are extra. In the beaten tracks bread and fresh beef may always be found, and each year there is less need of carrying the supplies formerly so essential. Chairs and tables, cots, knives and forks, and corkscrews have gradually penetrated to the remotest mountain hamlets. At the so-called foreign hotels at Nikko and other resorts, charges are usually

made at a fixed price for each day, with everything included, as at an American hotel.

Foreigners travelling away from the ports take with
them a guide, who acts as courier, cooks and serves the
meals, and asks one dollar a day and his expenses.
Thus accompanied everything goes smoothly and easily;
rooms are found ready, meals are served promptly, show-
places open their doors, the best conveyances await the
traveller's wish, and an encyclopædic interpreter is always at his elbow. Without a guide or an experienced
servant, even a resident who speaks the language fares
hardly. Like all Orientals, the Japanese are impressed
by a retinue and the appearances of wealth. They wear
their best clothes when travelling, make a great show,
and give liberal tips. The foreigner who goes to the
Nakasendo or to remote provinces alone, trusting to the
phrase-book, finds but little consideration or comfort.
He ranks with the class of pilgrims, and the guest-room
and the choicest dishes are not for him. The guide may
swindle his master a little, but the comforts and advan-
tages he secures are well worth the cost. All the guides
are well-to-do men with tidy fortunes. They exact commissions wherever they bring custom, and can make or
break landlords or merchants if they choose to combine.
Some travellers, who, thinking it sharp to deprive the
guides of these percentages, have been left by them in
distant provinces and forced to make their way alone,
have found the rest of the journey a succession of impositions, difficulties, and even of real hardships. After
engaging a guide and handing him the passport, the
traveller has only to enjoy Japan and pay his bill
at the end of the journey. The guides know more
than the guide-book; and with Ito, made famous by
Miss Bird, Nikko and Kioto yielded to us many pleasures which we should otherwise have missed. An acquaintance with Miyashta and his sweet-potato hash

made the Tokaido a straight and pleasant way; and Moto's judicial countenance caused Nikko, Chiuzenji, and Yumoto to disclose unimagined beauties and luxuries.

CHAPTER XV

NIKKO

OF all Japan's sacred places, Nikko, or Sun's Brightness, is dearest to the Japanese heart. Art, architecture, and landscape gardening add to Nature's opulence, history and legend people it with ancient splendors, and all the land is full of memories. "He who has not seen Nikko cannot say *Kekko*." (beautiful, splendid, superb), runs the Japanese saying.

With its forest shades, its vast groves, and lofty avenues, its hush, its calm religious air, Nikko is an ideal and dream-like place, where rulers and prelates may well long to be buried, and where priests, poets, scholars, artists, and pilgrims love to abide. Each day of a whole summer has new charms, and Nikko's strange fascination but deepens with acquaintance.

The one long street of Hachi-ishi, or lower Nikko village, ends at the banks of the Dayagawa, a roaring stream that courses down a narrow valley, walled at its upper end by the bold, blue bar of Nantaisan, the sacred mountain. Legend has peopled this valley of the Dayagawa with impossible beings — giants, fairies, demons, and monsters. Most of the national fairy stories begin with, "Once upon a time in the Nikko mountains," and one half expects to meet imp or fay in the green shadows. Mound builder and prehistoric man had lived their squalid lives here; the crudest and earliest forms of religion had been observed in these forest sanctuaries long before Kobo Daishi induced the Shinto priests to believe that their god of the mountain was but a manifestation of Buddha. Everything proclaims a hoary past—trees, moss-grown stones, battered images, crumbling tombs, overgrown and forgotten graveyards.

Each summer half the Tokio legations move bodily to Nikko, and temples, monastery wings, priests' houses, and the homes of the dwellers in the upper village are rented to foreigners in ever-increasing numbers. Nikko habitations do not yet bring the prices of Newport cottages, but the extravagant rate of three and even five hundred yens for a season of three months is a Japanese equivalent. Besides the foreigners, there are many Japanese residents and tourists—little men in hot, uncomfortable foreign clothes. with field-glasses strapped across one shoulder, and the freshest and tightest of gloves. The white-clad pilgrims throng hither by thousands during July and early August, march picturesquely to the jingle of their staffs and bells round the great temples, and trudge on to the sanctuary on Chiuzenji's shores within the shadow of holy Nantaisan.

Two bridges cross the Daiyagawa, and lead to the groves and temples that make Nikko's fame. One bridge is an every-day affair of plain, unpainted timbers. across which jinrikishas rumble noisily, and figures pass and repass. The other is the sacred bridge, over which only the Emperor may pass, in lieu of the Shoguns of old, for whom it was reserved. It is built of wood, covered with red lacquer, with many brass plates and tips, and rests on foundation piles of Titanic stone columns, joined by cross-pieces of stone, carefully fitted and mortised in. Tradition maintains that the gods sent down this rainbow bridge from the clouds in answer to saintly prayer. Its sanctity is so carefully preserved, that when the Emperor wished to pay the highest conceivable honor to General Grant, he ordered the barrier to the bridge to be opened that his guest might walk across.   Greatly to his credit, that modest soldier refused to accept this honor, lest it should seem a desecration to the humble believers in the sanctity of the red bridge.

Shaded avenues, broad staircases, and climbing slopes lead to the gate-ways of the two great sanctuaries—the mortuary temples and tombs of the Shogun Iyeyasu and his worthy grandson, the Shogun Iyemitsu.   The hill-side is shaded by magnificent old cryptomerias; and these sacred groves, with the soft cathedral light under the high canopy of leaves, are as wonderful as the sacred buildings.   Each splendid gate-way, as well as the soaring pagoda, can be seen in fine perspective at the end of long avenues of trees, and bronze or stone torii form lofty portals to the holy places.   The torii is a distinctively national structure, and these grand skeleton gates of two columns and an upward curving cross-piece are impressive and characteristic features of every Japanese landscape, standing before even the tiniest shrines in the Liliputian gardens of Japanese homes, as well as forming the approach to every temple.   The stone torii and the rows of stone lanterns are mossy and lichen-covered, and every foot of terrace or embankment is spread with fine velvety moss of the freshest green.   Although two hundred years old, the temples themselves are in as perfect condition and color as when built ; and nothing is finer, perhaps, than the five-storied pagoda with its red lacquered walls, the brass trimmings of roofs and rails, the discolored bells pendent from every angle, and a queer, corkscrew spiral atop, the whole showing like a great piece of jeweller's work in a deep, green grove.

Iyeyasu, founder of Yeddo, successor of the Taiko, and military ruler in the golden age of the arts in Japan, was the first Shogun buried on Nikko's sacred hill-side, and it was intended to make the mortuary temple before his tomb as splendid as the crafts of the day permitted.

His grandson, Iyemitsu, was the next and only other Shogun interred at Nikko, and his temple fairly rivals that of his ancestor.

At each shrine rise broad stone steps leading to the first and outer court-yards, where stand the magnificent gates, exquisitely carved, set with superb metal plates. and all ablaze with color and gilding. The eye is confused in the infinite detail of structure and ornament, and the intricacy of beams and brackets upholding the heavy roofs of these gate-ways. Walls of red lacquer and gold, with carved and colored panels topped with black tiles, surround each enclosure, and through inner and outer courts and gate-ways, growing ever more and more splendid, the visitor approaches the temples proper, their soaring roofs, curved gables, and ridge-poles set with the Tokugawa crest in gold, sharp cut against the forest background. At the lowest step his shoes are taken off, and he is permitted to wander slowly through the magnificent buildings on the soft, silk-bordered mats. Richly panelled ceilings, lacquered pillars, carved walls, and curtains of the finest split bamboo belong to both alike, and in the gloom of inner rooms are marvels of carving and decoration, only half visible.

Both temples were once splendid with all the emblems and trappings of Buddhism, redolent with incense, musical with bells and gongs, and resounding all day with chanted services. But after the Restoration, when the Shinto became the state religion and the Emperor made a pilgrimage to Nikko, Iyeyasu's temple was stripped of its splendid altar ornaments, banners, and symbols. and the simple mirror and bits of paper of the empty Shinto creed were substituted. In the dark chapel behind the first room there remains a large gong. whose dark bowl rests on a silken pad, and when softly struck fills the place with rising and falling, recurring and wavering, tones of sweetness for five whole minutes, while

Ito stands with open watch and warning finger, and the priest bends low and drinks in the music with ecstatic countenance. Iyemitsu's temple was spared, and there stand the rows of superb lacquered boxes containing the sacred writings. There, too, are the gilded images, golden lotus-leaves, massive candlesticks, drums, gongs, banners and pendent ornaments, besides the giant koros, breathing forth pale clouds of incense, that accompanied the rites of the grand old Buddhist faith.

Each temple has a fine water-tank in its outer court; an open pavilion, with solid corner posts supporting the heavy and ornate roof above the granite trough. Each basin is a single, huge block of stone, hollowed out and cut with such exactness that the water, welling up from the bottom, pours over the smooth edges so evenly as to give it the look of a cube of polished glass. The fountain at the Iyemitsu temple was the gift of the princes of Nabeshima, and its eaves flutter with the myriad flags left there by pilgrims who come to pray at the great shrine. All about the temple grounds is heard the noise of rushing water, and the music and gurgle of these tiny streams, the rustle of the high branches, and the cawing of huge solitary rooks are the only sounds that break the stillness of the enchanted groves between the soft boomings of the morning and evening bells. The noise of voices is lost in the great leafy spaces, and the sacredness of the place subdues even the unbelieving foreigner, while native tourists and pilgrims move silently, or speak only in undertones, and make no sound, save as their clogs clatter on stones and gravel.

It is impossible to carry away more than a general and bewildered impression of the splendid walled and lanterned courts, the superb gate-ways, and the temples themselves, but certain details, upon which the guides insist, remain strangely clear in memory. Over the doors of the stable where the sacred white pony is kept are colored carvings representing groups of monkeys with eyes, or ears, or mouth covered with their paws—the signification being that one should neither see, hear, nor speak any evil. In one superbly-carved gate-way is a little medallion of two tigers, so cunningly studied and worked out that the curving grain and knots of the wood give all the softly-shaded stripes of their velvet coats and an effect of thick fur. One section of a carved column in this gate is purposely placed upsidedown, the builder fearing to complete so perfect and marvellous a piece of workmanship. Above another gate-way curls a comfortable sleeping cat, which is declared to wink when rain is coming, and this white cat has as great a fame as anything along the Daiyagawa.

The strangest hierophant in Nikko is the priestess who dances at the temple of Iyeyasu. She looks her three-score years of age, and is allowed a small temple to herself, where she sits, posed like an altar image, with a big money-box on the sacred red steps before her, into which the pious and the curious toss their offerings. Then the priestess rises and solemnly walks a few steps this way, a few steps that way, poses before each change, shakes an elaborate sort of baby's rattle with the right-hand, and gesticulates with an open fan in the left-hand. The sedate walk to and fro, the movements of the rattle and fan constitute the dance, after which this aged Miriam sits down, bows her head to the mats, and resumes her statuesque pose. She wears a nun-like head-dress of white muslin, and a loose white garment, like a stole, over a red petticoat, the regular costume of the Shinto priestesses. She seems always amiable and ready to respond to a conciliatory coin, but the visitor wonders that the cool and shaded sanctuary in which she sits, with nearly the whole front wall making an open door, does not stiffen her aged joints with rheumatism and end her dancing days.

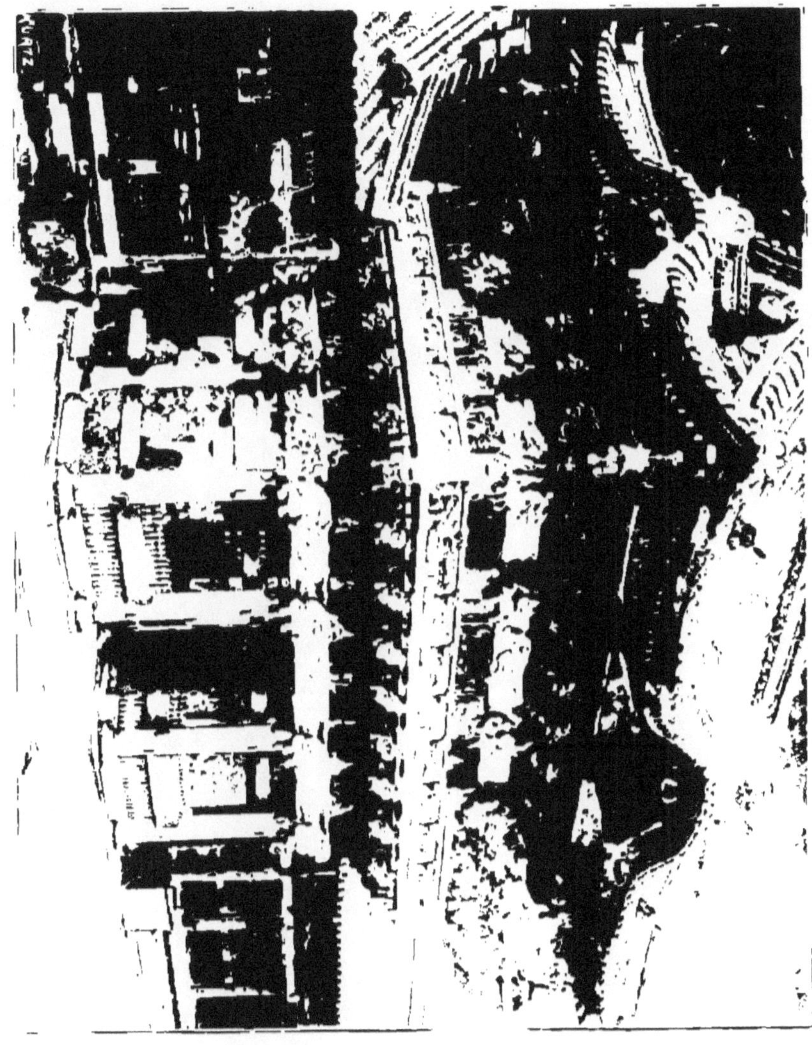

A green and mossy staircase, a greener and mossier balustraded walk, leads up and along the crest of the hill to the final knoll, atop of which stands the simple bronze urn containing the great Shogun's body. A more still and solemn, a more peaceful and beautiful resting-place could not be imagined, and the peculiar green twilight reigning under the closely-set cryptomerias, with those long stretches of stone balustrades and embankments, which the forest has claimed for its own and clothed in a concealing mantle of the greenest moss, subdue the most frivolous beholder to silence and seriousness.

On that velvety-green stair-way leading to Iyeyasu's tomb I met, one day, a scholar of fine taste and great culture, a man of distinction in his native West. " I am overwhelmed with the beauty and magnificence of all this," he said. " I must concede the greatness of any religion that could provide and preserve this, and teach its followers to appreciate it."

Afterwards, almost on the same step, a dear missionary friend stopped me, with eyes full of tears. " Oh !" she sighed, " this fills me with sadness and sorrow. These emblems and monuments of heathenism ! I see nothing beautiful or admirable in those wicked temples. They show me how hard it will be to uproot such heathen creeds. I wish I had not come."

A woodland path leads around the foot of the great hill on which the Shoguns' tombs are built, a path laid with large flat stones and set with a rough curbing of loose rocks and bowlders, covered—by the drip and damp and shade of centuries—with a thick green moss. This silent footway leads past many small temples, stone-fenced enclosures, moss-covered tombs and tablets, tiny shrines behind tiny torii, and battered, broken-nosed, and headless Buddhas. Half-hidden tracks, in that gloomy and silent cryptomeria forest, rough-set staircases, roads plunging into the deep shadow of the woods

entice the explorer to ever-new surprises. At deserted
and silent shrines heaps of pebbles, bits of paper, or
strips of wood painted with a sacred character attest
the presence of prayerful pilgrims, who have sought
them out to register a vow or petition. Tiny red shrines
gleam jewel-like in the far shadows, and fallen cryptomerias make mounds and ridges of entangled vines among
the red-barked giants still standing. Above a water-fall,
all thin ribbons and jets of foam, are more old temples,
where pilgrims come to pray and tourists to admire, but
where no one ever despoils the unguarded sanctuaries.
In one of these buildings are life-size images of the
gods of thunder and the winds. Raiden, the thunder-
god, is a bright-red divinity with a circle of drums
surrounding his head like a halo, a fierce countenance,
and two goaty horns on his forehead. Futen, the god of
winds, has a grass-green skin, two horny toes to each
foot, and a big bag over his shoulders. A fine heavy-
roofed red gate-way and bell-tower distinguish another
cluster of temples in this still forest nook, their altars
covered with gilded images. One open shrine, which
should be the resort of jinrikisha men, is dedicated to a
muscular red deity, to whom votaries offer up a pair of
sandals, beseeching him for vigorous legs. The whole
place is hung over with wooden, straw, and tin sandals,
minute or colossal. Then down through the wood, past
a hoary graveyard, where abbots and monks of Nikko
monasteries were buried for centuries before the Shoguns came, one returns to the Futa-ara temple and Iyemitsu's first gate-way.

In our wanderings we once happened upon an old
and crowded graveyard, with splendid trees shading the
mossy tombs and monuments. The stone lanterns,
Buddhas, and images were past counting, and one granite deity, under a big sun-hat, had a kerchief of red cotton tied under his chin. His benevolent face and

flaming robes were stuck all over with tiny bits of paper, on which the faithful had written their petitions, and the lanterns beside him were heaped with prayer-stones. A Hindoo-looking deity near by sat with uplifted knee, on which he rested one arm and supported his bent and thoughtful head.

A hundred stone representatives of Buddha sit in mossy meditation under the shadow of the river bank, long branches trailing over them and vines clambering about their ancient brows. Time has rolled some from their lotus pedestals, beheaded others, and covered them all with white lichens and green moss, and Gamman, as this row of Buddhas is named, is the strangest sight among the many strange sights of the river bank. Custom ordains that one should count them, and no two persons are believed to have ever recorded the same number of images between the bridge and Kobo Daishi's open shrine.

There is an eta village just below Nikko, peopled by these outcasts, who follow their despised calling of handling the carcasses of animals and dressing leather and furs. Their degradation seems to result not more from that Buddhist law which forbids the taking of animal life, than from the legendary belief that they are the descendants of Korean prisoners, long kept as executioners and purveyors for the imperial falcons. Colonies of etas lived for centuries without part or lot in the lives of their high-caste neighbors. After the Restoration, the power of the great nobles was curtailed, and with the gradual freeing of the lower classes from the tyranny of caste the eta became a citizen, protected by law. Prejudice still confines him to his own villages, but when he leaves them salt is no longer sprinkled on the spot where he stands to purify it.

The most harrowing situation of the old romances was the falling in love of a noble with a beautiful eta girl. Now the eta children attend the Government schools on the same terms as their betters. But this liberality was of slow growth, and in one province, where the stiff-necked parents withdrew their children because of the presence of these pariahs, the governor entered himself as a pupil, sitting side by side with the little outcasts in the same classes, after which august demonstration of theoretical equality caste distinctions were allowed to fade.

Nikko becomes a great curio mart each summer, the curios having, naturally, a religious cast; and bells, drums, gongs, incense-burners. images, banners, brocade draperies, and priestly fans make a part of every peddler's pack, each thing, of course, being certified to have come from the sacred treasuries near by. The souvenirs, which the most hardened tourist cannot resist buying, are the Nikko specialties of trays, cups, boxes, and teapots of carved and lacquered wood, and of curious roots, decorated with chrysanthemums or incised sketches of the Sacred Bridge. The Japanese eye sees possibilities in the most unpromising knot, and the Japanese hand hollows it into a casket, or fits it with the spout and handle that turn it into a teapot. All the village street is lined with these wooden-ware shops, alternating with photograph and curio marts.

Visitors to Nikko always buy its *yuoki*, a candy made of chestnuts and barley-sugar, which comes in slabs an inch square and six inches long, wrapped in a dried bamboo sheath, and put in the dainty little wooden boxes which make Japanese purchases so attractive. It is like a dark-brown fig-paste, and has a flavor of marrons glaces and of maple-sugar. Flocks of children, with babies on their backs. hover about the yuoki shop in upper Nikko, and if the tourist bestows a box on them, their comical bobs and courtesies, their funny way of touching the forehead with the gift during all the bowing, and the rapture with which they attack the bar of sweets express most eloquent thanks.

When rain or fatigue prevented our making any outdoor excursions, the village street furnished us with an all-day occupation. A mossy and abandoned rice-mill faced us across the road, with a tiny cascade dripping down from the leafy hill behind it, feeding its overshot wheel, and dropping by dwarf water-falls to the side of the road, whence it ran down the slope to add its singing to the water chorus that makes all Nikko musical. Pack-horses, farmers, pilgrims, and villagers went picturesquely by, each pedestrian tucking his kimono in his belt to shorten it, and holding a vast golden halo over his head in the shape of a flat, oil-paper rain umbrella.

A small garden separated our summer home at Nikko from our landlord's house, and from early morning, when his amados thundered open, until dark, when they rumbled shut, the whole conduct of Japanese household life lay before us. Our neighbors came out of doors betimes. A bucket of water from a tiny cascade filled the broad, shallow copper wash-basin, in which one by one they washed their faces. Meanwhile the kettle boiled over the charcoal fire, and some child ran down to a provision-shop for a square slab of bean-curd, which, with many cups of tea, a little rice, and shreds of pickled fish, composed their breakfast. Then the futons were hung over poles or lines to sun; the andons, pillows, and big green tents of musquito-nets put away; the tatami brushed off, and the little shop put in order for the day.

The women washed and starched their gowns, pasting them down on flat boards to smooth and dry ; sewed and mended, scrubbed and scoured in the narrow alcove of a kitchen all the morning; while the children trotted back and forth with buckets of water to sprinkle the garden, wash the stones, fill the bath-tubs, and supply the kitchen. The rice, after being washed and rubbed in the cascade, was soaked for an hour and then poured into the furiously boiling rice-pot. The brush fire under the stone frame of the kettle was raked out, and when the steam came only in interrupted puffs from under the cover, this was lifted to show a pot full to the brim of snowy-white grains. A soup had meanwhile been stewing, a fish had been broiled over charcoal, and, with tea, the noonday dinner was ready. At some hour of the day offerings of rice and food were mysteriously placed on the steps of the tiny shrine to the fox-god, chief ornament of the farther garden. Towards sundown came supper, and then the lighting of the lamps. Shadow pictures on the shoji repeated the actions and groupings within, the splash of water betrayed the family bath, and when all, from grandfather to baby, had been boiled and scrubbed, the amados banged, and the performance was over until sunrise.

CHAPTER XVI

CHIUZENJI AND YUMOTO

THE Inquisition should have been put in possession of the Japanese kago as a lesser punishment for heretics, so exquisite and insidious are its tortures. This kago is a shallow basket with a high back, slung from a pole carried on the shoulders of two men, and in the mountains and remote districts is the only means of travel, except by pack-horses. The Japanese double their knees and sit on their feet with great dignity and apparent comfort; but the greater size of the foreigner, his stiff joints and higher head, prevent his fitting into the kago; nor is he much better off when he gets astride, dangling his long legs over the edges. Moreover, he not only knows that he looks ridiculous, but suffers the pangs of conscience

FARM LABORERS AND PACK-HORSE

for imposing his weight on two small coolies no larger than the ten-year-old boys of his own land. There are a few arm-chairs on poles, in which one may ride, like the Pope, or an idol in a procession, but the long poles, springing with the gait of four bearers, often make the passenger sea-sick.

The pack-horse, a slow-moving beast, has a keeper who pulls him along by a cord, his extended head and reluctant gait making that seem the only motive power. Horse and leader wear straw shoes, and new pairs are strung around the high saddle for reshoeing the beast every few miles. Iron horseshoes are confined to the capital and the large ports, and the village blacksmith is unknown. Pack-horses wear a thick straw pad and a high saddle fashioned like a saw-horse, on which the rider sits aloft, so well forward that his feet hang over the creature's neck. This saddle is merely balanced, not girded on, and the animals are so sleepy, slow-footed, and stumbling, with a lurching, swinging gait like a camel's, that riding one is really a feat.

From Nikko to Chiuzenji you must travel eight miles by kago, pack-horse, or on foot, the road leading past rich fields of buckwheat, millet, rice, and potatoes, farm-houses with thatched roofs, wayside shrines and tea-houses. The ascent of the two thousand feet to the higher region of the lake is chiefly included in one three-mile stretch, climbing by easy slopes and broad stair-cases to the high pass. At every few feet a stone step was built, or a tree trunk fastened with a forked stick and set with small stones. This stair-building, done ages ago, has become a part of the mountain. At short distances the staircase enters a little clearing with a rustic tea-house, or the usual tateba, built of poles, a few planks, branches or mats, and affording sufficient shelter for summer pilgrims and travellers. The keepers immediately put out cushions for guests on the edge of the platform that constitutes the floor of the one room, and bring the tray with its tiny tea-pot, thimble cups, and dish of barley-sugar candies. For the refreshment one leaves a few coppers on the tray, and in mountain jaunts, where the traveller walks to escape the kago and spare the coolies, these tiny cups of pale yellow tea are very stimulating. Each tateba commands some particular view, and even the pilgrim who is tramping the provinces and living on a few cents a day, will be found inditing poems to the different water-falls and gorges he looks down upon.

The head of the pass affords a magnificent view of the valley two thousand feet below, and presently the woodland path is following the border of the lake and comes out into the open of Chiuzenji village. Chiuzenji Lake, three miles wide and eight miles long, is surrounded by steep and thickly-wooded mountains, the great Nantaisan grandly soaring nine thousand feet above the sea, tapering regularly as a pyramid and forested to the summit. Nantaisan is a sacred mountain, a temple at its foot, shrines all along the ascent, and at the top an altar on which repentant murderers offer up their swords. Each August come hosts of pilgrims in white clothes and huge straw hats, with pieces of straw matting for rain-coats bound across their shoulders—devout souls, who, after purification in the lake, pass under the torii, say a prayer in the temple, and painfully climb to the summit. Only at such fixed seasons may visitors ascend the mountain, each one paying twenty cents for the privilege of toiling up its endless flight of steps. With these fees the priests keep the underbrush trimmed and the path well cleared, and where the holy guardian unbars the gate and motions one upward, begins the flight of stone stairs that extend, with few breaks or zigzags, straight to the top. The whole way is strewn with the cast-off sandals of the season, and great heaps of the waraji of past years lie here and there.

The pilgrims sleep in Government barracks in the village, a few coppers securing a mat on the floor and the use of the common fireplace. Their vow to Nantaisan being accomplished, they make the half-circuit of the lake, to visit the hidden shrines and temples of the forest shores, and then trudge to Yumoto for its hot sulphur baths and scenery, or home to their ripening rice-fields.

From across the water Chiuzenji village looks a small, yellow patch, lying between the unbroken green slope of Nantaisan and the great lake. Its five tea-houses rise straight from the water's edge, each with a triple row of outer galleries overlooking it. The way of life at the Tsutaya, Idzumiya, Nakamarya, and the rest is much more Japanese than in the frequented inns of Nikko. Chairs and tables are conceded to foreigners, but everybody must sleep on the floor, wash face and hands in the common wash-basin in the open court, and go about the house stocking-footed, or wear the stiff, heelless, monkey-skin slippers furnished by the inn. To call a servant one claps his palms, and a long-drawn "Hei!" announces that the rosy-cheeked mountain maid has heard, and the gentle swaying of the house proclaims that she is running up the stairs. The washing of rice, vegetables, fish, kitchen utensils, and family clothing goes on from the single plank of a pier running from the lowest floor of the house. Each inn has a similar pier, where sociable maidens chatter as they stir and wash the rice in bamboo baskets. The servants of the houses take the whole lake for wash-hand basin and tooth-brush cup, and the pier is a small-stage, upon which these local companies play their unstudied parts.

As the finest country walk in England is agreed to be that from Stratford to Warwick, so is the way from Chiuzenji to Yumoto the finest country walk in Japan, for its eight miles of infinite variety. First, the broad foot-path wanders for two miles along the shores of

Lake Chiuzenji, which, however, appears only in glimpses
of placid blue through the dense forest, all stillness, coolness, and enchantment. Then it emerges at the head of
the lake in a grove of pine-trees sheltering a rustic tea-
house, which overlooks the bit of low beach known as
the Iris Strand, and all the grand amphitheatre of mountains walling in Chiuzenji. Farther on are Hell's River
and the Dragon Head cascade, where a mountain stream
slides in many a separate ribbon down mossy ledges.
Thence the foot-path climbs to a high plain covered with
tall grasses and groves of lofty pines—the famous Red
Plain, dyed once with the blood of a conquered army,
and tinged with each autumn's frost to the same deep
hue again. From the border of this plain rise sombre
mountains, Nantaisan a giant among them, with green
and purple veils of shadows and a crown of floating clouds.
No sign of habitation or cultivation marks the high plain,
which, with its loneliness and its scattered pines, is so
much like the valleys of the high Sierras. Everywhere
else in Japan the country is wooded and shaded and cultivated from water's edge to mountain-top ; but in winter all the region above Nikko is deserted, and deep
snows in the passes shut it off from the rest of the world.
Tea-houses close, the people flee to the valley for warmth,
and only the coming of spring and the tourist restores it
again. Even those wizards, the Japanese farmers, do
not attempt to subdue these solitudes, whose wild beauty delights the whole people.

Beyond this lonely plain the way climbs seven hundred feet along the face of a precipitous hill to the level
of Yumoto Lake, which there narrows to a few feet and
slips down the rocks, a mass of foam, spray, and steam.
The lake—small, uneven, walled by perpendicular mountain-slopes and forests—is a still mirror of these superb
heights, one of which, Shirane-san, is a slumbering volcano. Vaporous sulphur springs bubble through the hot

crust of earth at the end of the lake, and boiling sulphur wells up, even in the bed of the lake itself, and clouds and heats the whole body of water so that no fish can live there. The two miles of winding forest - path, between the fall at one end of Yumoto Lake and the village of the same name at the opposite end, lead through an enchanted forest—a picturesque tangle of roots and rocks, covered with green moss, wound with vines, shaded with ferns, and overhung with evergreen branches.

Yumoto has two streets and a dozen tea-houses, whose galleries are hung with red lanterns, as if in perpetual fête, and an atmosphere nearly all sulphuretted hydrogen. One of the hot springs bubbles up at the entrance of the village, filling a tank about ten feet square, covered by a roof resting on four corner pillars. The sides are all open to the air, and an Arcadian simplicity of bathing arrangements prevails. Citizens and sojourners stroll hither, because the site commands a view of the thoroughfare, remove and fold up their garments, and sit down in the pool. When sufficiently boiled, they cool off occasionally on the edge of the tank, and then drop into the pool again. If the company prove agreeable, the bath occupies hours. More open-air pavilions are at the end of the village, where more bronze figures boil and cool themselves in the same exoteric fashion. The public bath - houses, that alternate with the tea-houses in the village streets, have roofs and sides of solid wood, except the street front, which is open and curtainless, and within which men, women, and children meet in the hot-water tanks, as at the market-place or street-corners in other countries. To a new-comer this extraordinary simplicity is startling, but if he stays long enough, he finds that the childlike innocence and unconcern of the people make a new code of the proprieties.

These infantile views of the Japanese as to bathing make even the great pay little attention to the seclusion

and inviolateness of the bath-room. In a high-class
Japanese house, or at the best tea-houses, this is an
exquisitely artistic nook, with cement walls and floors,
inlaid with fantastic stones and bits of porcelain. The
oval tubs are of pine, bound with withes, and white with
scouring. The doors are generally sliding paper screens
without locks, and the wooden wall, or door, if there be
one, is full of fantastic holes and tiny windows with no
curtain. Often the bath-house is a detached pavilion,
to which you are expected to walk in a special bath
gown, or ukata, meeting, on the way, household and
guests, who are always ready for a friendly chat. Europeans can hardly make a Japanese servant understand that in their order of arrangements, the bath and
the bath-room are for the use of one person at a time.
The Japanese wooden tub is vastly better than the zinc
coffins and marble sarcophagi in which we bathe. The
wood keeps the water hotter and is pleasanter to the
touch. One kind of tub has a tiny stove with a long
pipe in one end, and with a mere handful of charcoal
such a tub is filled with boiling water in the briefest
time. Many bathers have lost their lives by the carbonic
acid gas sent off by this ingenious contrivance. A Japanese hot bath is only a point or two from boiling. The
natives bear this temperature without wincing, and will
step from this scalding caldron out-of-doors, smoking
along the highway on a frosty day, like the man whom
Dr. Griffis describes. Our grave and statuesque landlord at Yumoto, who sat like a Buddha behind his low
table and held court with his minions, once appeared to
us stalking home in the starlight with all his clothes on
his arm. His stride was as stagey and majestic as ever,
there being no reason, in his consciousness, why he
should lay off his dignity with his garments, they representing to him the temporary and accidental, not the
real envelope of the pompous old soul.

PUBLIC BATH-HOUSE AT YUMOTO

At some of the great mineral springs there are now separate pools for men and women, in deference to foreign prejudice ; but more than one generation will pass before promiscuous bathing is done away with.

At all medicinal springs the baths are owned and managed by the Government and are free to the people. Here at Yumoto, men, women, and children walk into the one large room containing the pools, undress, lay their clothing in a little heap on the raised bench or platform running around the edge of the room, and step into the water ; and, as has been said, no one sees any impropriety in this custom. Women sit or kneel on the edges of the pool, scouring themselves with bags of rice-bran, and chattering with their friends in or out of the water. People stop at the open doors, or breast-high windows, to talk to the bathers, and conduct is as decorous, as reserved, and as modest as in a drawing-room. The approach of a foreigner sends all the grown bathers deep into the water, simply out of respect to his artificial and incomprehensible way of looking at natural things. They know, though they cannot understand, that the European finds something objectionable, and even wrong, in so insignificant a trifle as being seen without clothes.

At our tea-house in Yumoto our three rooms in the upper story were thrown into one during the daytime, making an apartment open to the gallery on three sides. Hibachis, or braziers, with mounds of glowing charcoal, tempered the morning and evening air, and all day we could sit on piles of futons, and enjoy the superb picture of mountains and lake before us. We were poled over the placid water in a queer ark of a boat, and the mountain-paths were always alluring, the roughest trail often passing under torii, or leading past some shrine, just when it seemed that no foot had ever preceded ours. At night, when the chilling air presses the sulphur fumes closer to earth, Yumoto streets resound with the wailing whistle of the blind shampooer, or amah. These amah are found everywhere—in the largest cities and in the smallest mountain villages—and, whether men or women, are never young, or even middle-aged. Theirs is an indefinite, unscientific system of massage, and their manipulations often leave their charges with more lame and aching muscles than before. But the amah are an institution of the country, and Yumoto streets would ring with their dreary music, and our screens would be slipped aside by many an ill-favored crone, as soon as it was time for the usual evening baths to be prepared at the tea-houses.

Upon another visit to Nikko and Chiuzenji in late October there was a more splendid autumnal pageant than the most gorgeous hill-sides of America had ever shown me. Frost had done its most wonderful work, and the air was exhilarating to intoxication. The clear and brilliant weather moved the coolies to frisk, play, and chant like children—even that dignified little man, Ito, relaxing his gravity to frolic like a boy, and to pry bowlders over the edges of precipices to hear them crash and fall far below. Chiuzenji looked a vast, flawless sapphire, and Nantaisan was a mosaic of richest Byzantine coloring. Kegon-no-taki, the fall of three hundred feet by which the waters of Chiuzenji drop to the valley in their race to the Daiyagawa, seemed a column of snow in its little amphitheatre hung with autumn vines and branches. But we dared not remain, for already Yumoto was closed and boarded up for the season, and on any day the first of the blockading snows of winter might shut the door of the one tea-house left open at Chiuzenji, and end the travel from the Ashiwo copper-mines.

CHAPTER XVII

THE ASCENT OF FUJIYAMA

IT was in the third week of July that we made our long-talked-of ascent of Fujiyama. There were nine of us, all told, four stalwart men, three valiant women, and two incomparable Japanese boys, or valets. For forty miles we steamed down the old line of the Tokaido, drawing nearer to the sea in its deep indentation of Odawara Bay, and to the blue bar of the Hakone range that fronts the ocean. At Kodzu we took wagonettes and rattled over the plain and up a valley along the To-kaido, children being snatched from under the heels of the horses, and coolies, with poles and baskets over their shoulders, getting entangled with the wheels all the way. A Japanese driver is a most reckless Jehu, and the change to jinrikishas, after the wild ten-mile charge up the valley, was beatific. Ascending a narrow cañon, and rounding curve after curve, we saw at last the many lights of Miyanoshita twinkling against the sky.

Miyanoshita, the great summer resort, is the delight alike of Japanese and foreigner. It has excellent hotels kept in western fashion, clear mountain air, mineral springs and beautiful scenery, and it is the very centre of a most interesting region. All the year round its ho-tels are well patronized, the midwinter climate being a specific for the malarial poison of the ports of southern China. Famous, too, is the wooden-ware of Miyano-shita, where every house is a shop for the sale of Japan-ese games, household utensils, toys and trifles, all made of the beautifully-grained native woods, polished on a wheel with vegetable wax. Exquisite mosaics of a hundred broken patterns amaze one with their nicety of finish and cheapness, and no one escapes from the village without buying.

Guides and coolies had been engaged for us at Miyanoshita, and at six o'clock, on the morning after our arrival, the three kagos of the ladies were carried out, and the four cavaliers, the two boys, and six baggage coolies followed. The broad path zigzagged upward to the narrow, knife-edge ride of the mountain range known as the O Tomi Toge pass. From its summit we looked back along the checkered green valley to Miyanoshita and Hakone Lake, with the Emperor's island palace. Looking forward across a checkered plain, we saw Fujiyama rise straight before us, its obstinate head still hidden in clouds. Dropping quickly to the level of the plain, we reached Gotemba, and, changing to jinrikishas, were whirled away to Subashiri, six miles distant.

Trains of descending pilgrims and farmers, perched high on the backs of pack-horses, smiled cheerfully at the procession of foreigners bound for Fuji, and at each rest-house on the way women and children, petrified with astonishment, stood staring at us. Black cinders and blocks of lava announced the nearness of the volcano, and the road became an inky trail of coal-dust through green fields. Banks of scoriæ, like the heaps of coal-dust around collieries, cropped out by the road-side, and the wheels ground noisily through the loose, coarse slag. The whole of Subashiri, crowding the picturesque street of a typical Japanese village, welcomed us. In the stream of running water, on either side of the broad highway danced, whirled, and spouted a legion of mechanical toys, some for the children's pleasure, and others turning the fly-brushes hung over counters of cakes and sweetmeats. The place looks in perpetual fête, with the hundreds of pilgrim flags and towels fluttering from each tea-house, and at the end of the street is a torii, leading to an ancient temple in a grove, where all Fuji pilgrims pray before beginning the ascent of the mountain. In the light of the afternoon, the double row of thatched houses and the street full of bareheaded villagers looked like a well-painted stage scene. Meanwhile the sun sank, and in the last crimson glow of its fading the clouds rolled away, and Fuji's stately cone stood over us, its dark slopes turning to rose and violet in the changing light.

We rose with the sun at four o'clock, looked at Fuji, all pink and lilac in the exquisite atmosphere of the morning, snatched a hasty breakfast and set off, the women in their kagos and the men on mettlesome steeds that soon took them out of sight along the broad cindery avenue leading to the base of the slanting mountain. In that clear light Fuji looked twice its twelve thousand feet above the sea, and the thought of toiling on foot up the great slope was depressing. Instead of a fifteen-mile walk, it looked fifty miles at least. All along the forest avenue moss-grown stone posts mark the distance, and at one place are the remains of a stone wall and lantern-guarded gate-way setting the limit of the mountain's holy ground. From that point the soil is sacred, although horses and kagos are allowed to go a mile farther to a mat-shed station, known as Umagaye-shi (Turn Back Horse). Thence the great Fuji sweeps continuously upward, and a tall torii at the head of the stone staircase marks the beginning of the actual ascent, the holy ground on which only sandaled feet may tread.

In the mat-shed the kagos were stored for a two days' rest, luggage was divided and tied on the backs of the coolies, who were as gayly fringed as Indians on the war-path, with the many pairs of straw sandals tied at their waists and hanging from their packs. The coarse cinders cut through boot-soles so quickly that foreigners tie on these waraji to protect their shoes, allowing eight pairs of the queer galoshes for the ascent and descent of Fuji. From Umagayeshi, the path goes up through woods and stunted underbrush and on over bare cinder and lava, pursuing the even slope of the mountain without dip or zigzag to break the steady climb. Three small Shinto temples in the woods invite pilgrims to pray, pay tribute, and have their staff and garments marked with a sacred seal. Beyond these temples, ten rest-houses, or stations, stand at even distances along the path, the first, or number one, at the edge of the woods, and the tenth at the summit. Priests and station-keepers open their season late in June, before the snow is gone, and close in September. In the midsummer weeks the whole mountain-side is musical with the tinkling bells and staffs of lines of white-clad pilgrims. Notwithstanding their picturesqueness, these devotees are objectionable companions, as they fill tea-houses and mountain stations, devour everything eatable, like swarms of locusts, and bear about with them certain smaller pilgrims that make life a burden to him who follows after. Nearly thirty thousand pilgrims annually ascend Fujiyama. These pious palmers are chiefly from the agricultural class, and they form mutual pilgrimage associations, paying small annual dues, from the sum of which each member in turn has his expenses defrayed. They travel in groups, each man furnished with his bit of straw matting for bed, rain coat, or shelter. They carry, also, cotton towels marked with the crest of their pilgrim society, to be hung, after using, at temple water-tanks, or as advertisements of their presence at the tea-houses which they patronize. At each new shrine they visit the priests stamp their white clothing with the red seal of the temple.

Fujiyama is invested with legends, which these pilgrims unquestioningly accept. It is said to have risen up in a single night two thousand years ago, when a great depression appeared to the southward, which the waters of Lake Biwa immediately filled. For a thousand years pilgrims have toiled up the weary path to pray at the highest shrine and to supplicate the sun at dawn. Fuji-san, the goddess of the mountain, hated, it is said, her own sex, and stories of devils, who seize women and fly off into the air with them, still deter all but the most emancipated Japanese women from making the ascent. It was after Fuji-san had quarrelled with all the other gods that she set up this lofty mountain of her own, where she might live alone and in peace. No horse's foot is allowed to fall on the steep approaches to her cloudy throne, and even the sand and cinders are so sacred, that whatever dust is carried down on the pilgrims' feet by day is miraculously returned by night. Even to dream of the peerless mountain is a promise of good-fortune, and Fuji, with the circling storks and the ascending dragon, symbolizes success in life and triumph over obstacles.

Until the year 1500, Fuji wore a perpetual smoke-wreath, and every century saw a great eruption. The last, in 1707, continued for a month, and threw out the loose cinders, ashes, and lumps of baked red clay that still cover the mountain. Ashes were carried fifty miles, damming a river in their path, covering the plain at its base six feet deep with cinders, and forming an excrescence on the north side, which still mars the perfect symmetry of the cone.

Umagayeshi, or Turn Back Horse, is four thousand feet above the sea, and the other eight thousand feet are surmounted in a distance of fifteen miles. We desired to reach Station Eight by four o'clock; either to sleep there until three o'clock the next morning, or to push on to the tenth and last station, rest there, and see the sun rise, from the door-way of that summit rest-house. Our two Colorado mountaineers had faced the slope like chamois, and were leaping the rocks walling the first station, before the female contingent had left the torii. Of the fifteen coolies accompanying us, three were assigned to each woman, with orders to take her to the top if they had to carry her pickaback. After an established Fuji fashion, one coolie went first with a rope fastened around the climber's waist, while another pushed her forward. Aided still further by tall bamboo staffs, we were literally hauled and boosted up the mountain, with only the personal responsibility of lifting our feet out of the ashes.

For the first three or four miles, the path led through a dense, green bower, carpeted with vines, and starred with wild flowers and great patches of wild strawberries. Scaling moss-covered log steps, we passed through temples with *gohei*, or prayer papers, hanging from the gates and doors, and bare Shinto altars within. At one shrine, the sound of our approaching footsteps was the signal for blasts from a conch-shell horn and thumps on the hanging drum, and the priests, in their purple and white gowns and black pasteboard hats, gave us a cheerful welcome, and many cups of hot barley-tea. At our request, they stamped our clothing with big red characters, the sacred seal or crest of that holy station, and sold us the regulation pilgrim's staff, branded with the temple mark. The old priest, to dazzle us with his acquirements, and to show his familiarity with foreign customs, glibly placed the price of the alpenstock at " Sen tents."

The forest ended as suddenly as if one had stepped from a door-way, and a sloping dump of bare lava and cinders stretched upward endlessly ; the whole cone visible, touched with scudding bits of thin white clouds. Every dike and seam of lava between the forest edge and the summit was clearly seen, and the square blocks of rest-houses, though miles away, stood out on the great ash-heap as if one could touch them. It was apparent that the walk would be merely a matter of perseverance. There are no dizzy precipices, no dangerous rocks, no hand-over-hand struggles, nor narrow ledges, nor patches of slippery stone—only a steadily ascending cinder path to tread. Above the forest line, nothing interrupts the wide views in every direction, and the goal is in plain sight.

After we had passed the third station, the scudding clouds closed in and hid the summit, and we trudged along, congratulating ourselves on our escape from the glaring sun while we were out on the open lava slope. Station Number Four was closed and its roof in partial ruins, where a rolling stone had crashed in during the winter, but at the next two huts we rested, in company with a sturdy mountaineer, his wife and baby, who were going up to open Station Number Nine for the summer. The baby was strapped on its father's back, its little bare toes sticking out from its tight swaddling-gown and curling up in comical balls as the wind grew colder. Our two veterans of Pike's Peak were far ahead, merely white spots on the dark, chocolate-brown slope, but we all intended to overtake them and come in with them at the end of the day.

Suddenly the drifting clouds swept down, curling along the dark lava, like steam, and wrapping us in a gray mist that blotted out everything. Another gust of wind brought a dash of rain, and hurried us to the lee wall of a closed hut for shelter. The shower came harder and faster, and the baggage - coolies with water - proofs and umbrellas were far in advance, invisible in the mist. We pushed on, and after climbing a hundred yards in loose ashes, found ourselves on the sliding track of the descent. We struck away blindly to the right and mounted straight upward. A seam of hard lava soon gave us secure foothold, but presently became a net-work of tiny cascades. My cheerful little coolie, in his saturated cotton suit, tried to encourage me, and passing the rope around a horn of lava at one breathing-stop, pointed upward, and assured me that there was clear sunshine above. Glancing along the sloping lava-track, we saw a foaming crest of water descending from those sunny uplands, and had barely time to cross its path before the roaring stream came on and cut off retreat. ·

After two hours of hard climbing in the blinding rain and driving wind, we reached the shelter of Station Number Eight, chilled and exhausted. This hut, a log-cabin faced with huge lava blocks, its low roof held down by many bowlders, and its walls five feet in thickness, consists of one room about twelve by thirty feet in size. Two doors looked sheer down the precipitous mountain-slope, and a deep window, like that of a fortress, was set in the end wall. The square fireplace, sunken in the floor, had its big copper kettle swinging from a crane, and the usual stone frame for the rice-kettle. When the doors were barred and braced with planks against the fury of the storm, the smoke, unable to escape, nearly blinded us. Our dripping garments and the coolies' wet cotton clothes were hung to dry on the rafters over the fireplace, where they slowly dripped. The master of Number Eight had opened his rest-house only five days before, and with his young son and two servants found himself called on to provide for us with our retinue of seventeen servants, for four young cadets from the naval college in Tokio, storm - bound on their way down the mountain, and a dozen pilgrims—forty-two people in all.

Warmed, and comforted with a stray sandwich, we were glad enough to go to bed. Each of us received two futons, one of which made the mattress and the other the covering, while basket-lids served for pillows. The floor was cold as well as hard, and the rows of cotton towels hung on the walls by preceding pilgrims fluttered in the draughts from the howling blasts that shook the solid little hut. The shriek and roar and mad rushes of wind were terrifying, and we were by no means certain that the little stone box would hold together until morning. One hanging-lamp shed a fantastic light on the rows of heads under the blue futons, and the stillness of the Seven Sleepers presently befell the lonely shelter.

CHAPTER XVIII

THE DESCENT OF FUJIYAMA

From Saturday until Tuesday, three endless days and as many nights, the whirling storm kept us prisoners in the dark, smoke-filled rest-house. What had been the amusing incidents of one stormy night became our intolerable routine of life. Escape was impossible, even for the hardy mountaineers and pilgrims at the other end of the hut, and to unbar the door for a momentary outlook threatened the demolition of the shelter. A tempest at sea was not more awful in its fury, but our ears became finally accustomed to the roar and hiss of the wind, and the persistent blows it dealt the structure. The grave problem of provisioning the place in time confronted us, and after our one day's luncheon was exhausted, it became a question how long the master of the station could provide even fish and rice for forty people.

The two boys, or valets, brought by their sybarite masters, like all Japanese servants out of their grooves, were utterly helpless, and lay supine in their corners, covered, head and all, with futons. The altitude, the cold, or the dilemma paralyzed their usually nimble faculties, and our coolies were far more useful. We could not stand upright under the heavy beams of the roof, and as the floor planks had been taken up here and there to brace the doors with, walking was difficult in that dark abode. While we grew impatient in our cage, the four little naval cadets sat, or lay, quietly in their futons, hour after hour, talking as cheerfully as if the sun were shining, their prospects hopeful, and their summer suits of white duck designed for the Eighth Station's phenomenal climate. Throughout our incarceration the coolies dozed and waked under their futons, sitting up only long enough to eat, or play some childish game, and dropping back to reckon how much per diem would accrue to them without an equivalent of work. When we found that the smoky fireplace offered some warmth, we sat around the sunken box with our feet in the ashes and handkerchiefs to our eyes to keep out the blinding smoke.

In that intimate circle we learned the cook's secrets, and watched him shaving off his billets of dried fish with a plane, stewing them with mushrooms and seasoning with soy and saké. This compound we found so good that our flattered landlord brought out hot saké and insisted on an exchange of healths. We noticed that in the midst of this hospitality he went and made some offering or other at his little household altar, and, writing something in a book, returned more benign and friendly than ever. The preparation of red bean and barley soups, two sweetened messes that only a Japanese could eat, and the boiling of rice seemed never to stop. Twice a day the big copper caldron was set on its stone frame half full of boiling water. When it bubbled most furiously over a brushwood fire, a basketful of freshly washed and soaked rice was poured in. In a half-hour the caldron was filled to the top with the full, snowy grains, ready for the chopsticks of the waiting company.

Each night the master of the hut prophesied clear weather at five o'clock in the morning, and each morning he prophesied clear weather for five o'clock in the afternoon, but the wind howled, the sleet swept by in clouds, and hail rattled noisily on roof and walls. The second afternoon the master of the summit rest-hut appeared at the window, and, more dead than alive, was drawn in by the excited coolies, who helped chafe his limbs and pour cups of hot saké between his lips. The story of his battle with the storm on the open, windswept cone satisfied us all to wait for the clearing. An empty rice-box had forced him to attempt the journey to revictual his station, and we wondered how soon our landlord would be compelled to the same desperate effort.

On the third morning the visiting boniface and four wood-choppers decided to attempt the descent, and when the door was unbarred, the pale daylight and a changed wind, that entered the dim cave where we had been imprisoned, foretold a clearing sky. As the clouds lifted, we could see for miles down the wet and glistening mountain to a broad, green plain, sparkling with flashing diamonds of lakes, and gaze down a sheer ten thousand feet to the level of the sea. It was a view worth the three days of waiting. The summit loomed clear and close at hand, and our western mountaineers made two thousand feet of ascent in thirty minutes, the rest of us following in a more deliberate procession, as befitted the altitude. The coolies, in bright yellow oil-paper capes and hats, trooped after us like a flock of canaries, gayly decorating the dark lava paths. At the edge of the summit, on the rim of the crater, we passed under a torii, climbed steep lava steps and entered the last station — a low, dark, wretched, little wind-swept cabin, with one small door and a ten-inch fireplace, where saké was warming for us.

Hardly had we arrived when the wind rose, the clouds shut down, and again the rain drove in dense and whirling sheets. The adventurous ones, who had pushed on to the edge of the crater to look in, were obliged to creep back to safety on their hands and knees, for fear of being swept over into that cauldron of boiling clouds and mist. It was no time to make the circuit of the crater's rim with its many shrines, or descend the path-way, guarded by torii, to the crater's bed. We hurried through the formalities at the temple, where the benumbed priest branded the alpenstocks, stamped our handkerchiefs and clothing, and gave us pictured certificates of our ascent to that point. Then began a wild sliding and plunging down a shoot of loose cinders to Station Number Eight, where the landlord produced a book and read our three-days' board bill from a record of many pages. Everything was chanted out by items, even to the saké and mushrooms that had been pressed upon us as a courtesy, and it was only after many appeals for the sum total that he instinctively ducked his head and named fifty-eight dollars for the seven of us. Then ensued a deafening attack of remonstrances from men and valets, threats and invectives in Japanese and English, lasting until the inn-keeping Shylock agreed to take thirty dollars, received this moiety cheerfully, and bade us adieu with many protestations of esteem.

Rubber and gossamer rain-cloaks were worse than useless in that whirlwind, and haste was our one necessity. Dress skirts were sodden and leaden masses, and mine being hung as an offering to Fuji-san, a red Navajo blanket replaced it, and enveloped me completely. A yellow-clad coolie securely fastened his rope, and we slipped, and plunged, and rolled down a shoot of loose cinders. Sinking ankle-deep, we travelled as if on runners through the wet ashes, sliding down in minutes stretches that it had taken us as many hours to ascend, and stopping only at one or two rest-houses for cups of hot tea, while we staggered and stumbled on through rain that came ever harder and faster.

At Umagayeshi, where the dripping party waited for more tea, the sun came gayly out and seemed to laugh at our plight. The sudden warmth, the greenhouse steam and softness, were most grateful to us after our hardships in the clouds. At Subashiri we put on the few dry garments we had been fortunate enough to leave behind us. The tea-house windows framed vignettes of Fuji, a clear blue and purple cone in a radiant, clouddappled sky. With the prospect of a hot day to follow, it was decided to push on to Miyanoshita, travelling all night, the kagos being as comfortable as the flea-infested tea-house, and the men of our party being obliged to walk on until they reached dry boots and clothes. Though the coolies grumbled, stormed, and appealed, they had enjoyed three days of absolute rest and full pay at Number Eight, and the walk of forty-five miles, from the summit to Miyanoshita, is not an unusual jaunt for them to make.

At Gotemba's tea-house we found our companions in misfortune—the little midshipmen—whom we joined in feasting on what the house could offer. The old women in attendance, yellow and wrinkled as the crones of ivory *netsukes*, were vastly interested in our Fuji experiences and dilapidated costumes, and gave us rice, fish, spongecake, tea, and saké. At midnight we roused the coolies from their five-hour rest, and prepared for the fifteen-mile journey over O Tomi Toge pass. The little midshipmen slid the screens and beckoned us up to the liliputian balcony again. "It is the night Fuji" said one of them, softly, pointing to the dark violet cone, striped with its ghostly snow, and illuminated by a shrunken yellow moon that hung fantastic above O Tomi Toge's wall.

With our commander-in-chief perched high on a pack-horse, whose chair-like saddle left his rider's heels resting on the neck of the animal, and the kago coolies slipping and floundering through the bottomless mud of the roads, we once more started on our way. The whole country was dark, silent, and deserted, and the only audible sound was the chatter of our army of coolies, who chirped and frolicked like boys out of school. The night air over the rice-fields was warm and heavy, and seemed to suffocate us, and fire-flies drifted in and out among the rushes and bamboos. Deep, roaring streams filled the channels that had been mere silver threads of water a few days before. The coolies could barely keep their footing as they waded waist-deep in the rushing water, and at every ford we half expected to be drowned.

At the summit of the pass we dismounted, and the coolies scattered for a long rest. The sacred mountain was clear and exquisite in the pale gray of dawn ; and while we watied to see the sun rise on Fuji, a dirty-brown fog scudded in from the sea, crossed the high moon, and instantly the plain faded from view and we were left, isolated Brocken figures, to eat our four-o'clock breakfast of dry bread and chocolate, and return to the kagos. Everywhere we encountered traces of a heavy storm, the path being gullied and washed into a deep ditch with high banks, whose heavy-topped, white lilies brushed into the kagos as we passed. Half asleep, we watched the green panorama unfolding as we descended, and at eight o'clock we were set down in Miyanoshita. Nesans ran hither and thither excitedly, to bring coffee and toast, to prepare baths, produce the luggage we had left behind, and mildly rehearse to the other domestics the astonishing story of our adventures. By noon, when we came forth arrayed in the garb of civilization, we were heroes.

For weeks after we returned to the plain, the treacherous Fujiyama stood unusually clear and near at hand. "The summer Fuji," its dark-brown slopes only touched with a fine line or two of snow, is less beautiful than "the winter Fuji," with its glistening crown; and our Mount Rainier, whose snows are eternal, whose wooded slopes shadow the dark-green waters of Puget Sound, is lovelier still. But though we have the more glorious mountain, the snow, the rocks, the forest, we have not the people instinct with love of poetry and nature; we have not the race-refinement, and the race-traditions, that would make of it another Fuji, invested with the light of dream and legend, dear and near to every heart.

CHAPTER XIX

THE TOKAIDO—I

As the kago gave way to the jinrikisha, the jinrikisha disappears before the steam-engine, which reduces a *ri* to a *cho*, and extends the empire of the commonplace. The first railroads, built by English engineers and equipped with English rolling-stock, have been copied by the Japanese engineers, who have directed the later works. The Tokaido railway line, built from both ends, put Tokio and Kioto within twenty-four hours of each other. The forty miles of railroad between Yokohama and Kodzu were completed in 1887, bringing Miyanoshita, a long day's journey distant, within three hours of the great seaport. The long tunnels and difficult country around Fujiyama, and the expensive engineering work at each river delayed the opening of the whole line until 1889. Before the iron horse had cleared all picturesqueness from the region three of us made the jinrikisha journey down the Tokaido.

The Tokaido having been the great post-road and highway of the empire for centuries, with daimios and their trains constantly travelling between the two capitals, its villages and towns were most important, and each supplied accommodations for every class of travellers. All the world knew the names of the fifty-three post stations on the route, and there is a common game, which consists in quickly repeating them in their order backward or forward. As the railroad touched or left them, some of the towns grew, others dwindled, and new places sprang up. Each village used to have its one special occupation, and to ride down the Tokaido was to behold in succession the various industries of the empire. In one place only silk cords were made, in another the finely-woven straw coverings of saké cups and lacquer bowls; a third produced basket-work of wistaria fibres, and a fourth shaped ink-stones for writing-boxes. Increased trade and steam communication have interfered with these local monopolies, and one town is fast becoming like another in its industrial displays.

May is one of the best months for such overland trips in Japan, as the weather is perfect, pilgrims and fleas are not yet on the road, and the rainy season is distant. The whole country is like a garden, with its fresh spring crops, and the long, shaded avenue of trees is everywhere touched with flaming azaleas and banks of snowy blackberry blossoms. The tea-house and the tateba everywhere invite one to rest and watch the unique processions of the highway, and away from foreign settlements much of the old Japan is left. Tea is everywhere in evidence in May. It is being picked in the fields, carted along the roads, sold, sorted, and packed in every town, while charming nesans with trays of tiny cups fairly line the road.

From Miyanoshita's comfortable hotel the two foreign women and the Japanese guide started on the first stage of the Tokaido trip in pole-chairs, carried by four coolies each. The *danna san*, or master of the party, scorning such effeminate devices, strode ahead with an alpenstock, a pith helmet, and russet shoes, while the provision-box and general luggage, filling a kago, followed after us. We were soon up the hill in a bamboo-shaded lane, and then out over the grassy uplands to the lake of Hakone. The singing coolies strode along, keeping even step on the breathless ascents, past the sulphur baths of Ashinoyu and to the Hakone Buddha—a giant bass-relief of Amida sculptured on the face of a wall of rock niched among the hills. The lonely Buddha occupies a fit place for a contemplative deity—summer suns scorching and winter snows drifting over the stony face unhindered. A heap of pebbles in Buddha's lap is the register of pilgrims' prayers.

At Hakone village, a single street of thatched houses bordering the shore of Hakone lake, the narrow footpath over the hills joins the true Tokaido, a stone-paved highway shaded by double rows of ancient trees, a forest aisle recalling, for a brief journey, the avenue to Nikko. The chrysanthemum-crested gates of the Emperor's island palace were fast shut, and Fuji's cone peeped over the shoulders of encircling mountains, and reflected its image in the almost bottomless lake—an ancient crater, whose fires are forever extinguished. Here we tied straw sandals over our shoes and tried to walk along the smooth flat stones of the Tokaido, but soon submitted to be carried again up the ascent to Hakone pass, which looks southward over a broad valley to the ocean. Pack-horses, with their clumsy feet tied in straw shoes, were led by blue-bloused peasants, their heads wrapped in the inevitable blue-and-white cotton towel, along the stony road, that has been worn smooth and slippery by the straw-covered feet of generations of men and horses.

From the *Fuji no taira* (terrace for viewing Fuji), in the village of Yamanaka, we looked sheer down to the plain of Mishima and saw, almost beneath us, the town that would mark the end of our day's journey. The villages of Sasabara and Mitsuya have each a single row of houses on either side of the road replacing the shade-trees of the Tokaido, and, like all Japanese villages, they overflow with children, to whom *Ijin san*, the foreigner, is still a marvel.

Mishima is a busy, prosperous little town, with a gay main street and shops overflowing with straw hats, baskets, matting, rain-coats, umbrellas, tourist and pilgrim necessities. Shops for the sale of foreign goods are numerous, and besides the familiar cases of "Devoe's Brilliant Oil for Japan, 150° test," American trade is advertised by pictures of the Waterbury watch, and long hanging signs declaring the merits of the American time-keepers sold at three *yen* apiece. Even the chief of the jinrikisha men, who came to make the bargain for wheeling us down the Tokaido, pulled out such a watch to tell us the time of day.

Mishima's best tea-house, where daimios rested in the olden time, is a most perfect specimen of Japanese architecture, full of darkly-shining woods, fantastic windows, and tiny courts. In one of our rooms the tokonoma held a kakemono, with a poem written on it in giant characters, and three tall pink peonies springing from an exquisite bronze vase. In another, smiled a wooden image of old Hokorokojin, one of the household gods of luck, and on a low lacquer table rested a large lacquer box containing a roll of writing-paper, the ink-box, and brushes. These, with the soft mats, a few silk cushions, a tea-tray, and tabako bon, were all that the rooms contained, until our incongruous bags and bundles marred their exquisite simplicity. The landlord, with many bows and embarrassed chucklings, greeted us there, and presented a most superb, long-stemmed Jacqueminot rose, whose fragrance soon filled the whole place.

When we went out for a walk all Mishima joined us; and with a following of two hundred children and half as many elders, we turned into the grounds of an old temple shaded by immense trees and protected by an ancient moat. The brigade clattered after us across the stone bridge of a great lotus pond, where the golden carp are as large and as old as the mossy-backed patriarchs at Fontainebleau and Potsdam, and snapped and fought for the rice-cakes we threw them as if it were their first feast. Farther in the temple grounds gorgeously-colored cocks with trailing tails, and pretty pigeons are kept as messengers of the gods, and a toothless old man makes a slender living by selling popped beans to feed them. Prayers for rain offered up at this temple always prevail, and we had barely returned to the tea-house before a soaking storm set in and restricted us to our inn for entertainment.

The large matted room, or space at the front of the tea-house, was at once office, hall, vestibule, pantry, and store-room. At one side opened a stone-floored kitchen with rows of little stone braziers for charcoal fires, on which something was always steaming and sputtering. Chief-cook, under-cooks, and gay little maids pattered around on their clogs, their sleeves tied up, hoisting water from the well, and setting out trays with the various dishes of a Japanese dinner. There is no general dining-room, nor any fixed hour for meals in a Japanese inn. At any moment, day or night, the guest may clap his hands and order his food, which is brought to his room on a tray and set on the floor, or on the ozen, a table about four inches high. Rice is boiled in quantities large enough to last for one, or even two days. It is heated over when wanted, or hot tea is poured over the cold rice after it is served. Our guide cooked all our food, laid our high table with its proper furnishings, and was assisted by the nesans in carrying things up and down the stairs. In a small room opening from the office two girls were sorting the landlord's new tea just brought in from the country. They sat before a large table raised only a few inches from the floor, and, from a heap of the fragrant leaves at one end, scattered little handfuls thinly over the lacquer top. With their deft fingers they slid to one side the smallest and finest leaves from the tips of the new shoots of the plant, and to the other side the larger and coarser growth, doing it all so quickly and surely that it was a pleasure to watch them. In another corner of the office two other little maids were putting clean cases on all the pillows of the house. The Japanese pillow is a wooden box, with a little padded roll on top, which is covered with a fresh bit of soft, white mulberry-paper each day. The bath-room was as accessible as the kitchen, without a door, but with glass screens, and one large tank in which three or four could sociably dip together. Here were splashing and talking until midnight, and steam issued forth continually, as guests and the household staff took their turn. The landlord requested the masculine head of our party to use a special tub that stood in an alcove of the office, a folding-screen about three feet high being set up to conceal him from the populous precincts of office, corridor, garden, and main street. A too vigorous sweep of his stalwart arm, however, knocked down his defence, and dropping to his chin in the water, he called for help ; whereupon the two maids, who were sorting tea, ran over and set the barrier up again, as naturally as a foreign servant would place the fire-screen before a grate.

In old Tokaido days the home bath-tub was often set beside the door-step, that bathers might lose nothing that was going on. Government regulations and stern policemen have interfered with this primitive innocency, except in the most remote districts, and these Oriental Arcadians are obliged to wear certain prescribed fig-leaves, although they curtail them as much as possible in warm weather, and dispense with them when beating out wheat ears in their own farm-yards, and treading the rice-mill in-doors. Privacy is unknown to the lower classes, and in warm weather their whole life is lived out-of-doors. With their open-fronted houses, they are hardly in-doors even when under their own roofs. On pleasant mornings women wash and cook, mend, spin, reel, and set up the threads for the loom on the open road-side, and often bring the clumsy wooden loom out-of-doors, throwing the bobbins back and forth, while keeping an eye on their neighbors' doings and the travelling public. One runs past miles of such groups along the Tokaido, and the human interest is never wanting in any landscape picture.

From Mishima southward the country is most beautiful, Fujiyama standing at the end of the broad valley with the spurs of its foot-hills running down to the sea. This Yoshiwara plain is one wide wheat-field, golden in May-time with its first crop, and the Tokaido's line marked with rows of picturesque pine-trees rising from low embankments brilliant with blooming bushes. In the villages each little thatched house is fenced with braided reeds, enclosing a few peonies, iris-beds, and inevitable chrysanthemum plants. The children, with smaller children on their backs, chase, tumble, and play, cage fire-flies, and braid cylinders and hexagonal puzzles of wheat straws ; and in sunshine or in rain, indifferently stroll along the road in the aimless, uncertain way of chickens.

Beyond the poor, unfragrant town of Yoshiwara, a creaking, springing bridge leaped the torrent of a river fed by Fuji's snows and clouds. In the good old days, when the traveller sat on a small square platform, carried high above the shoulders of four men, to be ferried over, these bearers often stopped in the most dangerous place to extort more pay—which was never refused. Above the river bank the road climbs a ridge, traverses the tiniest of rice valleys, and then follows the ocean cliffs for hours. This Corniche road, overhanging the sea, presents a succession of pictures framed by the arching branches of ancient pine-trees, and the long Pacific rollers, pounding on the beach and rocks, fill the air with their loud song. At sunset we came to the old monastery of Kiomiidera, high on the terraced front of a bold cliff. Climbing to a gate-way and bell tower worthy of a fortress, we roused the priests from their calm meditations. An active young brother in a white gown flew to show us the famous garden with its palm-trees and azaleas reflected in a tiny lake, a small waterfall descending musically from the high mountain wall of foliage behind it. Superbly decorated rooms, where Shoguns and daimios used to rest from their journeys, look out on this green shade. The main temple is a lofty chamber with stone flooring and gorgeous altar, shady, quiet, and cool, and a corner of the temple yard has been filled by pious givers with hundreds upon hundreds of stone Buddhas, encrusted with moss and lichens, and pasted bits of paper prayers.

All through those first provinces around Fuji the garden fences, made of bamboo, rushes, twigs, or coarse straw, are braided, interlaced, woven and tied in ingenious devices, the fashion and pattern often changing completely in a few hours' ride. This region is the happy hunting-ground of the artist and photographer, where everything is so beautiful, so picturesque, and so artistic that even the blades of grass and ears of millet "compose," and every pine-tree is a kakemono study. Thatched roofs, and arching, hump-backed bridges made of branches, twigs, and straw seem only to exist for landscape effects; but, unhappily, the old bridges, like the lumbering junks with their laced and shirred sails, are disappearing, and, in a generation or two, will be as unfamiliar to the natives as they now are to foreigners.

CHAPTER XX

THE TOKAIDO—II

GREAT once was Shidzuoka, which now is only a busy commercial town of an agricultural province. The old castle has been razed, its martial quadrangle is a wheat field; and the massive walls, the creeping and overhanging pine-trees and deep moats are the only feudal relics. Keiki, the last of the Tokugawa Shoguns, lived in a black walled enclosure beyond the outer moat, but the modern spirit paid no heed to his existence, and his death, in 1883, was hardly an incident in the routine of its commercial progress.

The great Shinto temple at the edge of the town is famous for the dragons in its ceiling. The old priest welcomed us with smiles, led us in, shoeless, over the mats, and bade us look up, first at the Dragon of the Four Quarters, and then at the Dragon of the Eight Quarters, the eyes of the monster strangely meeting ours, as we changed our various points of view.

At the archery range behind the temple our danna san proved himself a new William Tell with the bow and arrows. The attendant idlers cheered his shots, and a wrinkled old woman brought us dragon candies on a dark-red lacquer tray, under whose transparent surface lay darker shadows of cherry blossoms. The eye of the connoisseur was quick to descry the tray, and when the woman said it had been bought in the town, we took jinrikishas and hurried to the address she gave. The guide explained minutely, the shopkeeper brought out a hundred other kinds and colors of lacquer, and children ran in from home workshops with hardly dried specimens to show us. All the afternoon we searched through lacquer and curio shops, and finally despatched a coolie to the temple to buy the old woman's property. Hours afterwards he returned with a brand-new, bright red horror, and the message that " the mistress could not send the honorable foreigner such a poor old tray as that."

The fine Shidzuoka baskets, which are so famed elsewhere, were not to be found in Shidzuoka ; our tea-house was uninteresting, and so we set forth in the rain, unfurling big flat umbrellas of oil-paper, and whirling away through a dripping landscape. Rice and wheat alternated with dark-green tea-bushes, and cart-loads of tea-chests were bearing the first season's crop to market. The rain did not obscure the lovely landscape, as the plain we followed turned to a valley, the valley narrowed to a ravine, and we began climbing upward, while a mountain - torrent raced down beside us. One picturesque little village in a shady hollow gave us glimpses of silk-worm trays in the houses as we went whirling through it. The road, winding by zigzags up Utsonomiya pass, suddenly entered a tunnel six hundred feet in length, where the jinrikisha wheels rumbled noisily. On cloudy days the place is lighted by lamps, but on sunny days by the sun's reflection from two black lacquer boards at the entrances. The device is an old one in Japan, but an American patent has recently been issued for the same thing, as a cheap means of lighting ships' holds while handling cargo.

On the other side of Utsonomiya pass the road winds down by steep zigzags to the village of Okabe, noted for its trays and boxes made of the polished brown stem of a coarse fern. We bought our specimens from an oracular woman, who delivered her remarks like the lines of a part, her husband meekly echoing what she said in the same dramatic tones, and the whole scene being as stagey as if it had been well rehearsed beforehand.

From the mountains the road drops to a rich tea country, where every hill-side is green with the thick-set little bushes. At harvest-time cart-loads of basket-fired, or country-dried, tea fill the road to the ports, to be toasted finally in iron pans, and coated with indigo and gypsum to satisfy the taste of American tea-drinkers. In every town farmers may be seen dickering with the merchants over the tough paper sacks of tea that they bring in, and within the houses groups sitting at low tables sort the leaves into grades with swift fingers.

At Fujiyeda, where we took refuge from the increasing rain, the splashing in the large bath-room of the tea-house was kept up from afternoon to midnight by the guests, and continued by the family and tea-house maids until four o'clock, when the early risers began their ablutions. A consumptive priest on the other side of our thin paper walls had a garrulous shampooer about midnight and a refection later, and we were glad to resume the ride between tea fields at the earliest possible hour.

At Kanaya, at the foot of Kanaya mountain, the tea-house adjoined a school-house. The school-room had desks and benches but no walls, the screens being all removed. The teacher called the pupils in by clapping two sticks together, as in a French theatre. Spying the foreigners, the children stared, oblivious of teacher and blackboard, and the teacher, after one good look at the itinerants, bowed a courteous good-morning, and let the offenders go unpunished.

Up over Kanaya pass we toiled slowly, reaching at last a little eyrie of a tea-house, where the landlord pointed with equal pride to the view and to several pairs of muddy shoes belonging, he said, to the honorable gentlemen who were about piercing the mountain under us with a railway tunnel. Under a shady arbor is a huge, round bowlder, fenced in carefully and regarded reverently by humble travellers. According to the legend it used to cry at night like a child until Kobo Daishi, the inventor of the Japanese syllabary, wrote an inscription on it and quieted it forever. No less famous than Kobo Daishi's rock is the midzu ame of this Kanaya tea-house, and the dark brown sweet is put in dainty little boxes that are the souvenirs each pilgrim carries away with him.

Farther along the main road, with its arching shade-trees, the glossy dark tea-bushes gave way to square miles of rice and wheat fields. Here and there a patch of intense green verdure showed the young blades of rice almost ready to be transplanted to the fields, whence the wheat had just been garnered, the rice giving way in turn to some other cereal, all farming land in this fertile region bearing three annual crops.

A few villages showed the projecting roofs peculiar to the province of Totomi, and then the pretty tea-house at Hamamatsu quite enchanted us after our experiences with the poor accommodations of some of the provincial towns. A rough curbed well in the court-yard, with a queer parasol of a roof high over the sweep, a pretty garden all cool, green shade, a stair-way, steep and high, and at the top a long, dim corridor, with a floor of shining, dark *keyaki* wood. This was the place that made us welcome; even stocking-footed we half feared to tread on those brilliantly-polished boards. Our balcony overlooked a third charming garden, and each little room had a distinctive beauty of wooden ceilings, recesses, screens, and fanciful windows.

The most enviable possession of Hamamatsu, however, was O'Tatsu, and on our arrival O'Tatsu helped to carry our traps up-stairs, falling into raptures over our rings, pins, hair-pins, watches, and beaded trimmings. She clapped her hands in ecstasy, her bright eyes sparkled, and her smile displayed the most dazzling teeth. When we ate supper, sitting on the floor around an eight-inch high table, with little O'Tatsu presiding and waiting on us, not only her beauty but her charming frankness, simplicity, quickness, and grace made further conquest of us all. The maiden enjoyed our admiration immensely, arrayed herself in her freshest blue-and-white cotton kimono, and submitted her head to the best hair-dresser in town, returning with gorgeous bits of crape and gold cord tied in with the butterfly loops of her blue-black tresses. At her suggestion we sent for a small dancing-girl to entertain us, who, with a wand and masks, represented Suzume and other famous characters in legend and melodramas. When we left Hamamatsu, affectionate little O'Tatsu begged me to send her my photograph, and lest I should not have understood her excited flow of Japanese sentences, illuminated, however, by her great pleading eyes, she ran off, and, coming back, slipped up to me and held out a cheap, colored picture of some foreign beauty in the costume of 1865. When at last we rode away from the tea-house, O'Tatsu followed my jinrikisha for a long way, holding my hand, with tears in her lovely eyes, and her last sayonara broke in a sob.

A hard shell-road winds down to the shores of Hamana Lake and across its long viaduct. The jinrikishas run, as if on rubber tires, for nearly three miles over an embankment crossing the middle of the great lake, which at one side admits the curling breakers of the great Pacific. Until a few years ago this mountain-walled pool was protected from the ocean by a broad sand ridge, which an earthquake shook down, letting in the salt-waters. The Tokaido railroad crosses the lake on a high embankment, which was sodded and covered with a lattice-work of straw bundles, while seed was sown in the crevices more than a year before the road could be used. The whole railroad, as we saw in passing its completed sections, is solidly built with stone foundations and stone ballast, and intended to last for centuries. The Japanese seldom hurry the making of public works, and even a railroad does not inspire them with any feverish activity. Not until the last detail and station-house was finished was the line opened for travel, and following so nearly the route of the old Tokaido, through the most fertile and picturesque part of Central Japan, it keeps always in sight Fujiyama or the ocean.

In the course of the afternoon plantations of mulberry-trees came in sight. Loads of mulberry branches and twigs were being hauled into the villages and sold by weight, the rearers of silk-worms buying the leaves and paper-makers the stems for the sake of the inside bark. Climbing to one high plateau, we rested at a little rustic shed of a tea-house, commanding a superb view down a great ragged ravine to the line of foam breaking at its bowlder strewn entrance, and so on to the limitless ocean. One of the jinrikisha coolies preceded us to the benches on the overhanging balcony, and, kindly pointing out the special beauties of the scene, took off his garments and spread them out on the rail in the matter-of-fact, unconscious way of true Japanese innocence and simplicity of mind.

The guide-book calls the stretch of country beyond that high-perched tea-house "a waste region," but nothing could be more beautiful than the long ride through pine forest and belts of scrub-pine on that uncultivated plateau, always overlooking the ocean. At one point a temple to the goddess Kwannon is niched among towering rocks at the base of a narrow cliff, on whose summit a colossal statue of the deity stands high against the sky. For more than a century this bronze goddess of Mercy has been the object of pious pilgrimages, the pilgrims clapping their hands and bowing in prayer to all the thirty-three Kwannons cut in the face of the solid rock-base on which our lady of pity stands.

We reached the long, dull town of Toyohashi at dusk, to find the large tea-house crowded with travellers. Two rooms looking out upon a sultry high-walled garden were given us, and for dining-room a tiny alcove of a place on one of the middle courts. This room was so small and close that we had to leave the screens open, though the corridor led to the large bath-room, where half a dozen people splashed and chattered noisily and gentlemen with their clothes on their arms went back and forth before our door as if before the life class of an art school. The noise of the bathers was kept up gayly, until long after midnight, and no one in the tea-house seemed to be sleeping. By four o'clock in the morning such a coughing, blowing, and sputtering began in the court beside my room that I finally slid the screens and looked out. At least a dozen lodgers were brushing their teeth in the picturesque little quadrangle of rocks, bamboos, and palms, and bathing face and hands in the large stone and bronze urns that we had supposed to be ornamental only. Later, the gravel was covered with scores of the wooden sticks of tooth-brushes, beaten out into a tassel of fibres at one end, and with many boxes emptied of the coarse, gritty tooth-powder which the Japanese use so freely.

The last day of our long jinrikisha ride was warm, the sun glared on a white, dusty road, and the country was flat and uninteresting. Each little town and village seemed duller than the other. Wheat and rape were being harvested and spread to dry, and in the farm-yards men and women were hatchelling, beating out the grain with flails, and winnowing it in the primitive way by pouring it down from a flat scoop-basket held high overhead. Nobody wore any clothes to speak of, and the whole population turned out to watch the amazing spectacle of foreigners standing spell-bound until our jinrikishas had gone by.

At Arimatsu village we passed through a street of shops where the curiously dyed cotton goods peculiar to the place are sold. For several hundred years all Arimatsu has been tying knots down the lengths of cotton, twisting it in skeins, and wrapping it regularly with a double-dyed indigo thread, and then, by immersion in boiling water, dyeing the fabric in curious lines and star-spotted patterns. A more clumsy and primitive way of dyeing could not be imagined in this day of steam-looms and roller-printing, but Arimatsu keeps it up and prospers.

At sunset we saw the towers of Nagoya castle in the distance, and after crossing the broad plain of ripening rape and wheat, the coolies sped through the town at a fearful pace and deposited us, dazed, dusted, and weary, at the door of the Shiurokindo, to enjoy the beautiful rooms just kindly vacated by Prince Bernard, of Saxe-Weimar.

The Shiurokindo is one of the handsomest and largest of the tea-houses a foreigner finds, its interior a labyrinth of rooms and suites of rooms, each with a balcony and private outlook on some pretty court. The walls, the screens, recesses, ceilings, and balcony rails afford studies and models of the best Japanese interior decorations. The samisen's wail and a clapping chorus announced that a great dinner was going on, and in the broader corridors there was a passing and repassing of people arrayed in hotel kimonos.

As the wise traveller carries little baggage, the tea-houses furnish their customers with ukatas, or plain cotton kimonos, to put on after the bath and wear at night. These gowns are marked with the crest or name of the house, painted in some ingenious or artistic design; and guests may wander round the town, even, clad in these garments, that so ingeniously advertise the Maple-leaf, the Chrysanthemum, or Dragon tea-house. All guides, and servants particularly, enjoy wearing these hotel robes, and travellers who dislike to splash their own clothing march to the bath ungarmented, assuming the house gowns in the corridor after their dip. These ukatas at the Shiurokindo were the most startling fabrics of Arimatsu, and we looked in them as if we had been throwing ink-bottles at each other.

Until the long jinrikisha ride was over we had not felt weary, as each day beguiled us with some new interest and excitement; but when we stepped from those baby-carriages at the door of the Shiurokindo we were dazed with fatigue, although the coolies who ran all the way did not appear to be tired in the least. Their headman, who marshalled the team of ten, was a powerful young fellow, a very Hercules for muscle, and for speed and endurance hardly to be matched by that ancient deity. At the end of each day he seemed fresher and stronger than at the start, and he has often run sixty and sixty-five miles a day, for three and four days together. He led the procession and set the pace, shouting back warning of ruts, stones, or bad places in the road, and giving the signals for slowing, stopping, and changing the order of the teams. On level ground the coolies trotted tandem—one in the shafts, and one running ahead with a line from the shafts held over his shoulder. Going down-hill, the leader fell back and helped to hold the shafts; going uphill, he pushed the jinrikisha from the back.

The jinrikisha coolies make better wages than farm laborers or most mechanics. Our men were paid by the distance, and for days of detention each man received twenty-five cents to cover the expense of his board and lodging. They earned at an average one dollar and ten cents for each day, but out of this paid the rent of the jinrikisha and the Government tax. Where two men and a jinrikisha cover one hundred and eighty miles in four days they receive thirteen dollars in all, which is more than a farm laborer receives in a year. As a rule, these coolies are great gamblers and spendthrifts, with a fondness for saké. Our headman was a model coolie, saving his money, avoiding the saké-bottle, and regarding his splendid muscle as invested capital. When he walked in to collect his bill, he was clean and shining in a rustling silk kimono, such as a well-to-do merchant might wear. In this well-dressed, distinguished-looking person, who slid the screens of our sitting-room and bowed to us so gracefully, we hardly recognized our trotter of the blue-cotton coat, bare knees, and mushroom hat. He explained that the other men could not come to thank us for our gratuities because they had not proper clothes. In making his final and lowest bows his substantial American watch fell out of his silk belt with a thump; but he replaced it in its chamois case with the assurance that nothing hurt it, and that it was with the noon gun of Nagoya castle whenever he came to town.

CHAPTER XXI

NAGOYA

In this day of French uniforms, Gatling-guns, and foreign tactics, it is only in Nagoya that the garrison occupies the old castle; the fortress, with its gates and moats, remains unchanged, and the bugle-calls echo daily around the quaintly-gabled citadel. In the great parade-grounds outside the deep inner moat rise foreign-looking barracks and offices, and dumpy little soldiers in white-duck coats and trousers and visored caps stand as sentries on the fixed bridges, and in the portals of the huge, heavy-roofed, iron-clamped gate-ways. Of course these guards should be men in old armor, with spears and bows, and the alarms should be given on hoarse-toned gongs or conch - shell bugles, as in feudal days. Instead, the commandant of Nagoya has on his staff young nobles of old feudal families, who speak French, German, or English, as they have been taught in foreign military schools. A dapper little lieutenant, in spotless gloves and an elaborately - frogged white uniform, conducted us along the deep moat, over the bridge, and under the great gate of the citadel, whose stones, timbers, and iron clampings would defy a dozen mediæval armies. Gay chatter about *la belle Paris*, which the little lieutenant had learned to adore in his student-days, echoed under the yet more ponderous inner gate, and the ghosts of the old warriors must have groaned at the degeneracy of their sons.

Below the frowning citadel is an old palace, wherein the son of Iyeyasu, the first Prince of Owari, lived in state and entertained the Shogun's messengers. The empty rooms are musty and gloomy from long neglect, but the beautifully-carved and colored ceilings, and the screens and recess walls, decorated by famous artists with paintings on a ground of thinnest gold-leaf, remain the sole relics of his splendor.

The great donjon tower of the citadel, rising in five gabled stories, is surmounted by two golden dolphins, the pride of Nagoya. Made over two hundred years ago, each solid goldfish is valued at eighty thousand dollars, and many legends are attached to them. A covetous citizen once made an enormous kite wherewith to fly up and steal the city's treasures, but he was caught and put to death in boiling oil. The golden pets were never disturbed until one of them was taken down and sent with the Government exhibits to the Vienna Exposition in 1873. On the return voyage it sank to the bottom of the sea with the wrecked steamer *Nil.* Like the old lacquers and porcelain, the golden dolphin suffered no sea change, and, after a few months' immersion, was brought up and returned to its high perch on the tower, while all Nagoya rejoiced to see it flashing in the sun once more.

The donjon tower is a fine example of the old architecture, and the massive joists of keyaki would build barracks for twenty regiments. Inside the tower is an inexhaustible well, called the "Golden Water," which, in time of siege, would enable a rice-provisioned garrison to hold out for years. Up a stair-way of massive timbers one climbs, half in darkness to the top, to look down upon the broad Nagoya plain, the blue bay, and the busy port of Yokkaichi opposite, in the sacred province of Ise.

Commercially, Nagoya is best known as the centre of a great pottery and porcelain district. Seto in Owari being as famous as Staffordshire in England. In the Seto suburb porcelain clay is found, and silica exists in large quantities a few miles away. From the castle tower one sees the smoke of continuous lines of kilns surrounding the valley, and all the ware is sent in from these villages to Nagoya for distribution. Here the finest eggshell porcelain, rivalling the French ware, is made, much of it going to Yokohama to be decorated for the foreign market. Seto itself has given its name to all porcelain, and especially to the pale, gray-green ware so commonly used in Japanese households. Old green Seto ware is highly esteemed, both for its soft tinting and its peculiar glaze, suggesting jade or lacquer to the touch more than hard, kiln-burnt porcelain. The bulk of the commoner heavy porcelain is decorated here for the foreign market—men, women, and small boys mechanically repeating the monstrous designs in hideous colors, which they ignorantly suppose to represent western taste, and which the western world accepts as "so Japanese." Modern Owari is least desirable and least Japanese of all the wares of Japan, but as thousands of dollars pour annually into Nagoya for these travesties of national art, their manufacture and export will still go on. Recently the Seto potteries have been turning out large tea-caddies, with double or pierced covers, by tens of thousands, daubing them with the discordant colors of cheap foreign mineral paints. Across the ocean they are called Japanese rose-jars, although the rose was unknown in Japan until the entrance of foreigners, and the rose-jar and the *pot-pourri* it contains would greatly astonish a Japanese. But as Nagoya and Seto are made rich and happy by badly decorated porcelain tea-caddies, industry gains if art loses.

Thirty thousand Nagoyans are engaged in the manufacture of a cheap *cloisonné* enamel, ship-loads of plaques and vases with one unvarying hard, pale-blue ground being exported annually. The powdered porcelain from Seto's imperfect pieces forms the base of the enamel used, and the two industries work together economically.

In Nagoya town are shops filled with the charming Banko ware, made across the bay at Yokkaichi, which still retains all its old merits, unaltered by the demands of foreign markets. Banko teapots worked out of sheets of thin clay, pressed, folded, cut, and patterned in white mosaic or glazed designs in low relief, resemble nothing so much as bits of soft painted crapes stretched over hidden frames, and these fragile, unglazed pieces are all the more pleasing in the midst of Nagoya's keramic nightmares.

Nagoya being a little off the line of tourist travel, its

curio shops are not entirely stripped of their best things. As Owari's princes exchanged porcelains liberally with the daimios of Hizen and Kaga, some rare pieces of old Imari and Kutani are often chanced upon, as the impoverishment of great families, and the rage for foreign dress and fashions, tempts the better class to part with heirlooms. Whole afternoons wore on as we made our way into the graces of certain curio dealers, that they might disclose tneir jealously-guarded treasures. These old men of Nagoya have a real affection for the beautiful things of the past, made before any foreign demands had corrupted and debased the native art. Once convinced of the intelligent interest of their customer, the owners proudly open the go-down, and the swords, the lacquer, and the porcelains appear, and, lifted from their boxes, stripped of cotton and silk wrappings, are set forth. These old dealers are men wholly of the past, who meditate and smoke long over an offer, and if they agree to the price solemnly and slowly clap their hands as a ratification of the terms. Four times we passed by the largest curio shop in Nagoya, led by the tea-jars and boxes in the front to suppose that it was only the abode of a tea-merchant. When we had accidentally bought some choice tea there, we were invited back to a court, where two go-downs were crowded with old porcelains and lacquer. Near by was another shop where arms, armor, Buddhas, altar-pieces, saints, images, carvings, candlesticks, koros, robes, trappings, and all the paraphernalia of priests, temples, warriors, and yashikis were heaped up on the floor and hung overhead.

The coolies had been anxious about our rate of progress on the last Tokaido days, fearing to miss the great matsuri of the Nagoya year, which, celebrating the deeds of the founder and patron saints of the city, has been maintained with great pomp and splendor for centuries. The procession was to take four hours in passing, and our landlord engaged places for us in the house of a shoe-dealer in the main street. The dealer in *geta* and *dzori* dealt only in those national foot coverings, but, yielding to foreign fashions, had set up a sign of

"Shoes the Shop."

The sliding screens of the front wall of the room over the shop were removed, and bright red blankets thrown over the ledge and spread out on the eaves of the lower story. All the houses were open and decorated in this same way, and lanterns hung in rows from the eaves and from upright posts at the door-way.

The worthy shoe-dealer's blankets and lanterns were just like his neighbors', but when three foreigners appeared at the low balcony, then the multitude stopped and stared open-mouthed at that unusual spectacle, and we divided popular interest with the procession as long as we remained there. Policemen were perplexed between their duty of making the crowds move on and their own pleasure of having a look at the strangers. Soldiers from the garrison stared by hundreds, and the policemen requested them to depart, as well as the rustics and townspeople. Policemen rank much higher, in a way, than the soldiers, the guardians of the peace being nearly all descendants of the old samurai, the two-sworded, privileged retainers of feudal days, while the common soldier is enlisted from the farm laborers; and one quickly sees how much more regard the lower classes have for the *gunsa* than for the soldier.

The procession began with high ornamental wooden cars, or *dasha*, set on wheels hewn from single blocks of wood, and drawn by ropes, to which every pious person was supposed to lend a hand. Regular coolies were engaged for the steady wheel-horse work, and sang a wild chorus as men with stout sticks pried the clumsy wheels up for the first turn. The corner posts and upper railings of the dasha are lacquered in black or red, and finished with plates of open-work brass, or elaborately-gilded carvings. The sides are hung with curtains of rich old brocade or painted cloth, and the railed top is a stage, on which puppet-shows and tableaux represent scenes from mythology and legend. On one car Raiden, the red Thunder God, mounted on a rearing charger, shook his circle of drums, and Suzume. the priestess, repeated her sacred dance before the cave. Comic scenes took best with the audience, however. and the jolly old *shojo*, men who come up from the bottom of the sea for a revel on shore, wearing mats of bright red hair and gowns of gorgeous brocade, were received with greatest favor. They ladled out saké from a deep jar, and finally stood on their heads on the rim of the jar and drank from the depths. There were only twelve dasha in line, but they stopped every fifty feet while the puppets were put through their performances.

Succeeding the cars came a daimio's train, preceded by heralds in quaint, mediæval costume, and presenting every phase of the old-time parade. Chinese sages and instructors, Korean prisoners, falconers and priests walked in line after the daimios, who were mounted on horses half hidden in clumsy but beautiful old trappings. The men in white silk gowns and lacquer hats, who took the daimios' places at the head of the line, are descendants of those great families of the province, whose members have ridden in Nagoya's matsuri parades for centuries. After them came an endless line of men in armor, the suits of mail being either heirlooms of the wearers or provided from the rich stores of such things owned by the temple. The armor surpassed the treasures of curio shops, and the dents and cuts in the cuirasses and helmets attested their antiquity. Having sat from eleven o'clock until three in the upper room with the family of

THE SHOJO

the shoeman, we parted with elaborate expressions of esteem on both sides, and with such bows and prostrations from them that we wondered how our guide would contrive to slip a gift into their hands.

Nagoya maiko and geisha are celebrated throughout Japan for their beauty, grace, and taste in dress, and a geisha dinner is as much a property of Nagoya as the golden dolphins of the old castle. At ours we engaged two geisha to sing and play, and four maikos to dance in their richest costumes. As the guests were Japanese the feast was made a foreign dinner of as many courses as our guide and magician, Miyashta, could conjure from Nagoya's markets and the Shiurokindo's kitchen. Our three friends rustled in early, clad in ceremonial silk gowns, each with his family crest marked in tiny white circles on the backs and sleeves of his *haori*, or coat. At every praise of Nagoya, which the interpreter repeated to them on our behalf, they rose from their high chairs and bowed profoundly. At table the play of the knife and fork was as difficult to them as the chopsticks had once been for us, but they carried themselves through the ordeal with dignity and grace, and heroically ate of all the dishes passed them.

Towards the end of the dinner a gorgeous paroquet of a child appeared on our open balcony. Her kimono was pale blue crape, painted and embroidered with a wealth of chrysanthemums of different colors. Her obi, of the heaviest crinkled red crape, had flights of gray and white storks all over its drooping loops, and the neck-fold was red crape woven with a shimmer of gold thread. Her face was white with rice-powder, and her hair, dressed in fantastic loops and puffs, was tied with bits of red crape and gold cord, and set with a whole diadem of silver chrysanthemums. She came forward smiling with the most charming mixture of childlike shyness and maidenly self-possession, becoming as much interested in our curious foreign dresses as we in her splendid attire.

Presently, against the background of the night, appeared another dazzling figure — Oikoto, the most bewitching and popular maiko of the day in Nagoya. She, too, was radiant in gorgeously-painted crape, a red and gold striped obi, and a crown of silver flowers. Oikoto had the long, narrow eyes, the deeply-fringed lids, the nose and contour of face of Egyptian women. Her hand

and arm were exquisite, but it was her soft voice, her dreamy smile, and slowly lifted eyelids that led us captive. Oikoto san and the tiny maiko fluttered about the table, filling glasses, nibbling sweetmeats, answering questions, and accepting our frank admiration with grace incomparable. Two more brilliantly-dressed beauties entered, and with them the two geisha and their instruments. One of the geisha, O Suwo san, was still a beauty, who entered with a quiet, languid grace and dignity, and whose marvellous black eyes had magic in them.

The geisha struck the samisens with the ivory sticks, the wailing chorus began, and there succeeded a fan-dance, a cherry blossom-dance, and an autumn-dance, the four brilliant figures posing, gliding, moving, turning, rising, and sinking slowly before our enchanted eyes. One dance demanded quicker time, and the dancers sang with the chorus, clapping their hands softly and tossing their lovely arms and swinging sleeves. The three gentlemen of Nagoya joined in that pæan to the cherry blossoms and the blue sky, accenting the verse with their measured chanting; and one of them, taking part in a musical dialogue, danced a few measures in line with the maiko very well and gracefully.

The closing dance—a veritable jig, with whirls and jumps, rapid hand-clapping, and chanting by the maiko —ended in the dancers suddenly throwing themselves forward on their hands and standing on their heads, their feet against the screens.

"That is what we call the foreign dance: it is in foreign style, you know. You like it?" asked the interpreter on behalf of our guests; and our danna san had the temerity to answer that it was very well done, but that it was now going out of fashion in America.

After the seven dances the maiko stood in a picturesque row against the balcony rail and fanned themselves until supper was brought in for them and set on low tables, whereon were placed many cups and bowls and tiny plates, with the absurd bits and dolls' portions that constitute a Japanese feast.

The incongruous and commercial part of the geisha and maiko performance came in the shape of a yard-long bill, on which were traced charges of seventy-five cents an hour for each maiko, which included the two accompanists, and the jinrikisha fares to and from the entertainment. Unwritten custom required of us the supper for the performers, and a little gratuity or souvenir to each one.

When we begged the lovely Oikoto for her photograph, she proudly brought us one which showed that exquisite creature transformed into a dowdy horror by a foreign gown and bonnet, which the Nagoya photographer keeps on hand for the use of his customers.

CHAPTER XXII

LAKE BIWA AND KIOTO

AFTER the pace of the jinrikisha the slow train from Nagoya to Nagahama, on Lake Biwa, seemed to attain a dizzy speed. Rising continually, we reached a hilly region where the road-bed crossed a chain of tiny valleys, penetrated mountain-tunnels, and cut through pine forests and bamboo groves.

At Nagahama we rested in a lake-side tateba, content with the glorious view. and in no way eager to search for its famous *kabe* crapes. Lake Biwa. with long. wooded slopes running down to the shore, and mountains barring all the horizon, with smooth water and a blue sky. offers sixty miles of charming sail. Little thatched-roof villages, and the wide sweeping gables of temples show here and there in the solitude of pines, and the crest of one high promontory is girt with the white walls of Hikone castle. Many legends belong to this mediæval fortress, the scene of so many famous events, whose last daimio was murdered in Tokio by disaffected followers, soon after he negotiated, as prime-minister, the treaties of 1858.

At Otsu, at the lower end of the lake, the splendid old temple of Miidera and its monastery on the heights command the town and lake, and the soldiers' memorial column overlooks the eight great sights of Lake Biwa which are painted on half the fans, kakemonos, and screens of Japan. One of these eight wonders is Miidera, with its long and lofty avenues, the green twilight of its primeval groves, its yellow, moated walls and frowning gate-ways that hide in the enchanted forest; its ancient shrines, its terraces, and lichen-covered bell-tower, home of the legend of Benkei and his bell. Benkei was a muscular priest who lived on Mount Hiyeizan overlooking the lake. The other priests coveted the splendid bell of Miidera, which had been presented by the ruler of the kingdom of women living at the bottom of Lake Biwa to Hidesato for valiantly slaying a giant centipede that had frightened these ladies of the lake by its forays. The priests induced Benkei to steal the bell by promising him as much soup as he could eat, and he threw it over his shoulder and carried it to the top of the mountain. But its silvery tongue kept crying " I want to return." and the priests threw it down the mountain-side, over which it rolled, receiving many dents and scratches. to its old bell-tower. Near by it is the giant soup-kettle, in which the priests cooked Benkei's mess of pottage, and touching both relics of course verifies the legends. At the end of the monastery groves are large barracks. and troops of the chubby-faced. boyish-looking soldiers are always strolling through the arching avenues of the still old forest.

The greatest sight of Biwa, and one of the wonders of
Japan, is the old pine-tree of Karasaki, which has stood
for three hundred years on a little headland a couple of
miles above Otsu, with a tiny village and a Shinto temple all its own.   Its trunk is over four feet in diameter,
and, at a height of fifteen feet, its boughs are trained lat-
erally and supported by posts, so that it looks like a
banyan-tree.   The branches, twisted, bent, and looped
like writhing dragons, cover more than an acre of ground
with their canopy.   The tips of the boughs reach far
out over the water, and the sensitive Japanese hear a
peculiar music in the sifting of the rain-drops through
the foliage into the lake.   High up in the tree is a tiny
shrine, and the pilgrims clap their hands and stand with
clasped palms, turning their faces upward as they pray.
A heavy stone wall protects this sylvan patriarch from
the washing of storms and floods.

Under the branches a legion of small villagers, inti-
mating by pantomime their desire to dive for pennies,
untied their belts and dropped their solitary cotton garments as unconcernedly as one might take off hat or
gloves.   They frolicked and capered in the water as much
at home as fishes and as loath to leave it.   Fleeing from
this body of too attached followers, we were whirled
down the road to Otsu to eat the famous Biwa trout,
passing on the way a woman, who sat at ease in her bath-
tub by her own door-step, calmly scrubbing herself with a
bag of rice bran, and contemplating her neighbors, the
road, and the lake scenery the while.

On Mount Hiyeizan, by the ruined Buddhist temples
and monasteries, the American missionaries of different
denominations have a long-established summer camp,
where they enjoy a sort of Japanese Chautauqua circle,
their tents and buildings the only signs of habitation
where once stood hundreds of temples with their thousands of priests.

THE GREAT PINE-TREE AT KARASAKI

From the old temple of Ishiyama, east of Otsu, is seen the famous Seta bridge and Awatsu, where the lake takes on a wondrous silvery sheen when the sun shines and the wind blows, these being three more of the famous sights of Biwa. The grounds of Ishiyama contain what is known as a dry garden, where blackened rocks and rocks free from every green thing are piled fantastically with strange landscape resemblances. In the temple is a prayer-wheel, which is turned by thousands of pilgrims every summer, and in a small room off the temple a priest showed us the writing-box and ink-stone of Murusaki Shikibu, a poetess and novelist of the tenth century, whose work, the *Genji Monogatari,* is the great classic of its age. The remaining wonders of Lake Biwa are the flights of the wild geese, the return of the fishing-boats to Yabashi, and Mount Hira with the winter snows on its summit.

From Otsu over to the Kioto side of the mountains we went by train, rushing down the long grade and through tunnels to the great plain, where sits the sacred city, the capital and heart of old Japan, incomparable Kioto, Saikio, or Miako. We saw it in the sunset light, the western hills throwing purple shadows on their own slopes, and the long stretch of wheat fields at their base turned to a lake of pure gold. The white walls of the Shogun's castle, the broad roof of the old palace, and the ridges of temples rose above the low, gray plain of house roofs and held the sun's last level beams.

After the imitations and tawdriness of modern Tokio, the unchanged aspect of the old capital is full of dignity. After many long stays in spring-time, midsummer, and midwinter, Kioto has always remained to me foremost of Japanese cities. Yaamis, the foreigner's Kioto home, with its steep terraced garden, its dwarf-pine and blooming monkey-tree, its many buildings at different levels, its flitting figures on the outer galleries, is like no other hostlery. Yaami, proprietor of this picturesque hotel. is a personage indeed. He and his brother were professional guides until they made their fortunes. Their shrewd eyes saw further fortunes in a Kioto inn, where foreigners might find beds, chairs, tables, knives, forks, and foreign food, and they secured the old Ichiriki teahouse, midway on the slope of Maruyama, the mountain walling in Kioto on the east. The Ichiriki tea-house was the place where Oishi Kura no Suke. the leader of the Forty-seven Ronins, played the drunkard during the two years that he lived near Kioto, before he avenged the death of his lord. With it was bought an adjoining monastery, belonging to one of the temples on Mount Hiyeizan, and these two original buildings have expanded and risen story upon story, with detached wings here and there, until the group of tall white buildings. with the white flag floating high up in the midst of Maruyama's foliage, is quite castle-like. While the obnoxious foreign treaties are in force, no foreigners except those in Japanese employ are allowed to live in Kioto, or even to visit it without a passport, and this secures Yaami in his monopoly. As a matter of fact, Yaami is not the family name of the two pleasant and prosperous-looking men who walk about in silk kimonos, with heavy gold watch-chains wound about their broad silk belts, and who have the innocent faces of young children. save for the shrewdness of their eyes. Yaami is the corruption of Yama Amida (Hill of Buddha), which is the name of the hotel, and the two men belong to the Inowye family, a clan not less numerous in Japan than the Smiths of English-speaking countries. In parts of the house one finds relics of monastery days in dim old screens of fine workmanship, and there is a stone-floored kitchen, vast as a temple, with cooks serious as priests, wielding strange sacrificial knives, and who, in midsummer, wear an apron only, apparently as a professional badge rather than as a garment. The *momban*, or gate-keeper, sits, spider-like, in a web of his own, a mere doll's house by the gate-way. In olden times, and even to-day, in large establishments, the momban announces an arrival with strokes upon his gong, but this particular functionary corresponds more nearly to the Parisian *octroi*. All who enter the gates answer for themselves and pay tribute, or they are forever barred out. Even coolies disgorge their black-mail to the colony of fleet-footed brethren who hold a valuable monopoly at Ya-ami's gate, and in guilds and labor organizations the Orient is ages older and wiser than the Occident.

All of Maruyama's slope is holy ground and pleasure-ground. Tea-houses and bath-houses are scattered in between the great temples, and prayer-gongs and pious hand-clapping are heard in unison with samisens and revellers' songs. Praying and pleasuring go together, and the court-yard of the Gion temple at the foot of the hill is lined with monkey-shows and archery ranges, and in the riding-schools the adventurous may, for a few coppers, mount a jerky horse and be jolted around a shady ring. There, too, are many rows of images of fierce, red-cloaked Daruma, the Buddhist saint, who sailed across from Korea on a rush-leaf. He sat facing a wall for nine years, and wore off his lower limbs, and now his image, weighted with lead, is the target for merry ball-throwers, and is seen in every quarter of the empire.

From the airy galleries on Maruyama the city lies below one like a relief map. The river, the Kamogawa, crossed at intervals by long bridges, cuts the city in two. From each bridge a street runs straight on to the west-ward. By day these thoroughfares look like furrows ploughed through the solid plain of gray-tiled roofs; but at night they shine with thousands of lamps and lanterns, and their narrow, wavering lines of fire look like so many torchlight processions, and the river is one broad belt of light.

I first saw Kioto on the last day of the Gion matsuri, a festival which lasts for a month and brings all the population out-of-doors into one quarter during the evening. By dusk a babel of music and voices had arisen, which finally drew us down the steep and shady road, and through the great stone torii, to the Gion's precincts. The court-yard was almost deserted, and looking through the great gate-way to Shijo Street the view was dazzling and the shouts and chatter deafening. The narrow street was lined with rows of large white paper lanterns hanging above the house doors, and rows hanging from the eaves. Lanterned booths lined the curb, while humbler venders spread their wares on the ground in the light of flaring torches. Crowds surged up and down, every man carrying a paper lantern on the end of a short bamboo stick—the literal lamp for the feet—women bearing smaller lanterns, and children delighting themselves with gayly-colored paper shells for tiny candles. Boys marched and ran in long single files, shouting a measured chant as they cut their way through the crowd and whirled giant lanterns and blazing torches at the end of long poles.

From Gion gate to Shijo bridge the street was one wavering, glittering line of light, and crowded solidly with people. Where the street narrows near the bridge there is a region of theatres and side-shows, and there banners and pictures, drums and shouting ticket-sellers, and a denser crowd of people gathered. A loud shout and a measured chorus heralded a group of men carrying a Brobdingnagian torch, a giant bamboo pole blazing fiercely at its lofty tip. The crowd surged back to the walls as the torch-bearers ran by and on to the middle of Shijo bridge, where they waved the burning wand in fiery signals to the other bridges that the real procession was starting. More torches and lanterns, lines of priests in garments of silk and gauze, wearing strange hats, beating and blowing strange instruments ; and a sacred red chair, reason for all this ceremony, was borne on from the Gion to a distant Shinto sanctuary to remain until the matsuri of the following year.

From Shijo bridge to Sanjo bridge Kioto's river-bed is like a scene from fairy-land throughout the summer, and during the Gion matsuri the vision is enhanced. The tea-houses that line the river-bank with picturesquely galleried fronts set out acres of low platform tables in the clear, shallow stream. The water ripples pleasantly around them, giving a grateful sense of coolness to these æsthetic Japanese, who sit in groups on the open platforms, smoking their pipes and feasting under the light of their rows of lanterns. All the broad river-bed is ablaze with lights and torches, and on the dry, gravelly stretches a multitude of small peddlers, venders, and showmen set up their attractive tents and add to the general glitter and illumination. Hundreds linger and stroll on the bridges to admire the gay sight, for as only this people could have conjured up so brilliant a spectacle out of such simple and every-day means, so only they can fully enjoy its beauty and charm. All the children wear their gayest holiday clothes on such a great matsuri night, and the graceful women of the old capital, bare-headed, rustling in silk and gauze, their night-black hair spread in fantastic loops and caught with beautiful hair-pins, are worthy of their surroundings.

We left the bridge and wandered over the loose gravel and rocks of the river-beds, crossing by many planks and tiny bridges from one small island of shingle to another. There were countless fruit-stands, with their ingenious little water-fountains spraying melons and peaches to a dewy coolness and freshness, hair-pin stands glittering with silver flowers, and fan and toy and flower booths,

and all the while we wandered there the people watched
and followed with a respectful curiosity that amused but
could not annoy. Attracted by the beautiful face of a
young girl just within the curtained door of a side-show,
we paid the one cent entrance fee to see the conjurers.
The tent was empty when we entered, but such a stream
of natives poured in after us as to delight the proprietor
and encourage the musicians to pound out more violent
airs. A few miserable poodles were made to walk on two
legs and otherwise discomfort themselves at the bidding
of the beautiful girl, whose strange soft eyes and lovely
face were set off by an elaborate coiffure, a coronet of
silvery hair-pins, and a kimono of gray silk shot with
many tinsel threads. We foreigners found the faces and
holiday garb of the people more interesting than the performance, and the natives in turn seemed equally absorbed in watching us. Horse-shows, where daring but
terrified Japanese bestrode steeds and ambled three times
around the ring for a penny, puppet-shows, juggler-shows,
and peep-shows drew us in turn from one end of the river-
bed fair to the other, and when too weary to walk we
remounted to the bridge to admire afresh this feast
of lanterns, until at midnight we sought the groves of
Maruyama.

CHAPTER XXIII

KIOTO TEMPLES

KIOTO is seen at its best in summer-time. in the fulness
and color of its out-door life. Though the great plain of
the city bakes and quivers in the sun, the heat is no
greater than in other cities. The views from Maruyama
are always enchanting, and the sunset sky is not lovelier
than the dawn, when all the hill-side lies in cool, green

shade, when the opposite mountain-wall wears a veil of rose and lilac, and the air above the plain of gray roofs is full of filmy mists and tiny smoke-wreaths.

All travellers are abroad at sunrise or in the early morning, for by ten o'clock the sun blazes down with fury, and humane people keep their jinrikisha coolies and themselves in-doors. With the cooling dusk mosquitoes swarm from all these gardens and hill-side groves, and the victim fans and slaps until he creeps for safety under his mosquito-net, which, unhappily, does not exclude the nimble flea, whose ravages test both his endurance and his temper. At sunrise all the temples in Kioto open their gates for the first mass, and at dawn pilgrimages to these sacred spots may begin, the odor and silence of that dewy hour adding to their peace and sanctity.

All the way from Yaami's to the Yasaka pagoda and the Kiomidzu temple the hill-side is covered with temple and monastery grounds, the way leading through broad, tree-shaded avenues and narrow paths by bamboo groves or evergreen thickets. Wide, flagged walks and grand stair-ways follow the terraces to temples and bell-towers, screened by open-work walls and approached through monumental gate-ways made beautiful by carving, gilding and painting, inlaid metals, and fine tiles. Crossing from one temple enclosure to another, the walk extends for two miles along the brow of the hill through beautiful grounds. The park-like demesne of Higashi Otani, with its imperial tombs, adjoins Yaami's, and next it is the Kotaiji, with its noble avenues. At the end of one broad path-way, traversing the upper part of the Kotaiji grounds, the Yasaka pagoda, with its five stories of curving roofs and gables hung with old bronze bells, stands like a picture in the arching frame of green. These venerable pagodas, their walls covered with wondrous carvings and bracketings, faded to dim red and tarnished

gold, with the gray and white tiles of their picturesque
roofs half overgrown with mosses and vines, the topmost
ridge finished with a tapering, spiral piece of iron, delight the lover of the picturesque. Yasaka's cracked
and tongueless bells have long ceased to swing and ring
with every breeze, but they give an airy and fantastic
touch to the fine old structure. The pagoda dates from
the sixth century, and for twelve hundred years its four
altars have heard the prayers of faithful Buddhists. The
early light gilds its eastern wall, and the rich sunset
makes of it a palace of the imagination. To me it seemed
most beautiful one late afternoon, when, hurrying down
the steep steps of a narrow street behind it, I saw its
outlines, delicate and strong, against a glowing orange
sky.

All about the pagoda and the neighboring slopes of
Kiomidzu are potteries and shops for the sale of the
cheap porcelain and earthen-ware that pilgrims and visitors are prone to buy on their way to and from the temples.
The eminence is known as Teapot Hill, and the long,
steep street leading from Gojo bridge to the Kiomidzu
gates is lined on either side of its hilly half-mile with
china shops. There one may collect his three hundred
and sixty-five teapots in an hour, and few leave without
a souvenir of Kiomidzu porcelain, be it from Kanzan's or
Dohachi's godowns of exquisite wares, or from the long
rows of charming little open shops. Kiomidzu is the
centre of the porcelain-makers' district, as the manufacturers of faience are grouped together in the Awata
quarter, a mile beyond, and behind the little shop-fronts
and blank walls are busy work-rooms and burning kilns.
The founding of the Kiomidzu temple is lost in fable,
and its legends are many and confusing. All the Japanese rulers, warriors, and Shoguns have had something to
do with the place, and every foot of its enclosure is historic. It is the popular temple of the people, enshrin-

ing one of the thirty-three famous Kwannons of the empire, to which pilgrims flock by thousands, and where one sees the most active forms of the faith. Climbing the breathless hill-slopes and stone stair-ways the visitor reaches a giant gate-way, in whose shadow mendicant priests stand with extended bowl, straw hats concealing them to the shoulders, and their maize and purple garments hung with rosaries. There are two pagodas and innumerable stone lanterns and shrines, upon which the faithful toss pebbles as they pray. If the stone remains the prayer is answered, and the pilgrim proceeds with a lightened heart. The Hondo, or main hall, is a most ancient building, one half resting on the slope of the hill and the rest extending in a broad platform propped up by heavy timbers and scaffolding over the face of a precipice. From this platform jealous husbands used to hurl their wives; those who survived the fall of one hundred and fifty feet to the jagged rocks below being proved innocent of wrong-doing, and those who perished guilty. There are no rows of ticketed clogs at the steps of the Hondo, nor soft, clean mats within. The hall is open and benches are set before the altar, where the weary, dusty pilgrim may sit and, resting. pray. Votive tapers are brought to the shrine, and the low beams overhead are covered with votive pictures.

One fortunate afternoon we chanced upon a matsuri at Kiomidzu. All Teapot Hill was crowded with people, girls and children in their gayly-colored crapes and gauzes vying in brightness with the decorated houses. Priests, sitting on small, canopied platforms, hammered silver-toned gongs to call the faithful to give offerings. Coins were tossed in generously on the blankets where the priests sat, but they were not the thick modern copper sens, nor yet silver. Money-changers had their little stands along the via sacra, and in exchange for a sen the believers received a handful of ancient rins and half-rins. Thus provided, the pilgrim could bestow his pious alms on each group of priests, and if he followed the polite custom of wrapping any money gift in a bit of soft paper, the priests could not tell whether he had thrown silver or copper. Within the temple grounds tateba were crowded with feasters and tea-drinkers, dozens of fruit-stands were piled with slices of watermelon, and fans painted with Kiomidzu scenes were sold on every side.

Inside the temple itself the scuffle of clogs and mutterings of pilgrims drowned all sounds save the silvery notes of the gongs. On the image-covered altar, one hundred and ninety feet in length, veiled by clouds of incense, were dimly visible the gilded statue of the divine Kwannon, the special patroness of Kiomidzu, and the figures of the priests. It was not easy to pick one's way among the kneeling multitudes offering their fervent prayers oblivious to all surroundings. As one pilgrim departed the rest crowded forward, continuing the beseeching "*Namu Amida Butsu*" (Hear me, Great Lord Buddha) which they mutter so rapidly that only a long-drawn "*Na-na-na-na-na-a-a*" is audible as they press their palms together and wind their beads around their hands.

In the second temple, or Amida, were more candles, incense, and priests, and more kneeling people. At the end of the hanging platform of this temple is a small, latticed shrine dedicated to Kamnosube-no-Kami, the goddess who watches over lovers. He who would make sure of the affections of his beloved buys a printed prayer from the priest, rolls it into a narrow strip, and then, with the thumb and little finger of the right-hand, ties it to Kamnosube-no-Kami's grating, and implores her aid. If any other fingers are used to tie the knot, or if they even touch the prayer-paper, the charm is broken and the goddess is deaf. While we looked on

THE TRUE-LOVER'S SHRINE AT KIOMIDZU

one pretty creature in a red crape underdress and a dark-blue gauze kimono, who blushed most beautifully, bent her anxious face to the grating and deftly wound her fingers in and out. Following her a middle-aged coolie tossed in his fractional coin, rang, clapped, and tied his sentimental petition to the lattice.

Holiday crowds poured up and down the broad paved walks, wandered about the paths, or gathered in the pavilions, while new throngs toiled up the stone staircases to join in the festival. On the overhanging platforms sacred dances had been performed all day, giving place towards nightfall to the low tables covered with red blankets, around which companies picturesquely grouped themselves, while pretty nesans pattered back and forth to serve them. The whole scene was so spectacular and fascinating that we sat there watching the moving crowds and looking out over the city below us until the sun sank in clouds of splendid color, and twinkling lights began to creep upward from the streets.

Near the top of Teapot Hill a narrow lane diverges into a dense bamboo grove, where the feathery tips meet far overhead, and only a green twilight filters down to the base of the myriad slender columns. This bamboo grove is one of the finest in Kioto, and its cool shade is most grateful on a summer day. Beyond it is the famous Spectacle Bridge, a massive stone pile, whose two low arches are not unlike a bowed spectacle-frame. The lotus-pond which it crosses is surrounded in the early summer mornings with breakfasting parties, who sit there to see the splendid flowers open their cups with the first rays of the sun. When that show is over these flower-lovers wander through the farther confines of Nishi Otani, with its superb bronze gates and dragon-guarded tanks, and its imperial tombs hidden away in the quiet groves.

The chain of temples still lengthens southward, and

among the most ancient, surrounded with walls of Titanic bowlders, is the Dai Butsu temple, with its huge image of gilded wood, and its fallen bell, whose interior would make a temple in itself. A stone monument, the Mimizuka, covers the heap of thousands of human ears, cut by Hideyoshi's generals from the heads of enemies slain in the Korean expedition, salted and brought home as proof of prowess. Last is the Sanjiusangendo, or Hall of the Thirty-three Thousand Buddhas, which, with its rows and rows of tall gilded statues, is a curious place, but less like a sanctuary than a wholesale warehouse of sacred images.

Northward from Yaami's the chain of temples extends along the leafy hill-side, first among them being the great Chioin sanctuary, one of the largest, oldest, and richest in Kioto. Its colossal gate-way, its long avenues, great stone embankments, terraces, staircases, and groves of ancient trees proclaim its age and endless honors. Stretching over surrounding acres run the yellow walls of its monastery grounds and priests' houses. The Chioin's altar is a mass of carved and gilded ornaments surrounding a massive golden shrine, while the ceiling and walls of the vast interior are hardly less splendid. Occasional worshippers kneel in the vast matted hall muttering their prayers, but usually only a solitary old priest is seen industriously hammering at a drum, shaped like a huge, round sleigh-bell. From five o'clock in the morning until the temple closes at four in the afternoon the hard, mechanical *thunk, thunk* never stops. A nice old woman, who must be a professional mender, judging by her incessant patching and darning of blue-cotton garments, takes care of the shoes while visitors roam through the temple stocking-footed ; and proudly does she point out, among the bracketed eaves, the sun-umbrella which the great builder of the temple purposely left there. Back of the main temple are other shrines and suites of reception-rooms, with screens and ceilings decorated by famous artists, and quiet corners where abbot and priest may sit and look upon the exquisite little gardens.

If I were a good Buddhist I should say a prayer or two to the Chioin's great bell, an inverted cup of bronze eighteen feet in height, breathing music so sweet that it thrills the listener, and ringing so seldom that no one willingly misses its voice. This bell hangs by itself in a shady place at the top of a long stone staircase, and is struck from the outside by a swinging wooden beam that brings out soft reverberations without jar or clang. This huge hammer is unchained on rare days of the month at the sunrise hour, and in the stillness of dawn one cannot tell whence the sound comes. It is in the whole air ; under one's feet, or tingling and beating within one's body, while yet the ear seems to drink in the very ecstasy of sound.

About Nanjenji's lofty gate-way are clustering tea-bushes, and between its ancient shrine, its tombs, and picturesque bell-tower modern engineering has brought the aqueduct from Lake Biwa, the long tunnel emerging from the hill-side back of the buildings. Further on are Iyekando, with its lotus lake and verdant cemetery; Niyakuoji's pretty garden and cascade; and Shishigatami, Shinniodo, and Yoshida, each with its distinctive charm and interest.

The way from these sacred places, passing through the potters' district of Awata, and coming suddenly out on a level of rice fields, with Kurodani's pagoda and grove rising like an island from their midst, has been likened to the abrupt transportation from Rome to the Campagna. Kurodani is a beautiful old sanctuary, and the steep hill on which stands its great pagoda is an ideal Buddhist burial-ground. Tombs, stone tablets, and lanterns, and hundreds of images of Buddha, in stone and bronze, crowd against each other, and some priest or pilgrim, ever picturesque, is always moving up or down the broad gray staircase.

CHAPTER XXIV

THE MONTO TEMPLES AND THE DAIMONJI

As an evidence of the vitality of their faith the Monto Buddhists point to their great new temple in the southern part of the city. [This Higashi Hongwanji (Eastern Temple) was eight years in building, at an enormous cost, and is the largest temple in Japan. The squared trunks of keyaki-trees that support floor and roof are of a fine, close grain, that lasts for centuries without paint or preserving process. [A collection of thick black ropes hangs from the beams, all of them made from the hair of pious women too poor to offer other contributions. The largest rope is five inches in diameter and two hundred and fifty feet long, the hair, wound in a dozen separate strands around a slender core of hemp, having been given by three thousand five hundred of the pious maids and matrons of the province of Echizen. Here and there in this giant cable are pathetic threads of white hair, the rest being deep black. Each summer pious men came to give their days' labor to the temple when they had no money. The best workers in wood from several provinces, craftsmen descended from generations of wood-carvers, were brought together to labor for several years on the decorative panels, carving from solid blocks of hard keyaki wonderful birds and flowers, curling waves and dashing spray — designs full of movement and life.

This Shin, or Monto sect of Buddhists, is one of the richest and largest. Its temples are always built in the heart of cities, and always in pairs, a Nishi Hongwanji (Western Temple) and a Higashi Hongwanji (Eastern Temple) being found in Tokio, Kioto, and Osaka. At the Nishi Hongwanji of Kioto the vast interior discloses masses of carving, gilding, lacquer, damascening, and paintings on golden groundwork, and Monto altars are more splendid than those of any other sect. This Hongwanji is very rich, having been endowed with lands and mines in the days of Hideyoshi, its special protector, and the temple enclosure holds many relics of the Taiko. Connected with the temple is a great yashiki, or abbot's residence, and the wall-screens and superb ceilings, brought from Hideyoshi's castle at Fushimi, south of Kioto, to adorn the suites of reception-rooms, are finer than any in the imperial palace. The carved, gilded, and lacquered ceilings, the wonderful paintings on gold-leaf surfaces, the damascened mountings of the screens, the vast audience hall, the private rooms, the No pavil-ion, and the court where the enemies' heads were dis-played, are all magnificent. In a corner of the grounds is the pleasure-garden of Hideyoshi, a leafy, lake-cen-tred paradise, and a marvel of artistic arrangement, with its winding water overhung with wistaria arbors, crossed by picturesque bridges, reflecting its stone lanterns, thick-ets of oleander, bamboo, pine, palm, and banana trees, and the two beautiful miniature palaces within the maze. On a pine-covered knoll is the thatched summer-house, where the fierce yet poetic warrior sat in his armor to watch the moon rise over the trees and turn the lake to a silver shield at his feet.

The Hongwanji services are splendid and impressive ceremonies: the companies of gorgeously-clad priests, the chanting, the incense, the lighted tapers, the bells, the opening of the doors of the golden shrine to display the image of Buddha, all bearing a strange resemblance to the worship of Romish churches. The faithful kneel, touch themselves, and use the rosary in prayer; and high mass at the Hongwanji might almost be high mass at St. Mark's. Mass is celebrated at five o'clock on every morning of the year, and all day worshippers may come to kneel and pray before the altars. On the first and fifteenth days of each month special services are held at two o'clock in the afternoon, and every January recurs a week of prayer in honor of the founder of the Shin sect, when priests come from all parts of the empire to the mother-temple. The fortnightly afternoon services consist of readings from the sacred scriptures, and the chanting of Japanese and Chinese sacred poems by some twenty priests in black gauze stoles; a larger chorus, hidden behind the central shrine and altar, joining in and responding. The high-priest, in a cardinal and gold brocade kesa, sits directly facing the shrine, and at intervals touches the swinging plate of bronze used as a gong in the order of worship. The golden shrine, in a great gilded alcove, or chancel, bears countless gilded lotus flowers and candelabra, and slender columns of incense rise from the priests' low reading-desk. At the conclusion of the chanted service the doors of the shrine are opened, and the sacred image displayed in a silence broken only by low strokes on the gong. Then the priests file away, and the faithful, flocking into the vacant place behind the rail, and kneeling where the priests have knelt, prostrate themselves, rub their rosaries in their palms, and repeat with ecstatic fervor the invocation: "*Namu Amida Butsu*" (Hail, Great Lord Buddha).

Every year, on the temple steps, the contributions of rice from distant provinces are stacked high in their cylindrical straw bales, themselves emblems of abundance. This rice is sent as an annual tribute from different parts of the empire to the head-temple of the sect at Kioto, to be used for offerings in the sanctuaries, for the priests' food, and for alms to the poor.

The present high-priest has a longer genealogy than the Emperor, and is the seventy-third of his family, in direct succession, to live in the same Kioto yashiki. Besides his ecclesiastical rank, he is a nobleman of the first order, and moves in the imperial circle, his modern brougham with liveried men being often seen driving in and out of the palace enclosures in the western end of the city. Besides his temple services, he directs the large college which the Hongwanji maintains for the education of young men for the priesthood and for advanced philosophical studies for lay students. In its library is a vast literature of Buddhism, the scrolls of silk and paper in boxes of priceless gold lacquer facing the neatly-bound volumes of Sinnett, Sir Edwin Arnold, and other foreign writers. The college employs teachers of all European languages, and intends to send missionary workers to European countries. One of the priestly instructors, Mr. Akamatsu, spent several years in England, and has made comparative religions his great study. This admirable scholar is an admirable talker as well, and every student of Buddhism in Japan is referred to his vast stores of information. The breadth and liberality of Mr. Akamatsu's views are shown in his belief in the brotherhood of all religions, their likeness, and their convergence towards " that far-off, divine event, towards which the whole creation moves." It was he who drew up and translated that new canon of his faith, which introduced passages from the Sermon on the Mount, and who explained that these contained exactly the Buddhist tenets. The Shin Buddhists are called the Protestants of that faith. The priests may marry, and are not required to fast, to do penance, make pilgrimages, or abstain from animal food. They believe in salvation by faith in Buddha, and in those ever-higher transmigrations of the soul which finally attain Nirvana. Their priests maintain that the presence of Christian missionaries has made no difference with their people, the scholarly and intelligent seeing that the two faiths differ only in a few articles and practices. For the lower orders, these spiritual shepherds declare Buddhism to be the better religion, its practice for centuries having made the masses the gentle, kindly, patient, and contented souls that they are. One priest, sent to Europe to study the effects of Christianity, reported that vice, crime, and misery were greater there than in Japan, and that the belief of the west seemed less able to repress those evils than the belief of the east. These Monto priests, too, express broad views about the reciprocity of nations and the fair exchange of missionaries. Now that English clergymen and thinkers study Buddhism in the monasteries of Ceylon, avowing their acceptance of the articles with much sacred ceremony, Monto apostles may yet preach to the people of England and America. However this may be, the priests do not fear the proselyting labors of the Doshisha teachers in Kioto, and speak warmly of its good works, and particularly of its hospital and training-school for nurses.

In 1885 the first American missionaries came to Kioto, and as the sacred city is beyond the treaty limits, the college and hospital are maintained under the name of the Doshisha company, and the foreigners engaged in the work are ostensibly in Japanese employ. Back of the Christian Japanese, who stands as president of this company, are the rich Mission Boards, which furnish the money, and direct its expenditure and the method of work. Each teacher in the Doshisha school is really a missionary, and outside the class-room carries on active evangelical work. School buildings, hospital, and residences for the foreign teachers all front on the high yellow walls of the imperial palace grounds, significant testimony to the changes that have come, the barriers and prejudices that have given way. The school is crowded to its furthest capacity, the hospital is besieged, and physicians overworked. The teachers claim that all the students are Christians, that the new religion is spreading, and that the people are most anxious to know about it. While they do not affirm that Buddhism and the old religions are dying, the success of their work sustains their conviction. They have erected substantial brick buildings and comfortable dwellings, and have a general air of permanency. The choice of Dr. J. C. Berry as one of the pioneers in this enterprise was most fortunate ; his tact and urbanity having availed as much in dealing with the Japanese authorities as his zeal and ability in planning and promoting the work, and an exceptional staff has been gathered around him.

Of foreign missions in Japan there are the French Catholic, Russian - Greek, English and Canadian workers belonging to both Established Church and dissenting sects, while the Foreign Mission Boards of the United States have more than three hundred agents and teachers in Japan, nearly all of whom have families. Meanwhile, 191,968 Shinto temples, 14,849 Shinto priests, and the whole influence of the Government encourages this state religion, of which the Emperor is the visible head. There are 72,039 Buddhist temples, and 56,266 Buddhist priests and consecrated nuns proclaim that faith, while pilgrims to the thirty-three famous Kwannons of the empire do not lessen in number. A large fraction of the people profess no religion whatever, among whom are many of the younger generation of nobles, who, having studied and lived abroad, have adopted materialism, atheism, or agnosticism, like other foreign fashions. When an American devotee of theosophy expounded his occult science in a round of temple addresses he aroused a polite interest, but caused no excitement and attracted no body of followers. A Unitarian agent enjoyed greatest favor among the highest circles of the capital, his system of higher philosophy appealing strongly to those cultivated thinkers and men of letters.

The common people, like the ignorant of other races, do not at all comprehend the religion they do profess, observing its forms as a habit or a matter of blind convention, and celebrating its events with ceremonies and decorations, festivals and anniversaries, whose significance they cannot explain. Japanese streets suddenly blossom out with flags and lanterns at every door-way and along miles of eaves, and if you ask a shopkeeper what this rejoicing means, he will reply, "*Wakarimasen*," or "*Shirimasen*" (I do not know). Then some learned man tells you that it is the anniversary of the death of Jimmu Tenno, or the autumn festival, when the first rice of the garnered crop is offered to the gods by the Emperor in the palace chapel, by the priests at every Shinto shrine, and at every household altar in pious homes, or some other traditional occasion kept as a Government holiday. Closing the Government offices on Sunday, and making that a day of rest, was a matter of practical convenience merely, and the result of the adoption of a uniform calendar with the rest of the world, and a modern military establishment on foreign models.

One of the festivals of a religious character which is understood by the people, and is, perhaps, the most remarkable of all Kioto's great summer illuminations, is that of the Daimonji, at the end of the Bon Matsuri, or Festival of the Dead. According to Buddhist belief, the spirits of the departed return to earth for three days in mid-August, visiting their families and earthly haunts, and flitting back to their graves on the night of the third day. During the continuance of the Bon Matsuri, lanterns and paper strips are hung in front of those houses in which a death has occurred during the year, and burn-

ing tapers and bowls of food are set before the little
household shrines.   Alike in the backs of shops, in the
humblest abodes, and in villas and noble yashikis, lights,
offerings, and fragrant incense welcome back the dead.
In the cemeteries the bamboo sticks at each gravestone
are daily filled with fresh flowers, and on the night of
their return the spirits are guided to their resting-places
by the light of lanterns and oil-tapers burning throughout these cities of their silent habitation.   This beautiful custom, sanctified by the observance of many centuries, is tinged with little sadness, and the last night of
the Festival of the Dead is the great Festival of Lanterns, the most brilliant of the long, gay, fantastic Kioto
summer.

We were kindly invited by a Japanese gentleman to
witness the illumination from the upper story of a pa-
goda-like school-house, that rose high above all the roofs
in the heart of the city.   Two hundred children were
chirping and chattering in the open-sided class-rooms of
the lower floors, all eager to see the Daimonji, the great
signal-fires on the hills.   All sat on their heels in orderly rows, and silently bobbed to the mats at sight of us,
going on afterwards with their merry babble, which all
through the summer evening floated up to us in happy
chorus.

As dusk gave way to dark, we beheld a glimmer of
light like a waving torch on the side of the mountain
that stands like a tower beyond Maruyama.   Another
and another flash shone out against the dark face of
Daimonji-yama's long slope, until the flames joined and
lines of fire ran upward, touched, crossed, and finally
blazed out in the gigantic written character Dai, in outline not unlike a capital A.   Next a junk appeared in
fiery outlines on the slope north of the city; another
mystic character glowed on the next hill; and to the
north-west a smaller Dai showed, like the reflection of

the first huge symbol. Full in the west gleamed a torii, a pillared gate-way of fire. From every house-top and from the bridges came the shouts of enthusiastic spectators, and the children in the rooms below us twittered like a box full of sparrows. For centuries the priests of mountain temples have taught their simple parishioners to lay their gathered firewood in the proper lines, and regular trenches mark the course of each device. The longer lines of the big Dai are each a half-mile in length, and the five miles' distance of our point of view dwarfed them to perfect proportions. These fiery symbols burned for half an hour before they began to waver, and long after their images still danced and burned in our vision against the succeeding blackness.

Down in the city the crowds surged through the lanterned streets, each adding the illumination of his hand-lantern to the scene. The river-bed was all recrossing lines and arches of lights, and myriad points of uncovered flames were reflected in the waters. The hill-sides twinkled and glowed with the innumerable torches in the cemeteries, and thus, lighted back to their tombs by all the city and the hill-side, the Buddhist spirits rest until the next midsummer season recalls them to their joyous Kioto.

CHAPTER XXV

THE PALACES AND CASTLE

Kioto remains faithful to its traditions, and yields but slowly to the foreign fashions which absorb Tokio. Tokio has nineteenth-century political troubles, even demagogues and hare-brained students, that unruly young element, the *soshi*, keep it in a state of agitation, and sometimes appeal to the old two-handed sword, the dagger, and the cowardly bomb. But Kioto, devoted to its old order, maintains the reign of peace, while the arts flourish.

For the thousand years during which this ancient Saikio remained the home of the Emperor, and of his nominal subject, the Shogun, its western half was crowded with the life centering about the two rulers. The ancient Emperors were hidden within the vast palace enclosure, the centre of other large demesnes, whose yellow walls were marked with the five horizontal white lines which indicate imperial possessions. This collection of palaces and the yashikis of the kugés, or court nobles, were then surrounded by one exterior wall and moat, making an immense imperial reservation — a small isolated city. Within a few years this exterior wall has been destroyed, streets have been opened, and much of the space has been turned into a public park. The imperial palace buildings cover ten acres of ground, and are surrounded by twenty-six acres of ornamental park. In each of the four yellow outer walls is a richly roofed and gabled gate-way, as stately as a temple, the ends of the beams, the ridges, and eaves decorated with golden chrysanthemum crests. The great gate, opened only for the Emperor and his train, and through whose central passage only the sacred being himself may be borne, faces south, as does the throne, in accordance with the old superstitions of the East. The evil influences always threatening from the north-east are guarded against by many temples beyond that side of the palace.

In these days of departed greatness only the Daidokoro Mon (the august kitchen gate), a fine gabled structure in the western wall, is used. After the visitor presents the elaborate official permit, obtained by his legation from the Imperial Household Department of Tokio, and stamped after a personal inspection of the holder by the Kioto bureau of that department, there is much running

to and fro of ancient officials, much restamping and recording, before he is led through the precinct by an attendant.   Even with this guarantee, the severe and stately old guardians, in their ancient dress and tonsure, seem
to look on the intruder with suspicion.

The Japanese *gosho* is not exactly translated by the
word "palace," and is merely a greater yashiki, or spread-
out house, constituting the sovereign's residence.   This
gosho consists of so many separate roofed, one-story
wooden buildings as to make a small village.   Each room,
or suite of rooms, occupies a distinct building, its outside
gallery or veranda forming the corridor, and its sliding
screens the inner walls.   Each building has the great
sweeping roof of a temple, the belief in the divinity of
the Emperor, and his headship of the Shinto faith, requiring that his actual dwelling should be a temple, rigid-
ly simple as a Shinto shrine, with thatched roof and unpainted woods.   These clustered houses are the survival
of the old nomad camps of Asia, as the upward curving
gables of the roof are a permanent form of their sagging
tent-tops.   The palace has suffered from many fires, the
last occurring in 1854, but each rebuilding has followed
the original models, and the gosho looks just as it did
centuries ago.   The same straw mats, open charcoal braziers, and loose saucers of oil in paper lamp-frames, in-
viting a conflagration there as in the humblest Japanese
home.

The walk around the outer galleries and connecting
corridors takes half an hour, and one must go stocking-
footed, or in the curious slippers furnished by the guardians.   In summer the recessed and sunless apartments
are cool and dim, but winter makes them bitterly cold
and forlorn.   Except for two thrones, there is nothing
to be called furniture in the palace.   The silk-bordered
mats of the floor, the paintings on the sliding screens,
the fine metal plates on all the wood-work, the irregular-

ly-shelved recesses, quaint windows, curious lattices, and richly-panelled ceilings constitute its adornments. All the wonderful kakemonos, vases, and curios were stored in godowns when the Emperor left Kioto, and the seals have not since been broken. On the screens in the private apartments are many autograph poems, written by court poets or imperial improvisators. The tea-rooms and the garden tea-houses show how important were the long-drawn ceremonies of cha no yu in those leisurely days of the past.

The courts surrounding the state apartments are sanded quadrangles, their surfaces scratched over in fine patterns by the gardeners' bamboo rakes for the easy detection of strange footprints. In the court-yard before the old audience hall a cherry-tree, a wild orange-tree, and a sacred bamboo, all emblematic, grow at either side of the broad steps. In the middle of the wide, temple-like apartment commanding this court stands the sacred white throne of past centuries, a square tent or canopy of white silk, with rich red borders at the edges of the overlapping curtains. Two antique Chinese dogs guard the throne. On New-year's Day, and at rare intervals when the Emperor gave audience to his vassal jailer, the Shogun, he sat on a silk cushion within the closed tent, and only his voice was heard, speaking in the quavering, long-drawn tones still used by the actors in the No dance. The imperial princes stood at either side of the throne, the kugé and officials of the highest rank knelt on the steps, and the lowest officials in attendance, the *jige* or "down to the earth" subjects, prostrated themselves on the sands of the court, while the mournful and muffled tones of the sacred voice sounded.

When the Emperor gave his first audiences after the Restoration, in 1868, he occupied a newer throne in the Shishinden, a large audience hall with a lofty ceiling supported by round wooden columns. On the lower part of the rear wall are some very old screens painted with groups of Chinese and Korean sages. The floor is of polished cedar, and the throne is like that of his ancestors, but with the curtains rolled up from the front and two sides. It stands on a dais, guarded by the Chinese dogs brought as trophies from Korea, and holds

THE THRONE OF 1868.

within it a simple lacquered chair, with lacquer stands for the sacred sword and seal. After those audiences of 1868 the Emperor travelled to Tokio in a gold-lacquered *norimon*, or closed litter, guarded by a train clad in the picturesque dress and armor of centuries before, and equipped with curious old weapons. He, himself, wore voluminous silk robes and a stiff lacquer hat, and the faithful kugés were attired in gorgeous brocades and silks. When the Emperor and court returned to Kioto in 1878, to open the railway to the seaport of Hiogo-Kobé, he was dressed like a European sovereign, alighted publicly from his railway car, and drove to the palace in a smart brougham, escorted by troops with western uniforms and weapons.

The Shiro, or Nijo castle, half a mile south of the palace, where the Shoguns flaunted their wealth and power, is a splendid relic of feudal days. The broad moat, drawbridge, strong walls, and tower-topped gate-ways and angles date from the middle of the sixteenth century. The great gate-way inside the first wall is a mass of elaborate metal ornament, from the sockets of the corner posts to the ridge-pole, but the many trefoils of the Tokugawas have been everywhere covered by the imperial chrysanthemum. All the rooms, but especially the two splendid audience-chambers, with a broad dais before each tokonoma, are marvels of decorative art, rich in gilded screens, with exquisite paintings and fine metal work, wonderfully carved *ramma*, and sunken ceiling panels, ornamented with flower circles, crests, and geometric designs. But, alas! a hideous Brussels carpet, a round centre-table, and a ring of straight-backed chairs have crowded their vulgar way into these stately rooms, as into every government building and office, large shop, and tea-house in Kioto.

The Shoguns had the Kinkakuji, the Ginkakuji, and other suburban villas to which they might resort, and in which many of them ended their days as abbots and priests. The Emperors had only the exquisite Shugakuin gardens at the foot of Mount Hiyeizan for their pleasurings, until the Restoration gave all such rebel property to the crown. The Kinkakuji (the gold-covered pavilion) and the Ginkakuji (the silver-covered pavilion) stand at opposite sides of the city, each surrounded with landscape-gardens, from which nearly all Japanese gardens are copied. Both are as old as the Ashikaga Shoguns, and both are now monasteries. The Kinkakuji is the larger, and was even more splendid before it was despoiled of so many rare and historic stones and garden ornaments, but the place is still a paradise. Yoshimitsu, third of the Ashikaga Shoguns, built the Kinkakuji, and thither the great Ashikaga retired to end his life. This refuge figures in the many novels of the time of the Ashikagas, when the War of the Chrysanthemums, the Japanese War of the Roses, raged, and the Emperors with the kugés suffered actual want and privation. The memory of this third Ashikaga is abhorred, because he paid tribute to China and accepted from that country in return the title of "King of Japan;" but he so fostered luxury and art that some of his other sins are forgiven him. The pretty little palace at the lake's edge, with its golden roof and lacquered walls, has successfully withstood the centuries, and is still intact. In the monastery buildings near the gate-way are shown many wonderful kakemonos and screens, and in one court is a pine-tree trained in the shape of a junk, hull, mast, and sail perfectly reproduced in the feathery, living green needles of the tree. It is most interesting to see how the patient gardeners have bent, interlaced, tied, weighted down, and propped up the limbs and twigs to produce this model, with the slow labor of a century.

To the Ginkakuji retired the dignified Yoshimasa, eighth of the Ashikaga Shoguns, to found a monastery and to meditate, until with Murata Shinkio, the priest, and Soami, the painter, he evolved the minute and elaborate ceremonies of cha no yu. The weather-beaten boards and finely thatched roof of the first ceremonial tea-house in Japan, built before Columbus set sail for the Zipangu of Marco Polo, are greatly revered by Japanese visitors. Beautiful is the way to the Ginkakuji, past the high walls and gate-ways of monasteries, past the towering gates of countless temples, up their long shaded avenues, and on by bamboo groves and terraced rice fields. You buy wooden admission tickets for ten sen, which you give to a little acolyte, who opens the inner gate-way. This *chisai bonze san* (small priest) might have been twelve years old, but looked not more than five when I first knew him, and from shaven head to sandaled foot he was a Buddhist priest in miniature. This Shinkaku, leading the way to the lake with solemn countenance and hands primly clasped before him, suddenly broke forth into a wild, sing-song chant, which recited the names of the donors of the rocks and lanterns to the great Ashikaga Yoshimasa. He made us take off our shoes and creep up the steep and ancient stair-way of the Ginkakuji to see a blackened and venerable image of Amida. Morning, noon, and night service is said before the altar in the little old temple by the lake, and this small priest burns incense, passes the sacred books, and assists the wrinkled and aged priests in the observances of the Zen sect of Buddhists. Back of the monastery buildings is a lotus pond, where the great pink flower-cups fill the air with perfume, and every morning are set fresh before Buddha's shrine.

Going westward from Kioto the traveller crosses rice fields, skirts a long bamboo hedge, and comes to the summer palace of Katsura no Miya, a relic of the Taiko's days. An aunt of the Emperor occupied it until her recent decease, and to that is probably due its perfect preservation. An ancient samurai with shaven crown and silken garments receives, with a dozen bows, the handful of official papers that constitute a permit to visit the imperial demesne. Dropping his shoes at the steps, the visitor wanders through a labyrinth of little rooms, each exquisite, simple, and charming, with its golden screens and gold-flecked ceilings. The irregularly shelved recesses, the *chigai dana* of each room, the ramma, the lattices and windows. are perfect models of Japanese taste and art; and the Taiko's crest is wrought in silver, gold, and bronze on all the mountings, and is painted and carved everywhere. The open rooms look upon a lovely garden, and paths of flat-topped stones lead through the tiny wilderness of lake, forest, thicket, and stream; over old stone bridges, stained and lichen-covered, to picturesque tea-houses and pavilions, overhanging the lake. Stone Buddhas and stone pagodas stand in shadowy places, and stone lanterns under dwarf pine-trees are reflected in the curve of every tiny bay. It is an ideal Japanese garden, with the dew of a midsummer morning on all the spider webs, and only the low note of the grasshoppers to break the stillness.

Although all tourists spend a day in shooting the rapids of the Oigawa, it seems to me a waste of precious Kioto time and a performance out of harmony with the spirit of the place, although in May the blooming azaleas cause that wild and narrow cañon to blaze with color. The flat-bottomed boats dart through the seven-mile gorge and dash from one peril of shipwreck to another, just saved by a dextrous touch of the boatmen's poles, which fit into holes in the rocks that they themselves have worn. The flooring of the boats is so thin as to rise and fall with the pressure of the water, in a way that seems at first most alarming. The passage ends at Arashiyama, a steep hill clothed with pine, maple, and cherry-trees, which in cherry-blossom time, or in autumn, is the great resort of all Kioto, whose pleasurings there form the theme of half the geisha's songs and the accompanying dances. From the tea-house on the opposite bank the abrupt mountain-side shows a mat of densest foliage. A torii at the river's edge, stone steps and lines of lanterns lead to a temple on the summit, and down through the forest float the soft, slow beats of a temple-bell. The tea-house is famous for its fish-dinners, where *tai*, fresh from the cool, green river, are cooked as only the Japanese can cook them, and the lily bulbs, rice sandwiches, omelettes, and sponge-cake are so good that the place is always crowded.

Katsura no Miya is just below Arashiyama, and after one morning spent in the little palace, with its restful shade and stillness, our half-naked coolies ran with us through the glaring sunlight to the tea-house beside the cool waters of the Oigawa. They barely waited for us to step out of the jinrikishas before they plunged, laughing and frolicking, down the bank and leaped into the river, splashing and swimming there like so many frogs. They had run ten miles that morning, half of the way under a baking sun, the perspiration streaming from their bodies, and they plunged into the river as they were, taking off their one cotton garment and washing it, while they cooled themselves in the rushing waters. Then, lying down quite uncovered in their own quarters of the tea - house, they ate watermelon and cucumber, drank tea and smoked, until they dropped asleep in the scorching noonday of a cholera summer. In the late afternoon, when it was time to begin the long ride back to Maruyama, they limped out to us, lame and stiff in every joint and muscle, coughing and croaking like ravens. We felt that they must die in the shafts, but exercise soon relieved the cramped and stiffened limbs, and they trotted on as nimbly as ever over the hills to Kioto.

The coolie and his ways are matters of much interest to foreigners, but after a time one ceases to be amazed at their endurance or their recklessness. After the most violent exercise, *ninsoku*, the coolie, will take off his one superfluous garment and sit in summer ease in his decorated skin. Back, breast, arms, and thighs are often covered with elaborate tattooed pictures in blue, red, and black on the raw - umber ground. His philosophy of dress is a simple one. When the weather is too hot to wear clothes they are left off, and a wisp of straw for the feet, a loin-cloth, and a huge flat hat, a yard in diameter, weighing less than a feather, are enough for him. When there is no money to buy raiment he tattoos himself with gorgeous pictures, which he would never hide were there not watchful policemen and Government laws to compel him into some scanty covering.

The diet of these coolies seems wholly insufficient for the tremendous labor they perform—rice, pickled fish, fermented radish, and green tea affording the thin nutriment of working-days. Yet the most splendid specimens of physical health are reared and kept in prize-fighting condition on what would reduce a foreigner to invalidism in a week. I remember that while resting one hot morning under Shinniodo's great gate - way, my coolie, who by an unusually early start had been interrupted in his breakfast of one green apple, asked for some tea-money. I watched the hungry pony while he treated his companions to a substantial repast of tea and watermelon. Strengthened and recuperated, he came back, shouldered camera and tripod, and as he walked down the hot flagging, complacently picked his teeth with the sharp point of one tripod stick — a toothpick four feet long !

CHAPTER XXVI

KIOTO SILK INDUSTRY

KIOTO remains the home of the arts, although no longer the seat of government. For centuries it ministered to the luxury of the two courts, which gathered together and encouraged hosts of artists and artisans, whose descendants live and work in the old home. Kioto silks and crapes, Kioto fans, porcelains, bronzes, lacquer, carvings, and embroideries preserve their quality and fame, and are dearer and better than any other.

Silk is the most valuable article of export which Japan produces, and raw silk to the value of thirty millions of yens goes annually to foreign consumers, while the home market buys nearly seven millions of yens' worth of manufactured fabrics. The Nishijin quarter of Kioto and the Josho district, north-west of Tokio, are the great silk centres of Japan, and any silk merchant, fingering a crape gown, will tell instantly which of the rival districts produced it. Recently Kofu, west of Tokio, and Hachioji, twenty miles south, have become important centres of manufacture as well. The silk market has its fluctuations, its panics, and its daily quotations by cable; but raw silk has so inherent a value that it is a good collateral security at any bank, and the silk-broker is as well established and important a personage in the mercantile world of the Orient as the stock-broker in the Occident. Next to specie or gems, silk is the most valuable of commodities in proportion to its bulk, the cargo of a single steamer often representing a value of two million dollars in gold. The United States is the greatest consumer of Japan's raw silk. In 1875 fifty-three bales only of raw silk and cocoons were shipped to America. Three years later two thousand three hundred and thirty-six bales were sent, and in 1887 sixteen thousand eight hundred and sixty-four bales, while Europe took only fourteen thousand bales. Our share of the raw silk is nearly all consigned to Paterson. N. J. With the opening of this great foreign trade, silk is dearer to the Japanese consumer than twenty years ago; and while it still furnishes the ceremonial dress, and is the choice of the rich, cotton, and of late, wool, have taken its place to a great extent.

Everywhere the rearing of the worms goes on. The silk districts and villages are always thriving, prosperous, and tidily kept, forming peaceful and contented communities. Each house becomes both a nursery for the worms and a home factory, where every member of the family engages in the work. Wages in silk districts range from eight to twenty cents, in United States gold, for a day's work of eighteen hours, the higher price being paid to the most expert and experienced only. The houses are all spacious, kept most exquisitely clean, ventilated, and held to an even temperature. Sheets of paper coated with eggs, and looking like so much sandpaper, will in a few days fill the waiting trays with tiny white worms. The mulberry-leaves have to be chopped as fine as dust for these new-comers, which are daily lifted to fresh trays by means of chopsticks, the fingers being too rough and strong for such delicate handlings. For a week at a time the tiny gluttons crawl and eat, then take a day and night of sleep, maintaining this routine for five weeks, when, having grown large enough, they begin to wind themselves up in cocoons. Then the cauldron of boiling water and the whirling reel change the yellow balls into great skeins of shining silk, ready to be twisted. tied. and woven either at home or across the seas. Compressed into bales of a picul's weight, or 133½ pounds. the raw silk finds its way to market , or, woven in hand looms in the usual thirteen-inch Japanese widths, or in wider measures for the foreign trade, it is again sold by weight, the *momé* being the unit. One hundred and twenty momé are equal to one pound. Twenty-five yards of fine white handkerchief-silk weigh from 150 to 200 momé, and 100 momé of such silk varies in price from six to seven dollars, gold.

Steam-looms are fast supplanting the old hand-machines in Nishijin and Josho. The Government sent men to study the methods in use at Lyons and bring back machinery, and now there are filatures and factories in all the silk districts. Private corporations are following the Government example. At the Kwangioba no Shokoba the first exhibition of foreign machines, with instruction in their use. was given. To-day the lively clatter of the Jacquard loom is heard above the slow, droning noise of the hand-loom behind Nishijin's miles of blank walls. Slowly the weavers are abandoning the rude loom. which was probably in use. like gunpowder, at an age when Europeans clothed themselves in skins and lived in caves ; and the singing draw-boy is descending from his high perch, where he has so long been lifting the alternating handful of threads that make the pattern.

In a tour of the Nishijin factories, one scorching August day. we saw many of these primitive hand-looms, with half-clad weavers tossing the shuttles of silk and gold thread, their skin shining with the heat like polished bronze, and marked all over with the scars of moxa cones. Everywhere were gathered books upon books filled with samples of superb brocades. many of them more than a century old. Everywhere we were regaled with sweets and thimble-cups of lukewarm amber tea,

that seemed harmless as water, but murdered sleep.
Everywhere we found a new garden more enchanting
than the last, and everywhere the way in which work-
room and kitchen, living-room and sales-room were combined ; women, children, family, workmen, and servants
were ruled over by the master of the home and factory,
offered a curious study in political economy and patriarchal government.

Until the Emperor, and finally the Empress and court
ladies abandoned the national dress, the court-weaver of
brocade remained a considerable personage, for he and
his ancestors had been both tailors and dress-makers to
those august personages. We visited the beautiful garden and lantern-hung verandas of this artistic dictator,
and sipped tea, fanned the while by attentive maids,
while the stout, dignified, and prosperous head of the ancient house and our Japanese official escort conversed.
Afterwards we were shown the books of brocade and
silks manufactured for the imperial family and court.
The gorgeousness of some of these, especially the blazing red brocade, stiff with pure gold thread and covered
with huge designs of the imperial chrysanthemum, or
the Paulownia crest of the Emperor's family, fairly daz-
zled us. We saw the pattern of the old Emperors' ceremonial robes, and patterns designed by past Empresses
for their regal attire. Several of these were of a pure
golden yellow, woven with many gold threads; one design half covered with fine, skeleton bamboos on the
shimmering, sunshiny ground. The splendid fabrics that
bear the imperial crest may be woven only for the reigning family, and their furniture-coverings, draperies, and
carriage-linings are as carefully made and guarded as
bank-note paper. Squares of thickest red silk, wrought
with a single gold chrysanthemum, are woven for the
Foreign Office, as cases for state papers and envoys'
credentials. Rolls of the finest white silk were ready to

be made into undergarments for the Emperor, who, never wearing such articles twice, obliges his tailor to keep a large supply ready; and these garments that have once touched the sacred person are highly treasured by loyal subjects.

The weaver exhibited flaming silks covered with huge peonies, or fine maple-leaves, or circles of writhing dragons, which the outside million may buy if they choose, but not a sixteen-petalled chrysanthemum are they privileged to obtain from him in any way. In discussing the changeableness of the American taste, Kobayashi and his staff wondered that the mass of our people did not care for silks that would wear forever, rather than for the cheap fancies of the moment. The Japanese cling to the really good things that have stood the test of a century's taste, and Japanese ladies had a pride in wearing the brocade that had been theirs for a lifetime and their mothers' before them. In noble families inherited ceremonial dresses are as highly treasured as the plate and jewels of European families, though they are now seldom worn. Rolls of such silks and brocades were often presented by Emperor and Shogun to their courtiers, and the common saying, " He wears rags, but his heart is brocade," attests the esteem in which these *nishikis* (brocades) were held in olden times, and those *yesso nishikis*, with their reverse a loose rainbow of woof threads, are far removed from the thin, flat, papery, characterless stuffs known as Japanese brocades in the cheap foreign trade.

A heavy silk tapestry, peculiar to Japan, although suggested by Chinese models, is best woven now at the Dotemachi Gakko, an industrial school for girls, maintained by the Government. The art had nearly died out when the aged tapestry-weaver was brought to the school and given a class of the most promising pupils. The fabric is woven on hand-frames, the design being sketched on the white warp threads, wrought in with shuttles or bobbins, and the threads pressed down with a comb. Each piece of the design is made by itself, and connected by occasional cross threads, or brides, as in lace. The fabric is not dear, considering its superior beauty and durability, as compared to the moth-inviting tapestries of the Gobelins and Beauvais, and conventional and classic designs are still followed, the old dyes used, and gold thread lavishly interwoven.

The gold thread employed in weaving brocades and tapestries is either a fine thread wound with gold foil, a strip of tough paper coated with gold-dust, or threads wound with common gold-paper. The fineness and quality of the gold affect the cost of any material into which it enters, and in ordering a fabric or a piece of embroidery one stipulates closely as to the gold-thread employed. The fine gold-wires of Russian brocades are very rarely used, because of their greater cost. The manufacture of gold thread is an open secret, and women are often seen at work in the streets, stretching and twisting the fine golden filaments in lengths of twenty and thirty feet.

The old dyers were as much masters of their craft as the old weavers; and in trying to match the colors in a piece of yesso nishiki, I once went the round of Paris shops and dress-makers' establishments in vain. Nothing they afforded would harmonize with the soft tones of the old dyes. A distinguished American connoisseur, wishing to duplicate a cord and tassel from one of his old lacquer boxes, took it to a Parisian cord-maker. The whole staff looked at it, and the proprietor asked permission to unravel a bit, to decipher the twist and obtain some long threads for the dyer. But with months of time allowed him, he could not reproduce the colors nor braid a cord like the original, nor even retwist the Japanese cord he had unravelled.

Velvet-weaving is one of the old arts, but it was accomplished by the most primitive and laborious means, and the fabrics, dull and inferior to foreign factory velvets, do not rank among the more characteristic productions of Japanese looms. Kioto's painted velvets are unique, however, and charming effects are obtained by painting softly-toned designs on the velvet as it comes from the loom, with all the fine wires still held in the looped threads. The painted parts are afterwards cut, and stand in softly-shaded relief upon the uncut groundwork.

The crape guild of Kioto is as large, and commercially as important, in this day, as the brocade guild, whose members rank first among manufacturers. All crape is woven in *tans*, or lengths of sixty Japanese *shaku*, two and a half shaku being equal to an English yard. On the loom this material is a thin, lustrous fabric, hardly heavier than the gauze on which kakemonos and fan mounts are painted. It is so smooth and glossy that one cannot discover the smoother warp and twisted woof threads, alternately tight and loose, which give it its crinkly surface. When finished, the web is plunged into a vat of boiling water, which shrinks the threads and ensures the wrinkled and lustreless surface. Once dried the tans are tied like skeins, and lying in heaps, look like so much unbleached muslin. Crape must be dyed in the piece, and stretched, while damp, by bracing it across with innumerable strips of bowed bamboo. In the bath the pieces shrink from one-third to one-half in width, and a full tenth in length, but the more they shrink the more cockled is the surface. When finished the tan may measure from seventeen to twenty-four yards in length, but weight and not measure determines its value, and the scales are used instead of the yard-stick.

While the Chinese weave only the original Canton crape, with its heavy woof and firmly twisted threads,

the Japanese have produced a dozen kinds, each wrinkled, cockled, waved, and crinkled in different ways. The
great Joshu district produces not as many kinds of crape
as Kioto, and Nishijin's looms are busier each year, weaving crapes as light and thin as gauze, or as heavy and
soft as velvet; some costing only thirty or forty cents
a yard, and others two and three dollars for an arm's
length. The soft, thick, heavily - ribbed *kabe habutai*,

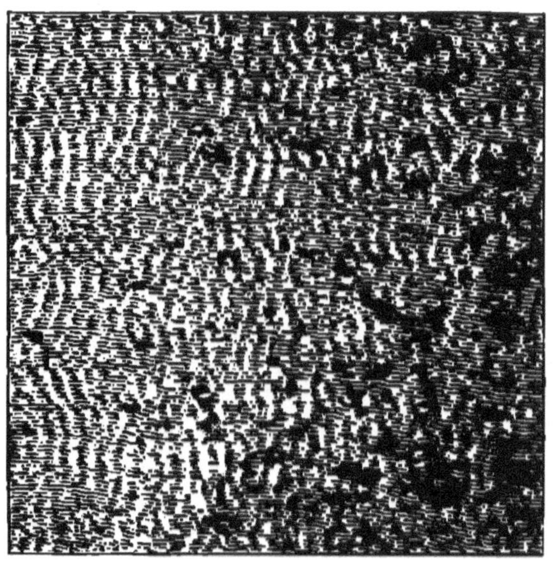

KABE HABUTAI

once kept for ceremonial gowns and the favorite gifts of
the great, is most expensive, having heavier threads and
larger cockles than other crapes, and never showing
crease or wrinkle. Plain crape, or *chirimen*, differs as the
fineness of thread and the closeness of weaving add to its
weight. *Ebisu chirimen* might be called *repoussé*, from
the scale-like convexities of its surface, and is a most
fascinating fabric. Finest and most exquisite of all is

the lustrous *kinu chirimen*, or crinkled silk, which shows only the finest lines and parallel ridgings marking its surface lengthwise. Used chiefly for the carelessly tied obi of the bath kimono, or as *obishime*, tied over the

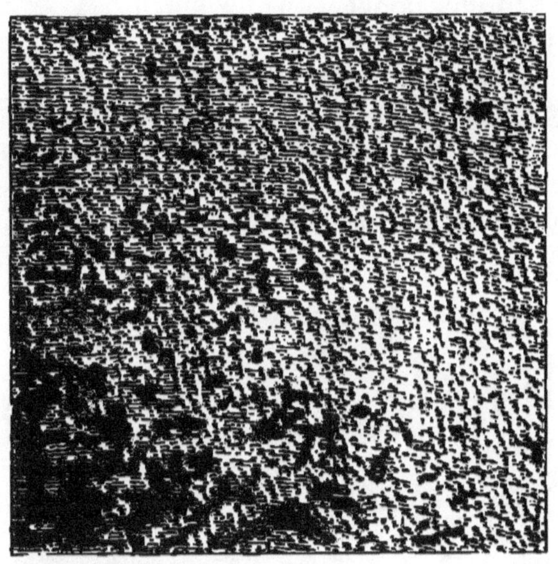

CHIRIMEN

womens' heavy satin and brocade obis to keep their stiff folds in place, these stringy scarfs add a last artistic touch of color to a costume. Kinu chirimen shrinks half its width, but loses nothing in length in the bath, and a tan a yard wide ranges from eighteen to twenty-eight dollars in price. *Kanoko chirimen* is plain crape dotted over with knots or projections in different colors, a result arrived at by processes similar to those employed at Arimatsu for dyeing cotton goods.

Yamamai, so little known outside the home market, is a most artistic fabric, roughly and loosely woven of the threads of the wild, mountain silk-worm, that is fed on oak-leaves. Yamamai has the natural yellow color of the cocoons, is considered both a cure and preventive of rheumatism, and is often worn at the command of foreign physicians. It is softer to the touch than the Chinese pongee, not being weighted with the clay dressing of Shantung pongees, while much heavier than the Indian tussores, all three of these fabrics being the product of the same wild oak-spinner.

The painted crapes of Kioto, specially designed for children's holiday dresses and obis, are works of art, in the manufacture of which the old capital holds almost a monopoly. All the elaborate processes of patterning

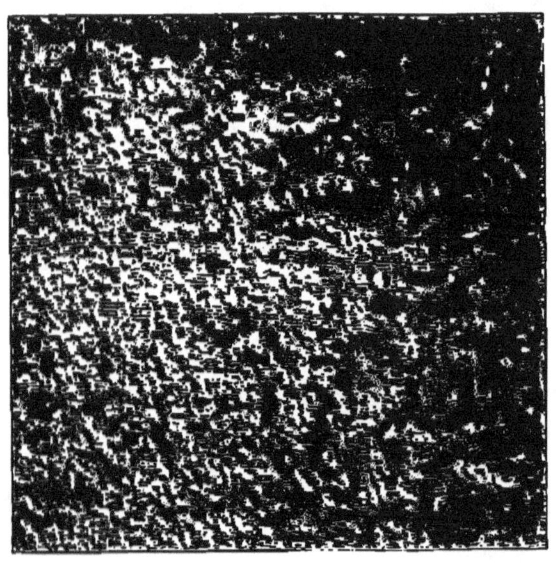

EBISU CHIRIMEN

such crapes were shown us one morning at Nishimura's great establishment. First, on a square of white crape, wrung out in water and pasted down at the edges on a board, the outline of the principal design was sketched in indigo. This line was then carefully covered by a thread of starch, drawn from a glutinous ball held upon the point of a stick, while the painter turned and tilted the crape to receive it. This starch, or "resist," as occidental dyers term it, is to prevent the spreading of the colors by capillary attraction, and the limits of every color must be carefully defined, unless the fabric is to be made one of those marvellous studies of blended and

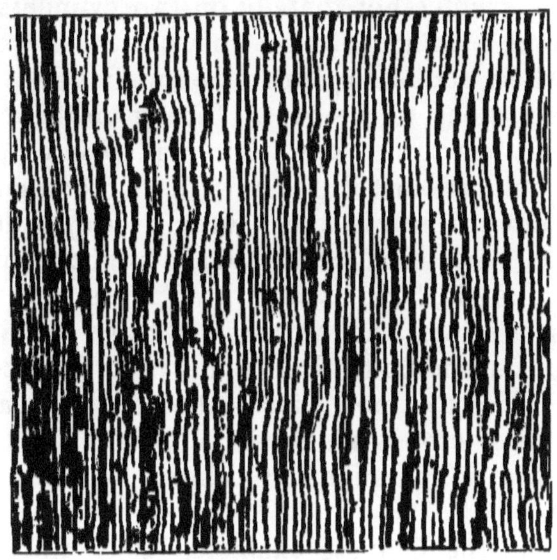

KINU CHIRIMEN

merging tints. As soon as the first color dried, the first starchy outline was washed out, and another drawn for the second color. After the removal of each "resist," the square was stretched on bowed bamboos and dried over a hibachi. The artist had purposely worked out his design with such cunning that it was only when the last touches in red had been given that we discovered the Daimonji's fires burning on the mountain-side, and a troop of men, women, children, and jinrikishas, all with glowing lanterns, figuring as silhouettes on Sanjio bridge.

When a whole tan of crape is to be painted, much of the design may be stencilled through perforated cardboard, but, in general, the best painted crapes display free-hand sketches, with patterns never exactly repeated, nor exactly matching at the edges. After the general outline is sketched, the tan, sewn together at the ends, is made to revolve horizontally on two cylinders, like a roller towel, passing before a row of seated workmen, each of whom adds a single color, or applies the "resist," and slips it along to the next. Sitting on the mats, the soles of his feet turned upward in his lap, in a pose that a circus contortionist might envy, each workman has a glowing hibachi at his knees, over which he dries his own work. And such work! Hazy rainbows on misty skies, flights of birds, shadows of trees and rushes, branches of pines and blossoming twigs, comical figures, animals, and fantastical chimeras, kaleidoscopic arrangements of the most vivid colors the eye can bear. These painted crapes are beyond compare, and the English and Dutch imitations in printed delaines fall absurdly short.

Following the Chinese example, Kioto silk-weavers now make silk rugs equalling the famous ones of Pekin. Even when new they have a finer bloom and sheen than the old prayer-rugs of western Asia, but their designs, first made from the suggestions of an American house, are neither Japanese, Turkish, nor at all Oriental, nor do they allow the best effects to be obtained. At two dollars a square foot, these thick, soft rugs make the costliest of floor coverings in a country where the cotton and hemp rugs of Osaka sell for a few cents a square foot, and the natural camel's-hair rugs of North China for eighteen cents a square foot.

CHAPTER XXVII

EMBROIDERIES AND CURIOS

THEIR range of stitches, their ingenious methods and
combinations, and the variety of effects attained with the
needle and a few strands of colored silk, easily place the
Japanese first among all embroiderers. Although China
taught them to embroider, they far surpass the Chinese
in design, color, and artistic qualities, while they attain
a minute and mechanical exactness equal to the soul-
less, expressionless precision of the best Chinese work.
They can simulate the hair and fur of animals, the
plumage of birds, the hard scales of fishes and dragons, the bloom on fruit, the dew on flowers, the muscles
of bodies, tiny faces and hands, the patterned folds of
drapery, the clear reflection of lacquer, the glaze of porcelains, and the patina of bronzes in a way impossible to
any but the Japanese hand and needle. Sometimes they
cover the whole groundwork with couched designs in a
heavy knotted silk, and this peculiar embroidery has the
name of *kindan nuitsuké*. With floss silk, with twisted silks, with French knots, and with gold and silver
thread, couched down with different colored silks, with
silk threads couched, and with concealed couchings, a
needle-worker attains every color effect of the painter;
nor does the embroiderer disdain to use the brush, or
to powder and spatter his designs with gold, nor to en-
croach upon the plastic art by his wonderful modelling
of raised surfaces, rivalling the sculptor with his counter-
feit faces. His invention and ingenuity are inexhaustible, and the modern craftsmen preserve all the skill of
their ancestors.

The oldest existing piece of Japanese needle-work is the mandalla of a nun, kept at Tayema temple in Yamato, which is certainly of the eighth century, although legend ascribes it to the divine Kwannon. Pieces of equal antiquity, doubtless, are in the sealed godowns of Nara temples, but very little is known of them. The latest triumphs of the art, pieces showing the limit of the needle's possibilities, are the ornamental panels and makemono executed for the Tokio palace, and other work by the same artists exhibited at Paris in 1889. This exhibition work was executed under imperial command at Nishimura's, the largest silk-shop in Kioto, a place to which every visitor is piloted forthwith. Solid brown walls, black curtained doors, and the crest of three hexagons are all that one sees from without; but the crest is repeated at door-ways across the street and around corners, until one realizes what a village of crape-weavers and painters, velvet-weavers and embroiderers, is set in the heart of Kioto by this one firm. The master of the three hexagons has taken innumerable medals, gold, silver, and bronze, at home and abroad, and, in response to every invitation to make a national exhibit, Government commands are sent him at Kioto. The blank outer walls and common entrance, the bare rooms with two or three accountants sitting before low desks, do not indicate the treasures of godown and show-room that lie beyond. In an inner room, with an exquisite ceiling of interlaced pine shavings, curtains, kakemono, screens, and fukusa are heaped high, while others are continually brought in by the small porters. In spite of the reputation and the artistic possibilities of the establishment, it sends out much cheap, tasteless, and inferior work to meet the demands of foreign trade, and of the tourists who desire the so-called Japanese things they are used to seeing at home.

For the old embroideries, those splendid relics of the

national life with its showy and picturesque customs, the buyer must seek the second-hand clothes-shops, the pawn-shops of the land. In the Awata district lives the great dealer who gathers in old kimonos, obis, fukusas, kesas, temple hangings, brocades, and embroideries from the godowns of nobles, commoners, priests, actors, saints, and sinners, to whom ready money is a necessity. Geishas and actors, with the extravagant habits of their kind, are often forced to part with their wardrobes, and the second-hand shops are half filled with beautiful and purely Japanese things which they have sacrificed. When I first beheld " my uncle " of Awata, his was a dark, ill-smelling, old clo' shop, with two bushy-headed, poorly-dressed attendants. Gilbert and Sullivan unwittingly made his fortune, and the old dealer could not at first understand why the foreign buyers, hitherto indifferent, should suddenly crowd his dingy rooms, empty his go-downs, and keep his men busy collecting a new stock. Three years after my first visit there was a large, new building with high-heaped shelves, replacing the dirty old house and its questionable bales tied up in blue cotton, and horribly suggestive of smallpox, cholera, and other contagions. Prices had trebled and were advancing steadily, with far less embarrassment of choice in the stock than formerly.

The gorgeous kimonos of actors and geishas offered at such shops far outnumber those richly-wrought gowns worn by women of rank at holiday times and at the palace, and most of the showy and gorgeously-decorative gowns displayed in western drawing-rooms have questionable histories. Even the stores of No dance costumes have been drawn upon, and choice old brocades are rarer now than good old embroideries. The priest's kesa, or cloak, a symbolic patchwork of many pieces, and the squares and bits from temple tables, for a long time offered exquisite bits of meshed gold-thread and colors, and on the back of such pieces one often found poems, sacred verses, and fervent vows, written by the pious ones who had made offerings of them to the temples.

The stores of fukusas seemed inexhaustible a few years ago, and I can remember days of delight in that ill-smell-

FUKUSA

ing old corner of Awata, when one out of every five fuku-sa was a treasure, while now there are hardly five good ones in a hundred of those needle pictures. The finest work was lavished on these squares of satin or crape,

which former etiquette demanded to have laid over the
boxes containing gifts or notes, both box and fukusa to
be duly admired and returned to the sender. These ceremonial cloths were part of the trousseau of every bride
of high degree, and old families possess them by scores.
The nicest etiquette ordered the choice of the fukusa,
and the season, the gift, the giver, and the receiver were
considered in selecting the particular wrapping. The
greatest artists have made designs for them, and a few
celebrated ones, bearing Hokusai's signature, are owned
by European collectors. The crests of the feudal families
become familiar to one from their constant repetition on
fukusas. Numberless Japanese legends, and symbols as
well, constantly reappear, and no two are ever exactly
alike in design or execution, however often one may see
the same subject treated. Equally popular are all the
symbols of long life—the pine, the plum, the bamboo; the
tortoise with the fringed shell that lives for a thousand
years; the peach that took a thousand years to ripen; the
stork, the old man and woman under the pine-tree hail-
ing the rising sun—and all, when wrapping a gift, equally convey a delicately expressed wish for length of days.
The fierce old saints and disciples, who with their dragons and tigers live on old Satsuma surfaces, keep company with the sages who rode through the air on storks,
tortoises, or carp, or stand unrolling sacred scrolls beneath bamboo groves. And the Seven Household Gods
of Luck, the blessed Shichi Fukujin, are on the fukusa
as well. There smile Daikoku, the god of riches, upon
his rice-bags, hammer and purse in hand; Ebisu, the god
of plenty, with his little red fish; Jurojin, the serene old
god of longevity, with his mitred cap, white beard, staff,
and deer; high-browed Fukurokujin, lord of popularity
and wisdom; Hotei, spirit of goodness and kindness,
sack on back, fan in hand, and children climbing and
tumbling over him; black-faced Bishamon, god of war

and force, holding his lance and miniature pagoda ; and
Benten Sama, goddess of grace and beauty, playing the
lute.

Takara Buné, the good-luck ship, the New-year's
junk, with dragon beak and silken sail, bearing rich
gifts from the unknown land, is another favorite subject.
To sleep with takara buné's image under one's wooden
pillow on New-year's night insures good-luck and good
dreams for the rest of the year. Quite as significant are
the *takara mono*, the ancient and classic good-luck symbols, which are the hat, hammer, key, straw coat, bag or
purse, sacred gem or pearl, the scrolls, the clove, the
shippo, or seven precious things, and the weights. These
emblems, introduced everywhere, fill flower-circles, or the
spaces and groundwork of geometrical designs, and are
always received with favor. The shojo, who have drunk
saké until their hair has turned red, the rats and the radish, the cock on the temple drum, poems in superb let-
tering, all ornament the fukusa, and there the mysterious
manji, or hook-cross, and the *mitsu tomoyé*, or three com-
mas curved within a circle, are continually reproduced.

This manji is the Svastika, or Buddhist cross of India, which appears in the frescos of the Pyramids and
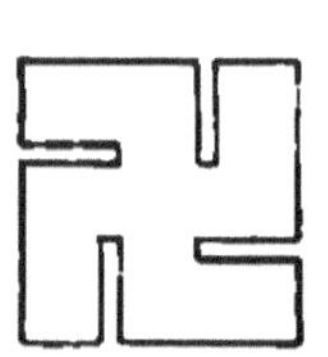
the Catacombs, in Greek art, in Etruscan
tombs, in the embroideries and missals of
mediæval Europe, in the Scandinavian design known as Thor's hammer, in old English heraldry, in the Chinese symbol called
the " tablet of honor," and on innumerable
temple ornaments.

Five of the old daimio families had the manji as their
crest, and it came to Japan from China and India, along
with the Buddhist religion. On old armor. flags, and war
fans it is constantly found, and it is the sign of life, of the
four elements, of eternity ; the portent of good-luck. the
talisman of safety from evil spirits, and an amulet against

threats or harm from any of the four quarters; while
the word "manji" is derived from the Chinese word
"mantse," meaning ten thousand.

The mitsu tomoyé is another universal symbol of innumerable meanings. It occurs on the crests of eight
daimio families; on temple drums, lanterns,
the ends of tiles, and on Daikoku's mallet. 
It is variously said to represent falling
snow, leaping flames, dashing water, and
clouds; the thongs of a warrior's glove,
uncurling fern-fronds, the down of seed
pods; the three great elements, fire, air, and water, the
origin of matter, the great principles of nature, an oriental trinity. On house-tiles and ridge-poles it invokes
protection from the three evils—fire, thieves, and flood,
and everywhere these two mysterious symbols confront
one.

Kioto abounds in curio-shops, ranging from the half-
mile long row on either side of the Manjiuji to the
splendid accumulations and choice art collections of
Ikeda, Hayashi, Kiukioda, Takada, and the bazaar at the
foot of Maruyama. At Ikedas, which is really an art museum filled with precious things, the processes of damascening and lacquering may be watched. It has been prov-
en of late that, when patrons will pay a price to warrant
the endless labor and care, as good lacquer may be made
to-day as formerly. Connoisseurs admit that they are
often deceived, and that they are able to tell the quality only, and not the age, of any really choice piece.
The new is as indestructible as the old, if carefully made.
A pin-point or a hot coal leaves no mark, a year's bath
in sea-water no trace, and amateur photographers have
found it proof against the acids and chemicals of devel-
oping fluids. Yet this substance, enduring as crystal, is
made by coat upon coat of an ill-smelling black varnish,
which, stirred in a tub with iron-filings, and set in the

sun to thicken and blacken, may be seen daily in the streets of any Japanese city. New lacquer is so poisonous to many persons that the curious are content to watch at a distance, while the workmen apply coat after coat, set the article in a moistened box to dry slowly, and grinding and polishing surface after surface, add those wonderful decorations that result in a trifle light as air and precious as gold or gems.

The "incense-shop" is one of the choicest and most truly Japanese of curio-shops. It looks, from the street, an every-day affair; but after propitiating the attendants by a purchase of perfume, the inner wealth is revealed in rooms filled with the choicest old wares. The salesmen tempt the visitor with rare *koros*, or incense-burners, and, in an elementary way, the master plays the daimio's old game of the Twenty Perfumes. He sprinkles on the hibachi's glowing coals some little black morsels in the shape of leaves, blossoms, or characters; scattering green particles, brown particles, and grayish ones, and showing the ignorant alien how to catch the ascending column of pale-blue smoke in the bent hand, close the fingers upon it, and convey it to the nose. You cannot tell which odor you prefer, nor remember which dried particle gave forth a particular fragrance. The nose is bewildered by the commingled wreaths and mixed cathedral odors, and the master chuckles delightedly.

There are certain curio-shops of an even more exalted kind, unknown to tourists, and reserved to Japanese connoisseurs and to those few eminent foreign residents who, in taste and appreciation, are Japanese. There, little tea-jars, ancient tea-bowls, and ornaments for the ink-box delight those to the manner born, and command great prices; and there one sees the precious iron pots of Riobondo lifted from brocade bags, and ancient pieces of wrought and inlaid bronze and iron, old helmets and swords, such as are to be found nowhere else.

Tokio and Osaka rival the Kioto makers of the finer modern metal-work, all three cities having been equal capitals and centres of wealth and luxury in the feudal days, when the armorer was the warrior's right-hand. The descendants of the ancient metal-workers of Kioto still labor at the old forges, and marvels of art, as well as of patient labor, come from the various workshops of the town. Both old and new designs are employed to beautify new combinations of metals, but at the present day the metal-workers' art expends itself on trifling things. Instead of adorning armor and weapons and fashioning their exquisite ornaments, the artists' taste and skill must be lavished on vases, placques, incense-burners, hibachis, water-pots, and flower-stands, and the countless cheap trifles and specimens of *bijouterie* made for exportation. In the coloring, cutting, and inlaying of bronze the Japanese are unrivalled; but for the great metal-work of the empire the student of native art must visit private collections and the treasures of the great curio-shops.

Feudal life invested swords and armor with their high estate, and gave the armorer his rank. The fine temper of the old blades has long challenged European admiration, and the sword-guards, the knife-handles, and the minute ornaments of the hilt are beyond compare. Sentiment, legend, and poetry glorify the sword, and the edict of 1871, which forbade their use as weapons, increased their value as relics, and brought thousands of them into the curio market. In rich and noble families they have always been treasured, but collections of fine blades are found in other countries as well, and the names of Muramasa and Masamuné and the Miochin family, are as well known as that of Benvenuto Cellini to connoisseurs of metal-work anywhere.

In the earlier uncommercial times little distinction was recognized in the comparative value of metals. Their fitness for the purpose required, and the effectiveness of their tints and tones for carrying out ornamental designs, were what the artist considered. One metal was as easily wrought by him as another. Iron was like clay in his competent hands, and he moulded, cut, and hammered as he willed, using copper, gold, silver, iron, tin, zinc, lead, and antimony simply as pigments, and combining them as a painter would his colors. The well-known *shibuichi*, or mixed copper and silver, and *shakudo* or mixed iron, copper, and gold, are only general names for the great range of tints and tones, shading from tawniest-yellow to darkest-brown and a purple-black, and from silver-white to the darkest steely-gray. Silver and gold were inlaid with iron, the harder metal upon the softer, and solid lumps of gold, silver, and lead are found encrusted in bronze in a way to defy all known laws of the fusion of metals. While good and even marvellous work is still done, the old spirit is gone, and the objects of to-day seem almost unworthy the art lavished on them.

The magic mirror is still manufactured in Kioto, and although the tourist is often assured that it does not exist, innumerable specimens prove that the face of a common polished steel mirror, of good quality, will reflect the same design as that raised in relief on its back. With small mirrors ten inches in diameter, as with the largest, in their elaborate lacquered cases, one may throw, with a ray of sunlight, a clear-cut image on wall or ceiling. The pressure of the uneven surface at the back, the varying density of the metal, and the effect of polishing, all combine to give this curious attribute to these *kagami*, which are gradually giving place to foreign glass and quicksilver.

CHAPTER XXVIII

POTTERIES AND PAPER WARES

THE porcelains of Kiomidzu, renowned as they are throughout Japan, figure lightly in the export trade lists, as compared to the immense shipments of decorated faience from the Awata district, for which there is such demand in foreign countries. On the main street of that quarter, which is the beginning of the Tokaido, the larger establishments cluster near together, and Kinko-zan, Tanzan, and Taizan attract one in turn. Latticed walls and plain gate-ways admit visitors to a succession of show-rooms, where they may wander and look. As it is the characteristic Japanese custom to consider every foreigner as a mere sight-seer, who puts tradesmen to trouble for nothing, the bushy-headed young men in their clean. cool cotton gowns make no effort to sell until he purchases something. Then he is led through further rooms to godowns or upper chambers, and their more desirable wares are displayed.

Kinkozan's specialty is the manufacture of the fine, cream-colored faience with a crackled glaze. which, when decorated in one way. is known as Kioto or Awata ware, and when covered with a blaze of color and gilding is the gaudily gorgeous, modern. or Kioto Satsuma. export-ed by ship-loads to America, where its crude hues and cheap effects are enjoyed. No cultivated Japanese, however, would ever give these monstrosities a place in his own home. In America these garish six-months-old vases and koros are even passed off as old Satsuma, to which softly-toned and simply-decorated ware it is no more like than is a Henri Deux *tazza* to a Limoges garden-stool. Kinkozan turns out also a coarse *shippoyaki*, or *cloisonneé* enamel, some on faience and some on copper ground; and the blue-and-white-gowned young man will lead one past garden and godown, and show one every stage and process of the manufacture of the different wares. The potters sit in little open alcoves of rooms, each with his low wheel and heap of clay before him. One old man sits with his feet doubled up before him, his right foot locked fast in the bend of the left knee, and the left foot laid sole upward on the right thigh, in the impossible attitude of so many Buddhas. This position he maintains with comfort for hours, and this lean, bald-headed, old man, wearing nothing but a loin-cloth and a pair of huge, round, owlish spectacles, is as interesting as his work. He puts a handful of wet gray clay on the wheel before him, making it revolve with a dexterous touch of the hand, while he works the lump of clay into a thick, broad bowl. With his fingers and a few little sticks he soon stretches the bowl upward, narrows it for a neck, broadens and flattens it a little at the top, and presently lifts off a graceful vase and sets it on a board with a row of others. In another place the workmen are grinding and working the clay; in another, preparing the glaze and applying it, and near them are the kilns in every stage. In a further garden the decorators are at work, each with his box of brushes and colors beside him, the vase being kept in half-horizontal position before him by a wooden rest. Each piece goes from one man to another, beginning with the one who sketches the designs in faint outline, thence passing to him who does the faces, to a third who applies the red, to a fourth who touches in the diaper-work and traceries, and so on to the man who liberally bestows the gilding. Lastly, two women slowly burnish the gold by rubbing it over with wet agates or carnelian.

At the other houses faience, in an infinity of new and strange designs and extraordinary colors is seen, each less and less Japanese. All these Awata potters work almost entirely for the foreign market, and their novelties are not disclosed to the visitor, nor sold in Japan, until they have had their vogue in the New York and London markets. From those foreign centres come instructions as to shapes, colors, and designs likely to prove popular for another season, and the ceramic artists abjectly follow these foreign models. All this helps to confuse a stranger; for, though the wares are named for the districts, towns, and provinces of their supposed nativity, he finds them made everywhere else — Satsuma, in three or four places outside of Satsuma; the Kaga of commerce, almost anywhere except in Kaga; while undecorated porcelain is brought from France by ship-loads to be decorated and sent out again, and everywhere the debasing effect of imitation and of this yielding to foreign dictates appears.

Cart-loads, car-loads, and ship-loads of screens go from the great ports to foreign countries, and in Kioto the larger proportion of these are manufactured. Whether *byobu*, the screen, is a purely Japanese invention, or a variation of the hinged door easily suggested to any primitive people who can watch Nature's many trapdoors and hinges, this people certainly makes most persistent use of it. Twenty different kinds may be seen in one's daily rides past the little open houses, but never does one discover the abominations in coarse gold thread on black satin grounds so common in our country and so highly esteemed. The four-fold or six-fold screen of a Japanese house has its plain silk, paper, or gold-leaf surface, covered with one large design or picture extending over the whole surface, instead of the narrow panels and patches of separate pictures which Western taste demands. In great establishments and monasteries there is a *tsui tate*, or flat, solid screen of a single panel, within the main door-way or vestibule—a survival of a Chinese fashion, intended less to baffle inquisitive eyes than to keep out evil spirits and beasts. Peculiar to Kioto are screens on which phosphorescent paint is used. A favorite design for these is the rice field at dusk, starred with flickering fire-flies, whose lights glow the more as the room darkens. A half century ago Gioksen, the artist, achieved great fame with these phosphorescent fire-flies; and recently the idea has been revived, with a fine promise of being vulgarized, growing coarser and cheaper in execution and poorer in quality, to meet the demands of the barbarian markets of the Occident. In the New-year week, when each family brings out its choicest screens, the display in the best streets is an art exhibition.

Screens of all sorts are more important in summer life than clothing, and, of necessity, are greatly relied on in the absence of garments. Screens with tiny windows in them shelter the undressed citizen and give him glimpses of the road, and screens with a variety of shelves and hooks bring a whole kitchen to the side of the hibachi on a windy day. Among summer screens, the commonest is the *sudare*, or curtain of reeds or tiny bamboo joints strung on threads. The waving of these strings and their tinkling sound are supposed to suggest the freshness of the stirring breeze, and the Japanese imagination transforms the bits of crystal, strung here and there, into cool rain-drops slipping down the bamboo stems. The taste of the foreign buyer has vulgarized the sudare, which is often a nightmare of crude design and worse color, weighted with glass beads of every color, and even made entirely of beads. The sudare in the streets of a Japanese town is almost as surely a sign of a shop where shaved ice and cooling drinks may be had.

as is our striped pole of the Occidental barber's premises.

Kioto fans are celebrated, but they are no better now than those of other cities, and prettier Japanese fans are sold in New York for less money than in Japan, because the enormous foreign demand keeps the best fan-painters and fan-makers of Kioto constantly employed on export orders. American importers send their buyers to Kioto and Osaka every spring to order fans for the following year. Designer and maker submit hundreds of models, and the buyer offers suggestions as to color and shapes. The men who execute these large orders seldom have an open shop or sales-room, and their places are known only to the trade. Thousands and hundreds of thousands of *ogi*, or folding fans, go annually from the port of Hiogo - Kobé to America, and as many more from Yokohama; while of the flat fans with handles, the *uchiwa*, the number is even greater. One American railroad company has for years taken a hundred thousand uchiwa each season for advertising purposes, one side being left plain, to be printed upon after they reach the United States.

The fan is the most ancient and important utility in Japan, and since Jingo Kogo invented the ogi, after the model of a bat's wing. men, women, and children have never ceased carrying one in their summer obi folds. Fans are the regulation gift upon every occasion and lack of occasion, and a large collection is acquired in the fewest summer weeks. Every large shop and tea-house has its own specially decorated and perfectly well-known uchiwa to be given to patrons. who in that way declare their wanderings; and at feasts each guest receives a plain white ogi, upon which poems, autographs, and sketches are to be traced by his fellow-guests.

Formerly. Kioto shops exhibited many more kinds of fans than at present. Among them were the court fans, or *hiogi*, made of twenty-five broad wooden sticks strung together, and wound with heavy silk cords, and as long as the Empress retained the old dress she and her ladies carried these heavy and useless articles. The *suehiro*, or wide-end fans of the priests, were a specialty of Kioto and Nara, and the suehiro accompanied every gift at New Years, weddings, and anniversaries, as certainly as the red and gold cords and oddly folded little papers now do. The *gumbai uchiwa*, heavy war fans, often with iron or bronze outer-sticks, went with each suit of armor; and the large oblong uchiwa, descending from priests to No dancers and to umpires in games and contests, were equally well-known productions of Kioto. Fans serve an infinite variety of purposes and speak a language in this land of their own, and no season or condition of life is without its ministrations. The farmer winnows his grain with a fan, the housewife blows up the charcoal fire with a fan, and gardeners, sitting for hours on patient heels, will softly fan half-open flowers until every petal unfolds. For specific gifts, specific designs and colors appear. One fan may be offered to a lady as a declaration of love. Another serves as her sign of dismissal, and the Japanese are often amused to see foreigners misapply the language and etiquette of fans.

Although gas and electricity light every Japanese city, and American and Russian kerosene come in whole cargoes, the manufacture of paper lanterns increases apace, for now all the quarters of the globe demand them. Constructing the flimsy frames is a sleight-of-hand process, and with the same deftness the old lantern-makers dash on designs, characters, and body-colors, with a bold brush. But one must live in Japan to appreciate the softened light of lanterns, and in the lavish and general nightly use of them learn all the fairy-like and splendid effects to be obtained with a bit of paper. some wisps of bamboo, and a little vegetable wax poured around a paper wick.

Cotton goods are largely manufactured in Kioto, and at all seasons the upper reaches of the Kamogawa's broad, stony bed are white with bleaching cloth. The Kamogawa's water, which is better for tea-making, for rice-boiling, and for mixing dyes than the water of any other stream in Japan, is also sovereign for bleaching, and its banks are lined for a long distance with dyeing establishments. The river-bed, paved with stones under each of its great bridges, is dreary, wind-swept, and colorless in winter-time, as compared to its summer brilliancy; but in January it is the place of the kite-flyers, and Hideyoshi's bronze-railed Shijo bridge—the southern end of the Tokaido, the centre from which all distances are measured—commands a view of an unexampled aerial carnival. Thousands of giant kites float upward, and the air is filled with a humming, as they soar, sweep, and circle over the city like huge birds. Kite combats take place in mid-air, and strings covered with pounded glass cut other strings, and let the half-animate paper birds and demons loose. Jinrikisha coolies on bridges and streets must dodge the hanging strings, and boys run over and into each other while watching their ventures; but the traditional kite-flying grandfathers whom one reads about in Western prints are conspicuous by their absence.

There is a game of battledore and shuttlecock much played at the same season by the girls, the battledore a flat wooden paddle ornamented with gaudy pictures of Japanese women. The game is a pretty one, and the girls are wonderfully graceful in playing it, the long sleeves and the flying obi-ends taking on expressive action when these charming maidens race and leap through its changes.

Kioto is not without its theatres and places of amusement, ever ready to beguile one from the sight-seeing and shopping rounds. Its great actor is Nakamura, and it maintains an academy for the training of maiko and geisha, where every spring there is a long-drawn-out festival of dances to help on the rejoicings of the cherry-blossom season. But its great place of amusement, its Vanity Fair, is the narrow theatre or show street running from Sanjio to Shijo Street, just beyond the bridges. This thoroughfare is lined all the way with rows of shops, labyrinthine bazaars, stalls, and booths, theatres, side-shows, peep-shows, puppet-shows, wax-works, jugglers, acrobats, wrestlers, trained animals, story-tellers, fortune-tellers, all exploited by the voice and drum of their loquacious agents at the door-way. No jinrikishas are allowed to run on this highway, and day and night, morning and midnight, it is filled with strolling people and playing children. In winter it is a cheering refuge from the wider, wind-swept streets, and in summer days it is cool and shady, the pavement constantly sprinkled, and the light and heat kept out by mat awnings stretched across the narrow road-way from roof to roof, in Chinese fashion. At night it is the busiest place in Kioto, even with the rival attraction of the river-bed; crowded with revellers, torches flaring, drums and gongs sounding, the high-pitched, nasal voices, of the show-men sing-songing their stories and programmes; and peddlers, pilgrims, priests, men, women, and children, and the strangers within their gates. making up the throng. Once when a giantess was on exhibition in a tent the spectators, instead of being awed by her heroic eight feet of height, were convulsed with laughter at sight of her. Every movement of the colossus sent them into fresh spasms. It was like a personification of some netsuke group to see this huge creature, with hair-pins like clubs, and clogs as large as a door-step, standing with folded arms, while pigmy visitors climbed up to perch like insects on her shoulders.

In this ever-open market one may buy the tailless cats of the country; forlorn, spiritless creatures, staying at

home and in-doors at night, and never going on midnight
prowls. Or, if he prefer, there are the wonderful long-
tailed Tosa chickens, fowls kept in tall, bamboo cages,
that their tail-feathers, measuring ten and twelve feet in
length, may make a graceful display. When they are let
out to scratch and wander about like other chickens,
their precious feathers are rolled up in papers and protected from any chance of harm. Japanese spaniels, or
Kioto *chins*, those little black-and-white, silky-eared pets,
with big, tearful, goggle eyes, and heads as round and
high as Fukurokojin's, are fashionably dear, ranging from
five to forty dollars each, even in their native town.

From the lower end of Theatre Street a covered way
leads to the fish-market of the city, a dark, cool, stone-
floored place, where more peculiar things may be bought,
and more picturesque groups may be studied, in the
strange Rembrandtesque light, than anywhere else in
Kioto. The foreign artists, who carry away scores of
sketches of Japanese life, seem never to find this fish-
market, nor in general to seize the best and least hack-
neyed subjects. Most of their pictures have been long
anticipated by the native photographers, and the foreign
artist repeats, with less fidelity, the familiar scenes and
subjects, with that painstaking western method that, to
the Japanese eye, leaves as little to the imagination as
the photograph itself.

CHAPTER XXIX

GOLDEN DAYS

NAMMIKAWA, the first *cloisonné* artist of the world, has
his home, his workshop, and his little garden in a quiet
corner of the Awata district. Most visitors never pass
beyond his ante-room, as Nammikawa holds his privacy

dear, and that small alcove with the black table gives little hint of what lies beyond. The more fortunate visitor follows the master through a dark recess to a large room with two sides open to the garden, and a tiny balcony overhanging a lakelet. He claps his hands, and big golden carp rise to the surface and gobble the mochi thrown them. In that little paradise, barely sixty feet square, are hills, groves, thickets, islands, promontories, and bays, a bamboo - shaded well, and a shrine, while above the farthest screen of foliage rise the green slopes of Maruyama.

A Japanese friend, who described Namikawa as "the most Japanese and most interesting man in Kioto," took us to drink tea with him in this charming garden, and, on the hottest afternoon of a hot Kioto summer, we noted neither time nor temperature until the creeping shadows warned us to depart. Old Japan seemed to re-live in the atmosphere of that garden, and a cha no yu was no more finished than the simple tea-ceremony the master performed there. By the old etiquette a Japanese gentleman never intrusted to any servant the making of tea for a guest, nor allowed the fine art of that simple, every-day process to be exercised unseen. The tea-tray, brought and set before the master, bore a tiny jewel-like tea-pot of old Awata, and the tiny *cloisonné* cups with plain enamelled linings were as richly colored as the circle of a tulip's petals, and smaller far. With them was a small pear-shaped dish, not unlike our gravy-boats, a beautiful bronze *midzu tsugi*, or hot-water pot, and a lacquer box holding a metal tea-caddy filled with the finest leaves from Uji tea-gardens. Taking a scoop of yellowed ivory, carved in the shape of a giant tea-leaf, our host filled the little tea - pot with loosely-heaped leaves, and having decanted the hot water into the little pear - shaped pitcher to cool a little, poured it upon the tea - leaves. Immediately he drew off the palest amber fluid, half filling each cup, and presented them to us, resting on leaf-shaped stands or saucers of damascened metal. The tea was only lukewarm when we received it, but as delicate and exquisitely flavored as if distilled of violets, as rich and smooth as a syrup, the three sips of it constituting a most powerful stimulant. In the discussion of tea-making that followed, our Japanese mentor explained to us that to the epicurean tea-drinkers of his country, boiling water was an abomination, as it scorched the leaves, drove out the fine fragrance in the first cloud of steam, and extracted the bitterness instead of the sweetness of the young leaves. " It may be well enough to pour boiling water on the coarse black tea of China's wild shrub," said this delightful Japanese, " but the delicate leaf of *our* cultivated tea-plant does not need it."

With the tea our host offered us large flat wafers of rice and fancy confections in the shape of most elaborate asters and chrysanthemums, too artistic to be eaten without compunction. The cups were refilled with the second and stronger decoction, which set every nerve tingling, and then only were we permitted to see the treasures of Nammikawa's creation. From box and silken bag within bag were produced vases, whose lines, color, lustre, and brilliant intricacy of design made them beautiful beyond praise. They were wrought over with finest traceries of gold, silver, and copper wires, on grounds of dull Naples yellow, soft yellowish-green, a darker green, or a rich deep-red, wonderful to behold, the polished surface as even and flawless as that of a fine onyx.

One by one some smaller pieces were brought in, in little boxes of smooth white pine, beautifully made and joined. Nammikawa opened first the cotton wadding, then the inevitable wrapping of yellow cloth, and lastly the silken covers, and handled with a tender rev-

erence these exquisite creations of his genius, every one
of which, when placed on its low teak-wood stand, showed
faultless. For two years his whole force was at work on
the two sixteen-inch vases which went to the Paris Exposition, and four years were given to the Emperor's
order for a pair for his new palace. These bore the
imperial emblems, and dragons writhed between chrysanthemums and through conventional flower-circles and
arabesques, and the groundwork displayed the splendid
red, green, russet, mottled gold, and glistening avanturine
enamels, whose secret Nammikawa holds. For it is not
only in his fine designs, but in the perfect composition
and fusing of his enamels and the gem-like polish that
this great artist excels all rivals.

In another garden, concealed by a bamboo hedge, is
the tiny laboratory, and the one work-room where less
than twenty people, all told, execute the master's de-

IN NAMMIKAWA'S WORK-ROOM

signs. One etches these patterns on the copper base. following Nammikawa's delicately traced ou'lines : another bends and fastens the wires on the etched lines. and a third coats the joinings with a red oxide that. after firing. unites the wires more firmly to the copper. Others dot the paste into the cell-like spaces. or sit over tubs of water. grinding with fine stones, with charcoal, and deer-horn the surface of the pieces that have been fired. Nammikawa adds the master-touches. and after conducting the final firing. himself gives them the last incomparable polish, after his men have rubbed away for weeks. These workmen come and go as they please. working only when the spirit moves them, and doing better work, the master believes. when thus left to their own devices. All of them are artists whose skill is a family inheritance, and they have been with Nammikawa for many years. The most skilful of these craftsmen receive one yen a day, which is extravagant pay in this land of simple living. and shows in what high esteem they are held. A few women are employed in the polishing and the simpler details. and. while we watched them. were burnishing a most exquisite tea-pot covered with a fine foliated design on pale yellow ground. This treasure had been bought by some connoisseur while the first rough filling of paste was being applied, and he had bided his time for a twelvemonth, while the slow processes of filling and refilling the cells. and firing and refiring the paste had succeeded one another until it was ready for the first grinding.

Fifty or sixty small pieces. chiefly vases. caskets. and urns, three and four inches high. and ranging in price from thirty to ninety yen each. are a whole year's output, and larger pieces are executed by special order at the same time with these. Nammikawa does not like to sell to the trade. and has been known to refuse the requests of curio merchants. making his customers pay more if he

suspects that they are buying to sell again. It is his
delight to hand the precious article to its new owner, en-
joining him to keep it wrapped in silk and wadding, and
always to rub it carefully to remove any moisture before
putting it away. He cautions visitors, when they attempt
to handle the precious pieces in his show-room, not to
touch the enamelled surface with the hand, the metal
base and collar being left free on each piece for that
purpose. Nor must two pieces of *cloisonné* ever be knocked together, as the enamel is almost more brittle than
porcelain. Curiously enough, this great artist uses no
mark nor sign-manual. "If my work will not declare itself to be mine, then the marking will do no good," he
says; and, indeed, his *cloisonné* is so unlike the crude
and commonplace enamels exported from Japan by ship-
loads for the foreign market, that it does not need the
certification of his name.

Nammikawa has the face of a saint, or poet—gentle,
refined, and intellectual—and his beautiful manner and
perfect courtesy are an inheritance of the old Japan.
His earlier days were not saintly, although they may
have been poetical. He was a personal attendant of
Prince Kuné no Miya, a brother of Prince Komatsu, and
cousin of the Emperor, and was brought up in the old
court life with its atmosphere of art and leisure. The
elegant young courtier was noted for his gayety and im-
providence. He remained in Kioto when the court moved
northward, and all at once ceased his dissipations, even
putting aside his pipe, to devote himself to experiments
in the manufacture of *cloisonné*, for which he had always
had a passion. In his laboratory there is a square
placque, a bluish bird on a white ground diapered with
coarse wires, which was his first piece. One can hardly
believe that only fifteen years intervene between this
coarse, almost Chinese, specimen of his work, and the
vases for the Emperor's palace. From the start he threw

himself into his profession with his whole soul and spirit. Incessant experiments in the solitude of his laboratory and work-room at night, and the zeal and patience of a Palissy at the furnace, conquered his province. He is still constantly studying and experimenting, and always fires his pieces himself, keeping long vigils by the little kiln in the garden.

Hurry and money-making he despises. Gazing dreamily out into his garden, Nammikawa declared that he had no ambition to have a large godown, a great workshop, and a hundred workmen ; that he always refused to take any large commissions or commercial orders, or to promise a piece at any given time. Neither good art nor good work can be commanded by money, he thought, nor did he want his men to work faster, and therefore less carefully, because greater prices are offered him for haste. It was his pleasure, he said, to take years for the execution of a single piece that might stand flawless before all connoisseurs, and receive its just reward of praise or medals. The latter are dearer to him than any sum of money, and in his own garden he finds happiness with them.

There is a Nammikawa of Tokio who is not to be confounded with this Kioto artist. The Tokio enameller has an entirely different style, a simple design thrown in a broad style upon an unbroken groundwork, easily distinguishing his work from any other ; but Nammikawa of Tokio deals directly with the trade, even contracting with foreign curio dealers for seasons of work, and makes replicas of his exquisite pieces by the score for them. Imitators of his style have arisen, and already many cheap pieces, copying his best models, can be purchased in foreign cities.

The idling most delightful of all in Kioto is going over and over again to the same places, doing the same thing repeatedly, and arriving at that happy and eminently Japanese frame of mind where haste enters not; time is forgotten, days slip by uncounted, and limits cease to be. The spring days, when the rain falls in gauziest mist—the rain that is so good for young rice— or summer days, when the sun scorches the earth and burns one's very eyeballs, seem to bring the most un- broken leisure and longest hours in any agreeable refuge.

Sitting on Yaami's veranda, with the great plain of the city wreathed in mists or quivering in heat, I have recognized my indebtedness to Griffis, Dresser, Mitford, Morse, and Rein, those authorities on all things Japan- ese, not to mention Murray and his ponderous guide- book, whose weight and polysyllabic pages strike terror to the soul of the new-comer. Griffis I read, until Tairo and Minamoto, Hideyoshi and Iyeyasu, grew as familiar as William the Conqueror and the Declaration of Inde- pendence; Dresser's text and illustrations were a con- stant delight and illumination, explaining the incompre- hensible and pointing to hidden things; and Morse's *Japanese Homes* laid bare their mysteries, and made ev- ery fence, roof, rail, ceiling, and wall take on new feat- ures and expression. Rein's is the encyclopædia, and he the recorder, from whose statements there is no ap- peal, and to him we turned for everything. It is only on the sacred soil that the student gets the true value and meaning of these books; while nothing so nearly expresses and explains the charm of the country as that prose idyl, Percival Lowell's *Soul of the Far East*, nor so perfectly fits one's moods on these long, leisure days, and Mitford's *Tales of Old Japan* are of ceaseless delight.

In this Japanese atmosphere the traveller feels what he misses through his ignorance of the vernacular, and is even inspired with a desire to study the language; but a little skimming of the grammar usually brings down that vaulting ambition. It is easy to pick up words and phrases for ordinary use, as all servants understand some

English, and every hotel and shop has its interpreter. Upper-class people, whom one meets socially, always speak English, French, or German. Scholars declare that the mastery of the language takes from twelve to thirty years, and the compiler of the standard lexicon modestly says for himself that forty years is not enough. With a few most illustrious exceptions, no foreigner, who has not learned Japanese almost before his own tongue, has ever been able to grasp its idioms so as to express himself with clearness and accuracy. The whole theory and structure of the language are so different from and so opposed to European speech—so intricate and so arbitrary, that the alien brain fails to grasp it. The lower, middle, and upper classes have each a different mode of expression, and the women of each class use a still simpler version. He who learns the court language cannot make himself understood by shop-keepers or servants. He who has acquired coolie-talk insults a gentleman by uttering its common words and inelegant expressions in his presence.

As if the differences between the polite and the common idioms and names for things did not make verbal complications enough, the imperial family and their satellites have a still finer phraseology with a special vocabulary for their exclusive use. Saké, or rice brandy, becomes *kukon* at court: a dumpling, which is a *dango* in the city, becomes an *ishi-ishi* when it enters the palace-gates; and a shirt, or *juban*, is transmuted to a *heijo* on an imperial back. Well-bred women say *o hiya* for cold water, and men always call it *mizu*. A dog not only gets the honorific prefix *o*, but if you call him, you say politely *o ide*, just as you would to a child; while the imperative *koi! koi!* (come, come,) is polite enough for the rest of the brute creation. Children say *umamma* for food, but if you do not say *omamma* instead, nesans will giggle over your baby talk.

Dialects and localisms contribute still further to confusion of tongues. A hibachi in Kioto is a *shibachi* in Yokohama, as a Hirado vase is a *Shirado* one. When you inquire a price, you say *ikura* for "how much" in Yokohama, and *nambo* in Kioto. All around Tokio the g has the sound of ng, or gamma nasal, and this nasal tone of the capital is another point of conformity with the modern French.

Everywhere in Japan an infinity of names belongs to the simplest things. Twenty-five synonyms for rice are given in Hepburn's smaller dictionary, all as different as possible. Rice in every stage of growing, and in every condition after harvesting, has a distinct name, with no root common to all. Endless mistakes follow any inexactness of pronunciation. The numerals, *ichi, ni, san, shi, go, roku, shichi, hachi, ku, ju,* are easily memorized, and learning to count up to one hundred is child's play compared to the struggle with French numerals. It is not necessary to say "four times twenty, ten, and seven," before ninety-seven is reckoned; that is simply *ku ju shichi,* or nine tens and a seven. Twenty is *ni ju,* thirty is *san ju,* fifty is *go ju,* and so through the list. The ordinal numbers have *dai* prefixed or *ban* added, and "fourth" is then *yo ban.* That *ichi ban* means "number one," and *ni ban,* "number two," surprises people who had supposed that Mr. Ichi Ban and Mr. Ni Ban owned the great Japanese stores that used to exist in two American cities. After learning the plain cardinal and ordinal numbers, the neophyte must remember to add the syllable *shiki* when mentioning any number of animals, *nin* for people, *ken* for houses, *so* for ships, *cho* for jinrikishas, *hai* for glasses or cups of any liquid, *hon* for long and round objects, *mai* for broad and flat ones, *tsu* for letters or papers, *satsu* for books, *wa* for bundles or birds. Any infraction of these rules gives another meaning to the intended phrase, and the slightest variation in inflection changes it quite as much. If you want three *kurumas,* you say "*kuruma san cho,*" and five plates are "*sara go mai.*" To say simply *saiyo* (yes), or *iye* (no), is inadmissible. The whole statement must be made with many flourishes, and frequent *de gozarimasus* adorn a gentleman's conversation.

If a curio dealer asks whether you wish to see a *koro,* and you look for the word in the lexicon, you find that koro means, according to Dr. Hepburn's dictionary, time, period of time, a cylindrical wooden roller used in moving heavy bodies, the elders, old people, tiger and wolf, *i.e.,* savage and cruel, stubborn, bigoted. narrow - minded, a road, a journey, a censer for burning incense, and the second or third story of a house. So, too, *kiku* may mean a chrysanthemum, or a compass and square, a rule, an established custom, the moment or proper time; fear, timidity, and a score of other things. The chief compensations of the language are its simple and unvarying rules of pronunciation, every syllable being evenly accented, every vowel making a syllable, and, pronounced as continental vowels are, giving music to every word.

The written language is the study of another lifetime. Having the Chinese written language as its basis, the Chinese, Japanese, and Koreans can all understand one another in this form common to all, though not in the spoken tongue. It is common to see Chinese and Japanese coolies writing characters in the air, in the dust, or in the palms of their hands, and seeming to make themselves intelligible in this classical sign language. The written language has the katagana, or square characters, and the hiragana, or "grass" characters, the latter simpler and more nearly corresponding to our script or running hand.

The efforts of scholars are now turned to Romaicising or transliterating the Japanese sounds and characters, and expressing them by the common alphabet of Latin and Anglo-Saxon people, basing it on phonetic spelling.

Volapuk, the new universal language of all nations, offers great difficulties to the Japanese, for although Schleyer, its inventor, kindly left out the *r*, which the Chinese cannot pronounce, he left in the *l*, which is a corresponding stumbling-block for the Japanese, who is seldom a natural linguist.

CHAPTER XXX

SENKÉ AND THE MERCHANTS' DINNER

IT required an elaborate negotiation extending through two weeks, as well as the tactful aid of an officer of the Kioto Kencho to arrange for me a cha no yu at the house of Senké, the great master of the oldest school of that art. Senké was about going to Uji to choose his teas; he was changing his teas; he was airing his godowns, and he sent a dozen other excuses to prevent his naming a day. Not until it had been explained fully to this great high-priest of the solemnity that I had studied cha no yu with his pupil, Matsuda, and that, knowing that Matsuda had first studied the *Hori no Uji* method, I was pursuing the art to its fountain-head, to make sure that no heterodox version of the Senké method had betrayed my inexperience, would he consent to receive me.

Senké is a descendant of Rikiu, the instructor and friend of Hideyoshi, the Taiko. For years they practised the "outward" rites together, and wrote poems to one another, until Hideyoshi admired Rikiu's beautiful daughter. Rikiu refused her to him, and estrangement followed. Rikiu had built a splendid gate-way for the Daitokuji temple, within which, as was the fashion of the time, he had placed a small wooden statue of himself. Taiko Sama, riding through with his train one day, was

told of the statue overhead. He declared it an insult to
him, the Shogun, and sent to Rikiu the fateful short sword,
the *wakazashi*, and the great master died the honorable
death of seppuku, or hara kiri.

"And the daughter? Did the Taiko get her after Rikiu's death?" we asked, as we sat waiting in Senké's
garden, listening to the many histories connected with the
place. "*Wakarimasen*" (I do not know), said our friend,
with that Japanese indifference to the end of a story that
so perplexes the western mind.

Senké has a lovely garden beyond the palace walls, and
reached by deserted streets, whose blank walls shelter
aristocratic homes. Crossing a court, we crept through
a small door in a large gate-way and entered this retreat,
whose floor was all irregular stones, covered evenly with
a soft, velvety, green moss. Upon this verdant surface
fell dappled shadows and an occasional ray of sunshine
from a canopy of maple, cherry, and pine branches, carefully clipped and trained so as to form an even tent-roof
over the whole enclosure. The stillness was unbroken,
though upon this strange paradise looked out a dozen
exquisitely simple tea-rooms, each isolated and sheltered
from the view of any other. Pupils come to Senké from
all parts of Japan, but even when every tea-room is in
use the same hush reigns. To subdue us to what we
were to work in, and to enhance Fortune's supreme favor of a cha no yu in the Taiko's manner, we were made
to wait and wait before we were invited into the cool
twilight of a large tea-room. The house has been burned twice since Hideyoshi's day, but each time has been
exactly reproduced, so that virtually we sat where the
Taiko had sat for many hours, and we used the veritable bowls, spoons, trays, and tea-caddies sanctified by
his touch three hundred years ago. The Taiko's crest
was on the simple, gold-flecked screens of the room, and
an autograph verse on a kakemono, and a single pink

lily in a bronze vase, were the ornaments of the tokonoma.

Senké, now past seventy years of age, receives few pupils himself, but neither he nor his handsome son of about thirty years is wholly incurious as to the strange fashions that have entered the country since the Restoration. We bowed with the profound solemnity of mourners, but with the vigilance of spies we watched Senké as he built the fire, laid on the white azalea charcoal, dropped some chips of sandal-wood, and boiled his historic iron kettle. Then followed the feast of many delicate dishes—tea; bean-soup, with bits of egg-plant; raw fish with shreds of *daïkon* and fresh ginger; tai-soup, with sea-weed and mushrooms; broiled *ai*, with *shoyu*; bamboo-soup; dried *Shikoku* salmon; broiled birds; Kaga walnuts, preserved in a thick syrup, and other dishes; each course accompanied by rice, and ending with barley-water. An old iron saké-pot and shallow red lacquer saké-cups were passed around with the various dishes, and we gravely pledged one another and the master who served us. When the dried fish was brought in my Kencho friend nipped off some choice bits with his chop sticks and offered them on a paper to our host, who ate them, and put the paper in his sleeve. At the end of the feast the first guest—the one sitting nearest the tokonoma—wiped all his bowls and dishes clean with paper, which he put in his sleeve, and we followed his example. With the thirteenth course we gathered up our tray of sweets and retired to the garden, waiting there until soft strokes on an old bell called us back to the room, which had been swept, and the picture and vase in the tokonoma changed. Senké, too, had replaced his dark gauze kimono by one of pale-blue crape, and sat in a reverent attitude. With infinite deliberation he went through the solemn rites, and duly presented us each with a bowl of green gruel more bitter

than quinine, twelve spoonfuls of powdered tea being
the measure used. This was his *koi cha*. The usu cha
was a less strong decoction, demanding a simpler ceremony, and was served in a bowl passed around for all to
sip from in turn. Previous study enabled us to note in-
telligently every movement of the old master, and the
significant position of each thumb and finger, hand, elbow, and wrist, as the venerable artist of cha no yu ex-
emplified the grace and niceties of the "outward"
school.

At the proper time we asked the history of the implements used in the ceremony. The *na tsume*, or tea-
bowl of Raku ware, in Jo-o shape, belonged to Rikiu,
Jo-o having been the teacher of Rikiu, and the arbiter
of the form of many implements of cha no yu. The
little bamboo slip with a flat, curved end, which lifted
the powdered tea from its box, was cut by Rikiu. It
bears no decoration or mark, and is of the ordinary
shape; but this commonplace *cha shaku* cannot be bought
for even two hundred dollars. The Emperor Komei,
father of the present Emperor, was taught by the elder
Senké, and bequeathed to his master various autographs
and an incense-box of great antiquity. Driven though
he is by the spirit of innovation and progress, the present Emperor occasionally enjoys a few quiet hours at
cha no yu. The Empress is most accomplished in its
ceremonial, and delights in the little poems which guests
are always expected to write for the host.

When the moment arrived for the production of these
tributes at Senké's tea, our Japanese friends dashed
them off in an instant, as if, with the return to their ceremonial silk gowns, they had returned to the habits of
thought of old Japan, when poetry filled the air. But
one of them whispered, to encourage us, "I have been
thinking it these two weeks."

With regret we saw *cha ire* (tea-caddy), *cha wan* (tea-bowl), *cha sen* (tea - whisk), and cha shaku (teaspoon), tied up in their precious brocade bags, and, with profound obeisances, we took leave of Senké, feeling that for a day we had slipped out of our century, and almost out of our planet, so unlike is the cha no yu to any other function in this irreverent, practical, and pushing era.

Of our friend, who had drained two of three bowls of it, we asked, "Does not this strong tea make you nervous, keep you awake, give you the *cha ni yotta*, or tea tremens?"

"Oh no," he answered; "I do not drink enough of it. I am very careful. But my friends, when they begin the study of English and foreign branches, find that they must stop drinking it. The English seems to bring into action many nerves that we do not use, and the drink is probably exciting enough in itself."

Foreign teachers say the same thing, and at the Doshisha school tobacco must be given up, though, next to tea, it is the great necessity of the Japanese.

Kioto's maiko and geisha performances are, of course, more splendid than those of any other city. The great training-school of maiko conforms to the classic traditions, and critics and connoisseurs assemble at the Kaburenjo theatre each spring when the famous Kioto dance, the Miakodori, is given by troops of maiko.

Did I not possess the ocular proof of a fan and a few souvenirs I could believe the fête which I saw to have been but a midsummer night's dream. A club of the great merchants of the city, wishing to do honor to two Tokio officials, devised a dinner. or geisha party. and included their American friends. The evening was one of the heaviest, hottest, and sultriest of the Kioto summer, and. after the sun sank in a bed of mist, swarmed with myriads of mosquitoes. Later, the full moon poured down a flood of silvery light that seemed to quiver with heat, yet, apparelled in our uncomfortable regulation costume, we found our way through the lanes to the dark gate-ways of Nishi Otani's long approach. The broad stone path lay marble-white in the moonlight between rows of gigantic trees, the tall stone lanterns looked like ghostly sentries, and fire-flies floated through the still, hot darkness. At the foot of the avenue a line of red lanterns hung glowing and motionless in mid-air, like so many strange fruits on the black branches. When we passed into the open, moonlighted court of the Gion temple and under its giant torii, we were received at a wide door-way by the master of the feast and the whole tea-house staff.

Above were our forty-four hosts of the evening, among whom were the court brocade-weaver, the great merchant of painted crapes, the maker of the incomparable enamels, the masters of the great potteries and bronze works, and a few artists. We bowed three or four times to each gentleman, who bowed twice as often to us, and we wondered how these quiet, grave, and gracious hosts, in their rustling garments of dark striped silks and their white *tabis*, could look so cool and fresh.

All the screens of the upper floor had been taken out, and three sides of the room were open to the night. We were conducted to seats at one end, the company gravely dropped upon the cushions ranged along either side, and the master of ceremonies, a great silk merchant and manufacturer, made a formal speech of welcome, and begged us to accept the poor repast they were about to offer. Every one bowed three times, a proper response was made, we all bowed again, and a file of nesans in dark silk gowns brought in tiny cups of tea. Then followed ten of the most famous maiko of Kioto, dazzling beauties, who advanced noiselessly, two by two, in exquisite kimonos of painted crape and obis of woven sunshine, and with coronals of silver hair-pins on their heads. As they drew near, all gliding with the same

slow grace, they knelt and set before us the ozens, or low
lacquer tables, holding cups, bowls, chopsticks, and nap-
kins. Two tiny maiko then entered with large trays of
sweetmeats, and the master of ceremonies lifted off with
his chopsticks and set before us sections of confection-
ery — waves and fan - tailed goldfish, an impressionist
sketch in sugar of rippling water filled with darting fish.
On Nabeshima and Owari plates, and in lacquer and porcelain bowls, were served innumerable courses—soups,
omelet, lily bulbs, chicken, small birds, jellies, many unknown and delightful dishes—and with each remove,
rice, lifted from a fine, red-lined, gold lacquer rice box
furnished with a big lacquer spoon worth six silver ones.
Tai, the sterlet of Japan, the arbitrary accessory of any
great feast, whose curiously shaped bones are symbols
of hospitality and abundance, was accompanied by a
peppery salad, and followed by more birds, by bamboo
sprouts, and a stew of *beche-de-mer*, before the appearance
of the *pièce de résistance*.

The maiko advanced in a broad line, two of them
bearing a large tray on which lay a magnificent carp,
still breathing, and with his scales shining as if just
drawn from the water. The master of ceremonies advanced, and, receiving the tray from the maiko, set it
on the mats and turned it slowly around for all to behold. As the maiko retired all leaned forward to watch
the noble carp, as it lay quivering on its bed of moss
and cresses, with a background of greenery like a true
Japanese garden. This custom of serving the living fish
at a feast is a survival of a traditional usage that foreigners seldom witness. Morsels of the fish were presently lifted from its back and passed to the company.
To us the performance was a kind of cannibalism possessing a horrible fascination, but the epicures uttered
sounds expressive of appreciation as they lingered over
the delicious morsels. A sudden jar or turning of the

tray made the carp writhe, and left upon us a sense of guilty consent and connivance which lasted for days.

Rice and eels were next served, another soup, more fowl, and then, with sponge-cake, fruits, and additional cups of tea, the feast concluded. Centuries ago the Portuguese taught the Japanese to make sponge-cake, and now they surpass in the art even a New England house-keeper with "faculty." With each course there had been an exchange of saké-cups and the drinking of innumerable healths, with amazing elaboration of etiquette. Each guest must accept the proffered pledge, extend it to be filled, touch the forehead, drink, empty, and return it to the giver, that he may repeat the same routine. The guests in their rustling garments moved about the mats, sitting before one and another in turn for a little chat and an exchange of saké-cups, and formal speeches and responses were made as well.

Throughout the feast the geishas twanged the koto and the samisen, and the maiko in painted crapes and gorgeous brocades danced with choral accompaniment. Their broad obis were tied in Osaka fashion, in long butterfly loops that spread the golden and glistening fabric all over the back of their scant, clinging kimonos. These lovely young creatures slowly posed, through dance after dance, bending, swaying, and turning with exquisite grace, moving their golden fans in time with the wail of the instruments and the plaintive burden of the song explaining the pantomime. It was a strange scene—the room, open to the summer night, hung round with crimson lanterns and lighted with the soft glow from the tall andons; the lines of sitting figures in their rich silk garments, and the dark faces lost in reverie as they followed the mazes of the golden-robed dancers.

After the dinner and between their dances the maiko seated themselves before the guests to entertain them with their wit and badinage, to fill the saké-cups, and to let the company admire them. Raiha was the name of one demure beauty, who inquired of us which one of them was loveliest according to our foreign standards. While we considered, some became coquettish and full of little Japanese airs and graces. but whatever sparkle and expression they threw into their eyes, the meekest look was given to the whole face by the broad touch of carmine on the lower lip. The final decision gave Raiha three of the foreign votes, and the one dissenter conformed when our Japanese friends assured him that she was the reigning professional beauty of Kioto. And we thought her shy, distinguished manners, her silver thread of a voice, and her demure eyes and smiles more charming even than her lovely face.

At midnight, when a monastery bell was softly booming from the mountain-slopes, we began our adieus. Nearly one hundred and forty bows were to be made by each of us, for, after bowing three or four times and saying "sayonara" to each of our hosts, we had to bid adieu to the lovely maikos and acknowledge the salutations of the tea-house attendants. When we sat down at the door-way to have our shoes put on, we were dizzy enough to be grateful for the fanning that the tea-house girls bestowed upon us. A chorus of sayonaras accompanied us as we followed the coolies with their long lanterns out through the torii and into the black shadows of the temple grounds.

CHAPTER XXXI

THROUGH UJI TO NARA

An early morning start, with many jinrikishas and tandems of coolies ; a wild spin through the streets, past shops, temple gates and walls ; by the innumerable toriis and lanterns forming arches and vistas in the groves of

PICKING TEA

Inari, the great temple of the fox-god, and we came out on the plain beyond Fushimi; then an irregular, hilly country, green with ancient pine and bamboo groves, every open valley and hill-side set with low, green mounds of tea-bushes; sandy, white roads, clear rushing streams, and we were in the heart of Uji, the finest tea district of Japan.

Groups of bobbing hats beside the tea-bushes, carts loaded with sacks and baskets of tea-leaves; trays of toasting tea-leaves within every door-way, a delicate rose-like fragrance in the air; women and children sorting the crop in every village; and this was the tea season in its height. Here were bushes two and three hundred years old yielding every year their certain harvest, and whole hill-sides covered with matted awnings to keep from scorching or toughening in the hot sun those delicate young leaves, which are destined to become the costly and exquisite teas chosen by the sovereign and his richest subjects.

Then we toiled up bush-covered steeps to cross elevated river-beds; rode through towered floodgates of dry watercourses. down to the green plain their lost waters had fed: through village streets, and past many a picturesque tateba, in one of which stood a little yellow Cupid in the sunshine that filtered through a wistaria trellis; and so on through ever-changing country scenes to the famous view of Nara's temples, trees, and pagodas.

Nara! A mountain-side covered with giant trees bound together by vines and old creepers; an ancient forest seamed with broad avenues, where the sunlight falls in patches and deer lie drowsing in the fern; double and triple lines of moss-covered stone lanterns massing themselves together, their green tops dim in the dense shadow: temples twelve centuries old; the booming of bells, and the music of running water.

Nara! The ancient capital, the cradle of Buddhism, and still the holy place of pilgrimages; its forest paths echoing the jingle of the devotees' ringed staffs, the mutter of their prayers, and the clink of their copper offerings at the temple gates. A place of stillness and dreams; an Arcadia, where the little children and the fawns play together, and the antlered deer eat from one's hand, and look up fearlessly with their soft human eyes. Old Shinto temples, where the priestesses dance the sacred measures of Suzume before the Sun Goddess's cave; temples where Buddha and Kwannon sit in gilded glory on the lotus, and lights, incense, and bells accompany the splendid ceremonies of that faith.

The great antiquity of Nara makes the magnificence of Nikko, with its Shogun's tombs, seem almost parvenu. It is the good-fortune of the older fane that its distance from the railroad—twenty-six miles—saves it from the rush of progress and the stream of tourists.

The founder of Nara rode up to the mountain on a deer to choose a residence for himself, and ever since the deer have been petted and protected. Groups of them, lying under the trees, permit themselves to be admired, and feeding parties turn their pretty pointed heads to look after the visitor. The does and fawns, however, hide in the dark fern-covered ravines. All through the forest and temple grounds are little thatched houses, where tea for man and corn-meal for deer are sold, together with the little carved images and deer-horn toys for which Nara is famous. It is a pity that the Japanese name for deer is such a harsh, unmusical word as *shika*, which even the little children, who toddle after the pretty creatures with out-stretched hands, cannot make musical. Plump little country maids, with their tied-up sleeves, are heard from sunrise until dusk calling up the deer to be fed—"*Ko! ko! ko! ko!*" (Come! come! come! come!) and at the word "Ko" even the fattest and heaviest stag lumbers forward and nibbles from their hands. Moving at leisure, these deer have a stiff, wooden gait, and seem badly-proportioned animals. It is when one leaps and bounds down some avenue, or across a clearing, that it shows its grace. The gentleness of these Nara pets is due, of course, to the long immunity from violence enjoyed by their race, beloved and protected by gods and men. Only once have they ever been harmed, and that blow was dealt by a young Japanese convert to Christianity, who struck at them as emblems of heathenism !

The atmosphere of Nara is serene and gentle—the true atmosphere of Japan. The priests are quiet, courteous old men, and the little priestesses, soft-footed and tranquil, dance in a slow succession of dignified poses. The Kasuga temple is a very cathedral of Shintoism, a place of many court - yards, surrounded by gates, and buildings painted bright Shinto red, with sacred straw ropes and symbolical bits of rice-paper hanging before the open doors. Venerable cryptomeria-trees, worthy of a California grove, stretch the great buttresses of their roots over the ground of the court-yard, and one thatched roof lovingly embraces the trunk of a crooked old tree that almost rests on it. Wistaria vines, thick, gnarled, and lichen-covered with the growth of years, hang in giant festoons from the trees, roll in curves and loops over the ground, and, climbing to the top of the tallest pines, hang their clusters of pale-green leaves like blossoms against the dark evergreens. A giant trunk, from which grow branches of the camellia, cherry, plum, wild ivy, wistaria and nandina, is a perpetual marvel. All through the woods the wistaria runs wild, leaps from tree to tree, and ties and knots itself in titanic coils.

In such lovely scenes the Kasuga priests lead an ideal existence. They marry, they raise families ; their little daughters perform the sacred dance in the temple for a

certain number of years, and they may leave the priesthood if they wish. All the brotherhood wear the loose,
flowing purple trousers, white gauze coats, and black,
helmet-shaped caps prescribed by the Shinto rules ; and
besides making the morning and evening offerings to
the gods, and conducting special ceremonies on the two
purification days of the year, they play the ancient flute
and drum, and chant a hymn while the sacred dance is
given. For a poetic, philosophical, meditative, or lazy man
nothing could be more congenial than this life. Hurry,
novelty, and the rush of events come not near Nara, which
is in the land "wherein it seemed always afternoon."

The pilgrims, who trudge from the most distant provinces with bell and beads and staff, make up the greater
number of visitors, and their white garments, straw sandals, cloaks, and hats, are of a fashion centuries old.
Bands of these votaries go through the temple courts,
in charge of voluble guides, who intone a description of
the places in the way of their craft the world over. One
or two old men seem always to be sauntering up the long
avenue, stopping frequently to rest, praying at every
shrine, and muttering to themselves praises of the sacred
place. Their wrinkled faces glow with pleasure, and
they delight in watching the deer, to whom the tinkle of
a pilgrim's bell or iron-ringed staff is always a promise
of cakes.

To the antiquarian, Nara is full of interest. The
temples, founded in the seventh and eighth centuries,
were the first Buddhist sanctuaries in Japan : Buddhism,
coming from India by way of China and Korea, having
found its first home here when Nara was the imperial
capital. Four empresses and three emperors held the
sceptre between 708 and 782, and all the region is historic ground. The great city, that covered the plain for
centuries after that imperial day, has shrunken to a small
provincial town, still eloquent of the past. The Shinto

temples, as their rules provide, have been rebuilt every twenty years, the original buildings being exactly duplicated each time, so that, in their freshness and perfect repair, they look now as they did a thousand years ago. The Buddhist shrines have been burned, rebuilt, half abandoned at times; and in recent years, since their lands were taken from them and their revenues withheld, have suffered seriously. The largest image of Buddha is the Nara Dai Butsu. The seated deity, 63 feet in height, was set upon his lotus pedestal in 749, and once the head of the statue fell off and was broken, and twice the temple burned and melted it. The temple enshrining the bronze deity is now dilapidated, and the huge corner beams and brackets of the roof are braced with timbers, so that an earthquake would be likely to over-set the holy place.

The great two-storied gate-way of the Dai Butsu temple has stood for eleven centuries and more, and is a picturesque, weather - beaten old structure, apparently strong enough to resist the assaults of another thousand years. Colossal Nio, with hideous countenances, stand on guard in niches, and within is a large green court-yard, and a closed gallery on the two sides that connect the gate-way with the temple—the cloister of a European cathedral. A huge bronze lantern, one of the earliest examples of such work, is said to have long contained the sacred fire brought from Ceylon. The great Buddha itself is disappointing, because seen too near. The face is sixteen feet long and over nine feet wide, and the expression is not calm, soulful, and meditative, as Buddha in Nirvana should be, but heavy and stolid, with a hard, unmeditative stare. The gilding with which the statue was once covered has worn away with time, leaving it as dark and blackened as befits its Hottentot countenance. On the great halo are images six and eight feet high that look like pygmies.

Behind the Buddha is a museum of antiquities connected in some way with the temple and its founders and patrons. Here are kept the carpenters' tools with which the first temple was built, and prehistoric-looking fragments of bronze and iron to which the stranger finds no clew. A door of the palace whereon Kusunoki, the Chevalier Bayard of Japan, wrote a farewell message with his arrow when he went away to his last battle, images, carvings, old armor, weapons, and trappings, afford the Japanese visitor much delight. But the real treasures of Dai Butsu are the relics left to it by one of the Nara Emperors, who built a substantial log storehouse in the enclosure, and bequeathed to the temple everything his palace contained. Palaces were small in those days, and their furnishings scanty; but the clothing, household effects, and ornaments of the dead benefactor were brought to this storehouse and carefully sealed up. Every summer, after the rainy season ends, the treasures are aired, the inventory verified, and the place sealed up again. Three of the greatest nobles of the empire are associated with the high-priest in the care of these Nara relics, and the storehouse can only be opened by an imperial order transmitted in the handwriting of the emperor. Only royal or greatly distinguished visitors may ask this privilege, as it is a great trouble and expense to get the guardians together. Its value as a collection and as a picture of the life of the eighth century is hardly appreciated by the Japanese, who chiefly reverence its sacredness as connected with the person of an early Emperor. An imperial commission, made up of officers of the imperial household and of art connoisseurs, examined, classified, and catalogued the treasures of the Nara and Kioto temples in 1888. Mr. Kuki, late Japanese minister to the United States, and president of this commission, had even this imperial treasure-house opened and the precious relics photographed. The commission and its staff numbered over twenty people, and the old guardians of the storehouse were much disturbed by this invasion of their carefully closed domain, which they would have resisted if they could.

On the hill above the Dai Butsu temple are other Buddhist sanctuaries; the Nigwatsudo and the Hachiman being devoted respectively to the goddess Kwannon and to Hachiman, god of war. Both are resorts for the summer pilgrims, and the droning of prayers, the clapping of hands and rattle of coins, are heard all day long. Stone terraces and staircases, mossy stone lanterns and green drinking-fountains make the old places picturesque, and the platforms afford magnificent views across to the bold mountain-wall in the west that divides Nara from Osaka's fertile rice plain. In the court-yards are sold maps, wood-cuts, and bunches of little cinnamon twigs that the pilgrims find refreshing, and there do captive monkeys perform grotesque antics. One may often see here the *Hiyakudo* (the hundred times going) performed by faithful pilgrims, who walk a hundred times around in the fulfilment of a vow.

Between these Buddhist temples and the Shinto shrines, hidden in their forest park, there intervenes a smooth, grassy mountain, called the Mikasayama, or "Three-hat hill," because of its three ridges. Every devout pilgrim climbs the delusive, velvety-looking slope to the stone at the third summit to look out upon the rich province of Yamato, "the heart of Japan," and the scene of so many battles, wars and sieges as to be also called "the cockpit of Japan."

Far as the eye can reach the valley is levelled off in rice fields. Tea-bushes stripe the more rolling country with their regular lines of thick, dark foliage; bamboo groves add a softer, more delicate green, and deepest of all are the tones of the pines.

Near the base of the hill, but high enough to command a wide prospect, runs a narrow road lined with little tea-houses and toy-shops where souvenirs are sold. Nara is famous for its cutlery and its India ink, and swords, daggers, knives and scissors are sold by shopmen who perform extraordinary feats to test the temper of their blades. India ink pressed into fantastic shapes, and writing - brushes made of deer's hair, are carefully tied up in the pilgrim's wallets, with the famous little Nara *ningio*, or images carved in wood. The Nara ningios always represent the legendary priests and people who founded Nara, and in these carvings the rural artists display great talent, giving wonderful expression to the tiny faces that are left rough faceted as first chipped off with the knife.

These tea - houses and shops interpose a neutral and worldly barrier between the cluster of Buddhist establishments at the one side and the region of Shintoism beyond. From the tea - house gates the road makes a curve off into the wistaria-tangled forest to conduct jinrikishas to the lower level, but the pilgrims descend, instead, four long flights of rough stone steps, that are wonderfully picturesque with these quaint moving figures and the queer little shops that hang to the borders of the stairs, climbing up and down the hill with them.

At the foot of the steps the road reappears, crossing a narrow creek-bed on a high bridge that gives one beautiful views of a dark little ravine, across which the trees nearly meet and the ancient creepers are looped and knotted. A little red shrine and a path lined with stone lanterns mark the beginning of the temple enclosure, dense woods rising at one side of the stone lanterns lighting the path to the ancient Shinto sanctuary of Kasuga, and open glades stretching out at the other. A few shops and tea-booths break the line of lanterns on one side ; the road is canopied with a great wistaria trellis, and a spring bubbles up in a stone basin in the midst of rock-work almost hidden in shade and moss. Weary pilgrims stop in this grateful shade to drink and to rest themselves at any hour of the day.

Passing the stall for the sacred white pony of the gods and some brightly-painted red wooden buildings, one enters a great court-yard with lanterns hanging from the eaves of the buildings and galleries surrounding its four sides, through whose doors are visible only a mirror and many-folded papers pendent from a straw rope. This symbolism suffices the believers, who kneel devoutly before it and toss in their coppers as a prelude to their prayers. Beside the shrine is the treasury of the temple, containing famous swords, the gold-mounted armor and helmets of great heroes, and lacquer-boxes holding precious writings and paintings. The queer saddles worn by the deer at the old matsuris are preserved, and yards of panoramic paintings on silk, depicting those splendid pageants of the old days, when the Emperor sent his representative down to witness the parade, and even the deer took part. The closed shrines, scattered through the forest, are quite as impressive as the holy of holies in this temple, and here the bareness and emptiness of Shinto worship strike the beholder. Each of the four little red chapels in a row has a fine bamboo curtain concealing the interior, and the middle chapel into which the pilgrims may look as they pay and pray, presents to their gaze only a screen painted with mythical beasts. A large covered pavilion in the court-yard was provided for the convenience of praying daimios in the time when piety was spectacular, and when the whole retinue of a great man assisted at his devotions. In another pavilion the towns-people burn beans and sow them abroad every winter to drive away evil spirits.

Every twentieth year the priests plant trees to furnish further timbers, but in Kasuga's court are two famous old cryptomeria, now too sacred to be felled even for such purposes, and one, enmeshed in the coils of a wistaria, is a marvel even in Nara. Without the square, heavy-timbered, red gate-way of the court two avenues meet, both lined with rows and rows of tall stone lanterns covered with moss and overhung with the dense foliage of the meeting trees. One avenue leads to a smaller temple, and the other, dropping by a flight of stone steps, turns to the right and descends in a long slope, bordered with regiments of stone lanterns, to a large red torii. Thence it pursues its way, bordered still with massive lanterns, for three-quarters of a mile to the greater torii, marking the limit of the sacred grounds and the beginning of the village streets. Other lantern lines, paths, and staircases join it, and a bronze deer, sitting among rough, mossy bowlders under a dense canopy of trees and creepers, pours a stream of pure spring-water into a granite basin. There are more than three thousand of these stone lanterns along the Kasuga approaches, all of them gifts from daimios, nobles, and rich believers; and in days when the temples were rich and faith prosperous, they were lighted every night. At present it is only during great festivals that wicks and saucers of oil are set in all the lanterns, but some sixty points of flame flicker nightly in the dense shadows by the Kasuga gate, giving most weird effects.

From Kasuga gate the upper avenue of lanterns leads to the Wakamiya shrine, dedicated to the early gods of the Shinto religion. Here the old custom of the sacred dance is kept up, and a group of young priestesses is in waiting to repeat the measures danced by Suzume before the Sun Goddess's cave in prehistoric times. The little ministrants are all between the ages of nine and twelve, timid, gentle, and harmless as the deer that often stray in and watch them. Their dress is the old costume of the imperial court — a picturesque lower garment or di-

IN THE KASUGA TEMPLE GROUNDS

vided skirt of the brightest cardinal-red silk, and a white kimono, with square sleeves and pointed neck filled with alternate folds of red and white. When they dance they wear loose kimonos of white gauze, painted with the wistaria crest of the Kasuga temple, the front of the gauzy garment half covering the red skirt, and the back pieces trailing on the mats. Their faces are plastered so thickly with white paint that they lose all expression, and, following the old fashion, their eyebrows are shaved, and two tiny black dots high up in the middle of their foreheads take the place of them. With lips heavily rouged, the countenance is more a mask than a human face. The hair, gathered together at the back of the neck, is tied with loops of gold paper, and then, folded in soft white paper, allowed to hang down the back. Long hair-pins, with clusters of wistaria and red camellia, are thrust across the top of the head, and fastened so that they stand out like horns over the forehead. In detail the costume is not pretty, but in its general effect it is singularly bright and picturesque.

One may have as many sacred dancers and as long a dance as he will pay for, and as soon as the money is received the two priests get into their ceremonial white gowns and high black hats, and, sitting before the ancient drums, chant, pound, and blow on doleful pipes an accompaniment for the little dancers. The sacred dance is solemn enough, and each dancer has a fan and a bunch of bells, from which hang long strips of bright-colored silks. They advance, retreat, glide to right and left, raise their fans, shake their sacred baby-rattles, and, with few changes in the measure, repeat the same figures and movements for a certain length of time. If one pays more money they repeat the same thing, and the priests can wail the endless accompaniment by the hour. To us the dance was simply a curious custom; but the devout old pilgrims, who have hoarded up their money for the journey for months and often years, feel it to be a solemn and sanctified service. It is pathetic to see their faces glowing and their eyes filled with tears at the fine spectacle that is so rare an event in their lives, and which crowns their summer pilgrimage to the old shrines of their faith.

CHAPTER XXXII

NARA

In the last week of June, the proprietor of the tea field beneath our veranda conducted a second picking of his stumpy little bushes. From sunrise until dusk rose a chorus of children's voices beyond the hedge. The first and best crop having been gathered weeks earlier with the first fire-flies, this hubbub accompanied only the gleaning after the harvesters. It was a pretty picture in the foreground of the magnificent view—these little blue and white figures in huge wash-bowl hats, with touches of bright red here and there in their costumes. The headman sat comfortably under a fig-tree, with no clothing to speak of, smoked his pipe, and watched the youngsters at work. When they toiled up to him with full baskets, he weighed the load with a rude steelyard and sent them back, so that some of the tea-pickers were always moving up and down the paths between the compact rows of bushes, and grouped about the patriarch under the fig-tree. The leaves were spread in the sun all day and carried off at night in large sacks and baskets. Walking out through the woods one day, with two little red-gowned priestesses from the Kasuga temple, we came upon a tiny village, and there found the same tea-leaves being toasted in shallow paper-lined baskets over charcoal fires. The attendants rubbed and tossed the fragrant leaves, that were soon dried enough to suffice for the home market.

Although secular occupations prosper, and Nara cutlery and ink rank high in public favor, the temple life of Nara is its real existence. Every day pilgrims and tourists passed before us in processions whose variety of people and costumes was endless. Yet in all the weeks the European coat and trousers only once appeared in those sacred aisles. Every morning two or more of the little red-robed priestesses came, hand in hand, to spend an hour or two beside my friend's easel. The old priests, in their white gowns and purple skirts, were very courteous and hospitable, and as our stay lengthened we grew to feel ourselves a part of the sacred community. The little priestesses carried us to their homes to drink tea, and the priests brought their friends to watch the methods of the foreign artist. Among the sight-seers and visitors to the Shinto shrines and their guardians were many Buddhist priests, whose shaved heads and black or yellow gauze gowns made them conspicuous. The priests of the two faiths seemed to fraternize and to treat each other with the greatest consideration. Their speech, as we heard it, was always so formal, so gentle, and so loaded with honorifics and the set phrases of politeness that there could never have been any theological controversies. A few Buddhist nuns, also, made pilgrimage to Kasuga's ancient groves; creatures unfeminine and unbeautiful enough in appearance to be saintly in the extreme. They wear white kimonos under gauze coats, with a skirt plaited to the edge of them—the same costume that priests wear—and they shave their heads with the same remorseless zeal. These bald-headed women give one a strange sensation, for in the absence of their dusky tresses their eyes appear too prominent, and it is easy to perceive an unnatural, snaky glitter in them. There are several nunneries near Nara and one in Kioto, but all the inmates assume the same priests' dress and shave their heads, and we inferred that all the six hundred Buddhist nuns in the empire were equally ugly.

At the edge of the little town of Nara is a large pond, wherein a court romance of the eighth century declares a lovelorn maiden to have drowned herself for sake of a fickle Emperor. Above this historic pond stands a fine old five-story pagoda, and the scattered buildings remaining from what was once a great Buddhist establishment. This Kobukuji temple dates back to the year 710, but has been burned and rebuilt again and again. After the downfall of the Shoguns, who were Buddhists, the restoration of the Emperor to power made Shinto the established faith. In the zeal attending the revival of Shinto, Buddhism was almost laid under a ban. Buddhist priests hid themselves, and Buddhist pictures, statues, and books were concealed. Moreover, the craze for foreign fashions induced a contempt for the old temples and pagodas. Two of the buildings of Kobukuji were torn down and the statues in them destroyed. Ropes were even placed about the beautiful old pagoda, which would have met the fate of the Column Vendome had not the saner citizens leagued together to preserve it. In this calmer day, the Japanese of whatever faith look upon this ancient pagoda, the old bell, and the venerable buildings of the Buddhist establishments as the pride of Nara.

The town of Nara is a well-kept little provincial settlement, but with nothing especially characteristic or interesting in its clean streets. One goes to see the black gnomes at work, kneading their dough of rapeseed-oil, soot, and glue, pressing it into moulds, baking it, and supplying the country with its best writing ink. While the Japanese india-ink is not equal to the Chinese ink, some of it is very expensive. It requires a connoisseur to tell why a stick the size of one's little finger should cost one or two dollars at the manufacturer's shop, while a cake three or four times as large, and apparently of the same substance, should be only a tenth of that price. The few curio-shops offer almost nothing to the most diligent searcher, and the town itself makes small claim upon the average visitors, who come to see the temples and enjoy the surroundings and the view from the sacred groves on the heights. In the little row of tea-houses along the brow of Mikasayama, one is in the midst of Nara's real life and atmosphere, and in the detached pavilions and houses scattered through their gardens the visitor is confronted with the most attractive phases of a Japanese traveller's existence. The exquisite simplicity and beauty of these tiny houses, with their encircling galleries, all the four sides open to the air and view, the silence of the garden, broken only by the trickling water as it falls from bamboo pipe to bronze basin or tiny lakelet, render it an Arcadia. For a small sum one may have one of these tiny houses to himself, a dainty box for cha no yu, and a doll's kitchen accompanying each pavilion. On sunny days the garden is a small paradise, with the moving figures of guests and attendants always giving a human interest to the picturesque bits of landscape. On rainy days the pictures are as many, but done in soberer tones. On those rainy June days, when there were few smart showers, but a steady, persistent, fine drizzle that left everything soaked with moisture, the domestics pattered about our garden from house to house, perched on their high wooden clogs, with their skirts tucked high above their bare feet, twirling huge oil-paper umbrellas above their heads. At night they came to close our amados noisily, and to hang up the mosquito-nets of coarsely-woven green cotton—nets the size of the room itself, fastened by cords at the four corners of the ceiling, and exhaling the musty, mildewed odor that belongs to so many things Japanese, and is so inevitable in the rainy season. From all the foliage mosquitoes swarmed by myriads, and a candle-flame attracted winged things that only an entomologist could name; insects so small and light that one breathed them; gorgeous golden-green beetles, rivalling their Brazilian congeners; and huge black stag-horn beetles that dealt one a sharp blow with the force of their coming. At night, too, the domestic rat asserted itself, and this pest and disturber of tea-house life ran riot in the empty chamber between the beautiful wooden ceilings

IN THE TEA-HOUSE

and the real roof. The thin wood acted as a sounding-board, and their scampering and racing, and the thud of the pursuing weasels, was an all-night and every-night affair. The Japanese themselves seem to feel no hostility towards rats and mice, and at Yaami's and at Nara the proprietor and staff sit quietly in the great office and kitchen-room, which are so nearly one, and allow these followers of Daikoku to scamper over their ledgers, between the groups on the mats, and to perform feats of racing and balancing on the rafters overhead.

The flimsiness of our little house, no less than the absurd walls and gates of the moated demesne, seemed to invite robbery, but in that Arcadia there were no robbers. The habitation was left alone for hours with every screen wide open, and countless things in view that might have tempted curious handling at least, but nothing was disturbed nor lost. There was no provision for locking the screens of any room, nor for making the amados proof against any amateur burglar, the need of such a protection never having been felt — a sufficient commentary on the people.

Nesans, coolies, and small boys were all so individual, so characteristically Japanese, so untouched by and unused to foreign influences, that they were an unceasing delight; and so unintentionally theatrical and picturesque that for day after day we felt ourselves to be living in a theatre, and Nara's hill-side to be one vast revolving stage. We had easily fallen into the serene and peaceful routine of Nara life, and become so interested in those surrounding us, that there was a real sadness on our own part when easel, camera, and koris were packed, and those simple, affectionate people bade us their tearful sayonaras.

It was a rainy morning, and the green rice plain looked greener under the gray sky as we rode away from Nara. Men and women were working in the fields, wading knee deep in the mud and water, stirring the muck around the young shoots, and tearing up the water-weeds with iron hooks. No other grain requires as much care as rice, and from the first transplanting from the seed-bed until the ears of grain are formed, there is continuous grubbing in the mire of the paddy fields. The legions of frogs that live in them share their abode with horrible slugs, snails, blood-suckers, and stingers of many kinds, against whose assaults the poor farmers wrap their legs knee-high with many thicknesses of cotton cloth. Following the level plain and skirting instead of surmounting the bold mountain-spur, all the twenty-six miles from Nara to Osaka ran through rice fields. Every little square of dyked paddy-field had its workers. In some the first ploughing was being done; in others the water was being worked into the soil; and, farther on, men and women, standing ankle-deep in the muck, were setting out the tiny green shoots. Here and there laborers were treading water-wheels to pump water from the lower to the higher levels, or with long sweeps dipping it slowly up from wells.

There are seven great Buddhist monasteries around Nara, all more or less in decay, but all possessing relics of great historic interest and value. Several of them show their white walls, like fortresses, high on the mountain-side, and in them linger the remnants of a once rich and numerous priesthood—their sacred retreats being so remote and inaccessible that not half a dozen foreigners have ever visited them.

Horiuji, half-way to Osaka, is the largest of these Nara monasteries, and its pagoda and Hondo are the oldest wooden buildings in Japan. Both were completed in the year 607, and both are intact, solid, and firm enough to endure for twelve centuries more. To students of Buddhism, Horiuji is a Mecca, on account of its wealth of scriptures, statues, pictures, and relics, dating from the time when that faith had just been introduced from China. To art connoisseurs its interest is unique because of its old Hondo, containing frescos executed by a Korean artist at the time of its erection, which, with one exception, are the only frescos proper in Japan, and among the few paintings executed on a surface erect before the artist. All other paintings in Japan — kakemono, panels of screens, and sections of ceilings or wall space—are done with the wood, paper, or silk lying on the floor before the seated artist. These Horiuji frescos are dim and faded, and only pale wraiths and suggestions of haloed saints, here a head and there a bit of drapery, can be made out. In recent years attention has been called to these works. By imperial command an artist came down from Tokio to copy them; and when the Imperial Art Commission came from their Nara work to inspect and catalogue the Horiuji treasures, Ogawa, their photographer, spent two days at work making flash-light exposures in the dark interior of the Hondo.

Among the sacred relics of Horiuji is the veritable eyeball of Buddha, the legacy of the holy Shotoku Taisho, the Emperor who founded Horiuji, and left to it statues of himself, carved by his own hand at different ages. Shotoku Taisho talked when he was four months old, and a little later conversed in eight languages all at once. It is therefore easy to believe that when this prodigy of legend was a year old, and, turning to the East, with clasped hands repeated the invocation of his sect — "*Namu Amida Butsu!*" (Hail, or Hear us, Great Buddha!) — he found this precious relic of Buddha's body, the eyeball, in his hands. That he knew it to be an eyeball is not the least part of the miracle, as it looks most like the tiny, discolored pearl of a common oyster. The eyeball of Buddha is shown every day at high noon, a special mass being chanted by the priest while the relic is displayed. For a consideration, and for the welfare of the temple treasury, the mass may be repeated at any hour. The celebrant, a very old priest, when called from the monastery, came in splendid apparel of brocade and gauze, and entering the little temple, knelt, touched a silver-voiced gong, and prayed before a gilded shrine with closed doors and a wealth of golden lotus ornaments. Then he slowly drew forth from an altar recess a large bundle, covered with rich red and gold brocade and tied with heavy silk cords, laid it reverently on a low table before the altar, and, with a muttered chant of prayer, untied and laid back bag after bag of old brocade, each lined with silk of some contrasting color and tied with thick cords. After the ninth bag was opened, an upright case, covered with more brocade, appeared, lifting which, the priest produced a little rock-crystal reliquary, and set it upon a golden lotus as a pedestal. The reliquary was in the shape of the conventional Buddhist tomb—a cube, a sphere, and a pyramid, placed one above the other—and the bits of flawless crystal were held together by silver wires. In the hollow sphere lay the dingy relic, that rattled like a pebble when it was turned for one to see it. The holy man never once paused in his muttered chant from the time he lifted the precious bundle from the altar until he had replaced the ten silken wrappings and set the sacred relic back in its niche.

In one of the buildings are queer oven-shaped humps in the floor, covering secret chambers, where for twelve centuries offerings of gold have been dropped for the rebuilding of the temples in case of fire. These hoards cannot be touched except on the occurrence of the calamity feared, and the priests even resisted the wish of the Imperial Art Commission to break open the vaults to examine the coins believed to be there. A Boston art connoisseur, who visited Horiuji a few years ago, and found its priests poor and its art treasures in need of care and restoration, started a fund for that purpose, and himself took in charge the rehabilitation of one precious old screen. Many valuable paintings, tattered, mouldered, and mildewed almost to extinction, were thereby rescued. Four other contributors have since subscribed generous amounts to this fund, all of whom, by strange coincidence, were from Boston.

On a hill back of the main sanctuaries is a most curious octagonal temple, filled with the votive offerings of those who have been restored to health, or received other answers to prayer. The outside walls are half-hidden by the hundreds of six-inch-square boards, upon which are painted the suffering pilgrims who have been cured, and a ledge is heaped high with awls, the conventional offering of the deaf whose hearing has been restored. Locks of hair, short swords, daggers, steel mirrors, and devices in coins are hung on the doors. The circular altar within the stone-floored temple, containing many old statues and sacred images, has its base completely plated with overlapping sword-guards, short swords, and little steel mirrors. Helmets and bits of armor are everywhere, and the long shell hair-pins of Japanese women have been offered in such numbers that, woven together with silk cords into curtains or screens, they hang like banners before and beside the altars. All around the walls and over the rafters, as far up into the darkness as one can see, hang short swords, ranged closely side by side, overlapping mirrors, guards, bows, arrows, curious weapons and pieces of armor, coins, and hairpins. Near this extraordinary place is a nunnery, where a family of holy women have the shaved heads and disfiguring garments of priests, their altars and images, their daily service, and the same routine of life in every way.

Rounding the last spur of hills and crossing a broad river, the road reaches the great Osaka plain, lying in a broad semicircle between the mountains and the shores

of the Inland Sea. On these vast alluvial flats rice is
still the main crop, and the saké made from it is considered the best in the empire. All over this emerald plain
the farmers could be seen at work, their wide hats showing like so many big mushrooms when the wearers, sunk
deep in the muck of the paddy fields, bent over their
work. On the prairie-like level of the plain the irrigating
system is simple and ingenious. Everywhere the farmers
were plastering up the little dikes that keep the water
within its limit and pattern the plain with a gigantic
check - work of narrow black lines and serve as foot-
walks from field to field. No fences or high barriers
break the even level. and those strange contrivances, the
primitive Persian water-wheels, may be seen every few
rods. This Persian wheel, with its row of hanging boxes,
is put in motion by a man who climbs it in treadmill
fashion, the boxes scooping up the water from the lower
level and discharging their burden into a trough at the
top, whence the stream flows from field to field by almost
imperceptible changes of level. The wheelman wears
only the loin-cloth prescribed by law and a wisp of blue
towel knotted about his head. Occasionally he fastens
a big paper umbrella to a long bamboo pole, and plants
it where it will cast a small shadow on him, but usually
he tramps his uncomplaining round in the blaze of the
tropical sun, a solitary and pathetic, but highly picturesque figure, isolated thus on the vast green plain. More
Oriental, even, are the groups at the wells, shaded by
straw mats or umbrellas on long poles, while they work
the same long well-sweeps as the shadoofs of the Nile.

Far off, like an island in this sea of green, rise the
castle towers and the pagoda - tops of Osaka, and for
hours we hardly seemed to gain upon the vision, but the
runners, saving themselves for a last effort and taking a
sip of tea in the suburbs, raced down through the streets
and over the bridges at a gait never before equalled.

CHAPTER XXXIII

OSAKA

OSAKA, the great commercial city of Japan, with its population of over 361,000 souls, stretches out its square miles of gray-roofed houses at the edge of the plain, where the waters of the Yodogawa reach Osaka Bay. Bars and shallows prevent large vessels from reaching the city, and Kobé-Hiogo, twenty miles across the arc of the bay, is its seaport. The branching river and the innumerable canals intersecting the city have given Osaka the name of the " Venice of Japan ;" as if a trading city, built on a level plain, with canals too wide and houses too low and dull in color to be in the least picturesque, could be considered even a poor relation of the " Bride of the Sea." The " Chicago of Japan " is a fitter title, for if no pork-packing establishments exist, the whole community is as energetically absorbed in money-making, the yen, instead of the almighty dollar, being the god chiefly worshipped, and Osaka's Board of Trade the most exciting and busy one in the empire.

Osaka has been prominent in the history of Japan from the very earliest times, and at the time of the Restoration the rebel Shogun made his last stand and fought his last battle at Osaka castle. The next great event in Osaka's annals was the flood of 1885, which was without parallel in this country of floods. During the last weeks of the rainy season of June the rain fell in torrents for more than a week, and a typhoon, sweeping the region, deluged the adjoining provinces. Lake Biwa rose many feet above its usual level, the rivers doubled and redoubled their size, and the whole Osaka

plain was a lake. The rivers having been raised arti-
ficially above the level of the surrounding country for
the irrigation of the rice fields, their banks and levees
melted away before the rush of waters, and the plain was
scoured by swift currents running eight and fifteen feet
deep over the rice fields. Farm-houses and villages dis-
appeared in a day, and the wretched people saved themselves and their few effects by taking to boats and rafts
or seeking refuge in trees. After two weeks of high-
water and continuing rains, the flood subsided and the
wreck was more apparent. A few farmers, by replanting
and careful tending, obtained crops that season, but
hundreds and hundreds of the homeless and destitute
were sheltered and fed in the unused barracks at Osaka
castle.

In the city itself only the castle and a few business
streets were left above water, and thousands of houses
and godowns were ruined; the mud-walls under the
heavy tiled roofs collapsing like card-houses in the
current. One hundred and forty-six bridges were carried away, and, for a time, boats were the only vehicles
and means of communication. The suffering and desti-
tution were terrible, and Osaka's many industries were
paralyzed. But in the shortest time after the subsidence
of the waters temporary bridges and ferries were established, embankments patched up, houses rebuilt, and
the city returned to its busy ways. Except for the mud-
stained walls and the heaps of drift and débris on roof-
tops, little reminded one of the disaster as we sped
through the stone-paved streets. House-boats went up
and down the river each evening with geisha and maiko
singing happily, and koto and samisen ringing on the air
till midnight. Jiutei's queer hotel, a foreign inn up-stairs
and a Japanese tea-house below stairs, was the scene of
as much feasting as ever, and the recuperative power of
Osaka's people surprised one at every turn.

The castle is the great show-place of Osaka, and although the palace, which was the heart of the great fortress, was burned in 1868, much remains to be seen. The area enclosed by the massive outer walls and the great moat is immense, and the clustered towers, and buildings, crowning the one elevation on all the Osaka plain, show commandingly from every point. The angles of the walls are sharpened and curve inward like the bow of a battleship, and on each corner remain quaint white towers with curving black roofs piled one upon another. The castle walls are wonders of masonry: single stones forty-six feet in length and ten or twelve feet square being built in on either side of the main gate. Other stones, twenty feet in height, and roughhewn as they came from the quarry, stand at angles of the walls like miniature El Capitans. Nearly all these titanic blocks are known to the Japanese by particular names, each with its legends attached; but the foreigner puzzles long to decide how those primitive builders brought such masses of granite from the quarries on the island of Kiushiu and placed them in these walls without the aid of steam or modern appliances. Three massive walls of defense, one within another, separate the castle proper from the surrounding barracks and parade-ground, and the headquarters are within the third enclosure. A dapper little lieutenant in spotless white uniform received our party at the temple-like headquarters building, one scorching August morning, and conducted us through a fourth wall, and up broad stone stair-ways to the lookout of the old citadel. His orderly ran ahead with field-glasses, and from that airy perch, three hundred feet above the city, we could look over an immense stretch of country and down upon the city roof-tops, from which the air rose quivering with heat. At eight o'clock in the morning at that high point the air was intensely hot, and the stones seemed to scorch our feet; yet up there was a well of deliciously cool water, an unfailing supply for the garrison at all times and through many sieges.

Returning to headquarters we met the commandant in such a beautiful snow-white uniform, covered with so many fine lines of white braid, as must make any man regret having to lay it aside for the dark and sombre winter regimentals. The bowing and interchange of conventionally courteous greetings between the commandant and the two Tokio officials whom we accompanied was a charming exhibition of the old etiquette, just a little modified by the new. The cool, shady room, where tea and cake and wine awaited us, had been built on the foundations of the old house where Hideyoshi lived, and its interior was panelled and ceiled with wondrous paintings and carvings brought from one of the Taiko's distant castles. Before it stood a pine-tree, planted by the daughter of that Napoleon of Japan, and there had been enacted the brilliant drama of feudal life which Judith Gautier has immortalized in *The Usurper*, a story which invests Osaka's castle with romance.

Then we spent two scorching hours in the gun-foundery and arsenal outside the castle walls, where the machinery was German from Chemnitz founderies, and the guns were made on Italian models. No foreigners were visible about the place, and the machinery was managed by Japanese workmen.

Next to its arsenal, Osaka takes pride in its mint, which is larger and better supplied with machinery than any of the Government mints in the United States. An army of workmen and workwomen in uniform tend the machines, and melt, cast. cut, stamp, weigh, and finish the coins, which, under the values of yens and sens, correspond exactly to our coinage of dollars and cents. The mint possesses a fine collection of coins, including the coins and medals of all countries, as well as a complete set of Japanese coins from the earliest days.

Another interesting Government institution is the bazaar for the exhibition and sale of goods of Osaka manufacture. All Japanese cities have these *hakurankwai* (exposition), but no other is on so great a scale and so crowded with beautiful things as this one. There one may see all that any workshop turns out or any dealer has for sale without the tedious process of bowing, taking off one's shoes, and sitting in tailor-fashion for an hour before the desired articles are shown. All the goods are marked in plain figures, and the fixed price obviates the bargaining and the rattle of the soroban. There is an admission fee of a few coppers, and a percentage is charged on all sales to support the institution. One may spend a day in the labyrinth of rooms studying Osaka's many industries; and everything, from gold and silver ware, crapes, brocades, lacquers, enamels, porcelains and carvings to food preparations, patent medicines, and imitations of foreign goods, is to be found there. There is even a department of plants and flowers, a hall of antiquities, a section of toys, acres of china shops, and specimens of everything made, sold, or used in that bustling city. Evening brings electric lights and a military band, and this industrial fair is made popular and profitable all the year round.

Osaka is the centre of great iron, copper, and bronze industries. Its artists decorate the finest modern Satsuma in microscopically fine designs, and the mark of Gioksen, of Osaka, on tiny vase or koro stamps the piece as the best example of the day. The soft yellow and richly-toned wares of Idzumi kilns find their market through Osaka, and the carving of teakwood into cabinets and stands, or mounts, for vases and tokonoma ornaments, is held almost as a monopoly by a great company of Osaka artisans. Its book trade and dry-goods trade are very great, and its chief silk-store, which is still purely Japanese, displays the choicest fabrics of

Kioto looms, and stuffs that only after much searching are seen elsewhere. The straw goods trade is an important one, and its paper industries are on an even greater scale. Fans are exported from Osaka by millions, the United States taking one fan for each inhabitant of the great republic.

Stamped leather is another product of Osaka, but is chiefly exported to Trieste, to be made up there and at Vienna into the pocket-books, portfolios, card and cigar cases that cost so much in American jewelry and stationery stores. At Toyono's, the largest leather factory, squares of stamped leather were shown us in more than a hundred designs of bugs, birds, and fish, covering the ground, each piece of leather being about twenty-four inches square, and selling at one or two dollars for the single piece. Larger pieces, stamped with large and elaborate designs in gold or colors, and used for the foreign trade as panels for wall decorations, mounted to ten and fifteen dollars each, the size and quality of the leather and work of the artist enhancing the price. The cost of one of the large square brass dies from which the impressions are made averages one hundred and fifty dollars. In the old days the two-feet-square surface of brass could be engraved in the finest all-over designs for half that sum. The leather is stamped from these dies by a hand-press, and after the stamping workmen sit on their heels and color the designs.

An industry peculiar to Osaka is the manufacture of floor rugs of cotton or hemp. These Osaka rugs were much esteemed in feudal days, when the daimio had the monopoly and sent them as gifts; but in these prosaic days a stock company and a large factory supply the home market and the great foreign demand for these inexpensive and pleasing articles.

Half the *kairos* sold in Japan are marked with an Osaka manufacturer's name, and in cold weather or in illness the possessor of the kairo calls Osaka blessed. For be it known that the kairo is a little tin box with perforated sides and a sliding top covered with cloth. *Kairo zumi* are three-inch paper cases filled with the finest persimmon-leaf charcoal. You light one end of a paper, drop it in the kairo, and blow it until it glows; slip the cover in and wrap the kairo in a handkerchief or special bag. The little charcoal stick will burn for three, or even six hours, giving a steady, even heat all the time. It comes in many sizes, is curved in many ways to fit closely to the body, and its weight is almost nothing. The commonest kairo, about four inches long by two inches high, costs three or five cents, according to the quality of cloth pasted over it, and each package of the zumi costs a cent and a half. On winter days one often sees the Japanese holding kairos in their hands, tucking them in their obis, and slipping them down their backs. They are serviceable in keeping dampness out of the piles of linen in house-keeper's closets, and at night they assume the function of the ancient warming-pan. In America it has been considered only as a toy, a muff-warmer, or a pocket-stove. But its best use is in the sick-room, where it will keep a poultice or hot cloth at an even heat for days. A chill, a cramp, or a rheumatic pain is charmed away by its steady, gentle heat; and in neuralgia, bound on the aching nerves, it soothes them. Headaches have been known to yield to it, and in sea-sickness the kairo overcomes the agonizing chills and relieves the suffering. Our heavy rubber hot-water bags, that are always leaking and suddenly cooling, may well be superseded by the little kairo.

Osaka has curio-shops that are small museums filled with the choicest industrial art of old Japan, and this rich commercial city rivals Tokio and Kioto in its amusement world, and has a theatre street a mile long. Its theatres, its wrestlers, its maiko and geisha are as

well known as its industries, and its jinrikisha runners
are reckoned the swiftest in the empire. The latter spin
over the stone-paved streets and bridges and round corners at a terrifying pace, all for six cents an hour, and
usually speed the departing guest to the station early
enough to allow him a half-hour at the little tea-houses
in the park, to eat cubes of the superlative Osaka sponge-
cake. The maiko and geisha of this southern capital are
renowned for their grace, beauty, and wit; their taste in
arranging the obi and dressing the hair; their cleverness
in inventing new dances; and the entertainments in
which they figure, under the lanterned awnings of the
house-boats as they float up and down the river at night,
are unique among such fêtes.

There are many rich and splendid temples in Osaka
that seem to have suffered little since the protection of
the Shogun and the court were withdrawn. Osaka, Tokio, and Kioto, the three capitals, are the three religious
centres; and the Buddhist establishments, the extensive
yellow-walled monastery grounds in the district beyond
the Osaka castle are worthy of a capital. The numbers
of priests in the streets, the thousands of summer pilgrims, and the scores of shops for the sale of temple ornaments, altar furnishings, rosaries, and brocade trian-
gles for the shelf of household images, give a certain
sacerdotal aspect to the busy town. One temple possesses
many relics of the Forty-seven Ronins, and at its annual
matsuri, when these are exhibited, the surrounding courts
are almost impassable with the crowds and the merry
fair. The twin Monto temples are splendid structures,
and priests from the Kioto Hongwanjis often assist in
their ceremonials.

As one approaches Osaka from Nara, Tennoji's roofs
and pagoda are seen at the same moment with the castle
towers. This pagoda is one of the few in Japan which
visitors are allowed to climb, and contains enough wood

and rough timber to build twenty like it after occidental methods. Such steep and clumsy stairs and ladders are harder to climb than mountains; for the climber crawls over and creeps under heavy beams, and fairly twists himself upward, getting an occasional peep down the dark well-hole, where the builders' secret is hidden. Visitors wonder how pagodas are made to stand in an earthquake country, and why these spindling edifices should be built up without regard to the inevitable tremble, until they see in the hollow chamber, or well, an exaggerated tongue or pendulum hanging from the topmost beams.

This tongue, made of heavy beams bolted together in a mass, is equal to about half the weight of the whole structure. It descends nearly to the base of the pagoda, and at the shock of an earthquake the large pendulum slowly swings, the structure sways, and settles back safely to its base.

In a tall sheathed bell-tower near the pagoda there is a most interesting shrine where parents hang the garments of sick and dying children. The whole interior is filled with little kimonos and bibs, and the long rope of the gong overhead is covered with them, while tearful women cluster round the priests in the small interior, and a continuous service seems to go on before the altar. In the court-yard a large stone water-tank, sunk a few steps and covered with a pavilion roof, contains a stone tortoise pouring a constant stream of water into the reservoir, on whose surface the faithful, buying wooden shavings or prayer-papers from the priests, cast these petitions and go away content.

Others fill little bottles with the water and carry it home as a specific against many ills. In a pond near by live hundreds of turtles. The *kamé* climb up on wooden platforms in the pond and sun themselves, but at the clap of the hand and the sight of popped beans floating about, the whole colony dive off and swim towards their benefactor.

All around Tennoji are the yellow walls of the monasteries, with miniature moats and heavy gate-ways, and this quarter is a religious city by itself, which was once a separate suburb with a population of 30,000.

<hr>

CHAPTER XXXIV

KOBÉ AND ARIMA

TRAVELLERS had cause to rejoice when the Tokaido railroad made it a twenty-four hours' journey on dry land from Tokio to Kobé, the foreign settlement adjoining the ancient town of Hiogo. It is almost always a miserable trip by water, notwithstanding the beauty of Fuji and the coast. Chopping seas, cross-currents, and unexpected pitchings and motions disturb the equilibrium even of an old sailor, and the trip to Kobé often lays him low, while smiling skies and seemingly smooth waters seem to make a mock of him. When typhoons sweep, the province of Kii is a magnet for them, and frightful seas rage around that point which guards the entrance to the Inland Sea.

Kobé, as the port of Osaka and Kioto, and the outlet of the great Yamashiro tea-district, is an important place commercially; its growth more than equalling Yokohama's since the opening of the port. Beginning with less than 10.000 native inhabitants in the town of Hiogo in 1868, it had risen to more than 80,000 in 1887. The foreign colony has increased in proportion, and in 1888 its foreign trade amounted to $42.971.976. Of this sum $24,667,906 were imports, and $18,304,070 were exports. Ships of all nations lie at anchor in its busy harbor, and the many American sailing vessels that come out loaded with kerosene return with cargoes of rags, camphor, and curios, by which general invoice name are included the cheaper porcelains, lacquers, fans, lanterns, toys, and trifles made for the foreign trade.

Kobé, lying at the head of the Inland Sea, sheltered from the ocean, and screened even from the land by the low range of mountains back of it, possesses the best and driest climate of any of the treaty ports now open for the residence of foreigners. The soil is sandy, and the site, facing southward, enjoys to the full the winter sun and summer winds. The town, beginning in lines of houses that run down from each velvet, green ravine in the abrupt hill-wall, slopes steeply to the water's edge, and there spreads out in a long Bund, one part of which, lined with foreign residences, banks, and consulates, is the pride of Kobé. This foreign Bund is much less picturesque than the native or Hiogo Bund, off which lie hundreds of curious junks, that at night display constellations of softly glowing lanterns on their masts, while the whole harbor and hill-side twinkle with open lights, and the electric search-lights of the men-of-war flash broad rays over the scene.

At the end of the native Bund Government buildings close the street, and the railway wharf and sea-wall follow a long point of land that runs far out into the bay, and is capped by a fortress with a round stone tower and a light-house. A double line of ancient trees marks the course of the Minatogawa, which centuries ago was turned from its proper channel and made to run along this high embankment. A steep slope of forty feet in some places leads from the level of the Hiogo streets to the banks of this watercourse, which are turfed over, shaded with rows and groves of pines and enormous camphor-trees, and made gay with garden-plots and picturesque tea-houses. The dry river-bed is a play-ground for legions of children, and during matsuris it is crowded with booths and side-shows. Hiogo, meaning "arsenal," figures prominently in ancient history, and here Kusunoki Masashige, that ideal hero and model of chivalric valor, fought the last battle of the War of the Chrysanthemums and established the sovereignty of the Emperor Go-Daigo in the fourteenth century. Kusunoki's memory is worshipped everywhere, but the Nanko temple in Hiogo is dedicated to his memory, and on anniversary days its matsuris are brilliant and picturesque affairs. Besides this great Shinto temple, Hiogo has a Buddhist establishment of equal importance—the Shinkoji, outside whose sanctuary sits a colossal bronze Buddha of serene, majestic countenance, its granite pedestal rising as an island in the midst of a lotus pond.

Properly speaking, the Minatogawa lies in Hiogo, but where ancient Hiogo ends and modern Kobé begins no mortal can see. The Motomachi, the main street of Kobé, winds its narrow length from the banks of the Minatogawa to the Foreign Concession, beyond which warehouses, tea - firing godowns, and foreign residences stretch and spread in every way outside the narrow limits of the tract conceded to alien residents in the treaties. Kobé means "head," or "gate of god," probably in reference to its position at the entrance of the Inland Sea. While so picturesquely placed it is the model foreign settlement of the East, and the municipal council — a mixed board of consular and native officials — has never allowed its right to that fame to be questioned. A pretty park down in the heart of the Concession, shaded with ancient camphor-trees and ornamented by hedges, groups of palms, thatched summer-houses, and a bell-tower, was once the execution - ground of Hiogo. A small temple that stood near it has given way to a large tea-firing godown, and native children tumble and play where the headsman used to bind mutilated bodies or ghastly heads to high poles and set them up at the corners, after immemorial usage. The park, or recreation-grounds for the foreign colony, lies, beside the long embankment of another elevated river-bed on the opposite side from the Minatogawa.

Every gap in the Kobé hills leads to some lovely little valley, and orange groves dot the hill-sides. In one green ravine are the falls of Nunobiki, where a clear mountain stream takes two long plunges down sheer granite walls, drops in foaming cascades past old rice-mills, and courses on over the sloping plain to the sea. The Moon temple shines, a white spot, far up towards the summit of the steep, green mountain, and, with the more accessible falls, offers the two favorite points for visitors' excursions. Farther along the brow of the hill stands the Gold Ball temple, a whitewashed structure, looking like an exaggerated country meeting-house, with its roof surmounted by a gilded sphere, and with nothing even suggesting Buddhism in its appearance. While it is an eyesore to every one else, the natives, who contributed the money to build this monstrosity of what they consider foreign architecture, are delighted with its unique and bizarre appearance. Around it lies a populous graveyard, many of the stones gray with the mosses of centuries. Others, newly erected, are family memorials, bearing the names of those members already buried there written in black characters, and the names of the living in red. It is a curious custom; but to the Japanese, who even point with pride to the red letters of their own names on these family monuments, it is rational and right. Cremation is the funeral rite preferred, and up a narrow valley behind the temple is the crematory, much used both by rich and poor. The process is simple and inexpensive, and the visitor always encounters some funeral train accompanying a body to that little white temple of fire, or some family group bearing the ashes down to the cemetery for final rest.

A line of tea-houses bands the brow of the hill; innumerable Shinto shrines lost among the pine-trees show their long lines of torii at the edges of the groves; and at another point the schools and homes of the large American missionary colony make a settlement quite to themselves.

Kobé is almost entirely given up to the trade in cheap goods for the foreign market. The streets are lined and the shops filled with such porcelain, bronze, paper, and lacquer monstrosities; such burlesques of embroidery and nightmares of color as crowd the Japanese stores in the cities of America, chief customers of this trade. One Chicago importing house takes more of such goods annually than the whole kingdom of Belgium, one of the oldest, richest, and most densely populated countries of Europe. The curio-shops proper have diminished in numbers as the rage for foreign trade increased, until there remains almost alone the establishment of an old samurai, who still retains the shaved crown and gun-hammer cue of his class. Despising modern ways and business signs, this one simply hung a huge sword over his gate-way and left his customers to stumble upon him accidentally, push their way through a rubbish and lumber-room, and pursue their unguided path across the garden. Of recent years even this old conservative has relented a little and made his entrance more plainly alluring; but formerly each comer felt the excitement of discovering some jealously hidden treasure-house. Within, there is still a room full of old saddles, state kagos, military trappings, and banners; a place crowded with spears, lances, and color standards; a chamber piled high with brocade gowns, uniforms and temple hangings; hundreds of carved and gilded Buddhas, divine Kwan-nons more or less battered and worn, and hoards of old porcelain, lacquer, bronze, and carvings. The last room looks upon a little garden with its inevitable miniature pond crossed by a stone bridge with stone lanterns, and stunted pines on the slope of a small mountain. Beyond this garden are more stores of armor, coins, and ancient things, and a second story doubles the whole lower labyrinth of the place. An army might be equipped from this magazine of military stores, or a pantheon fitted out with Buddhas, Kwannons, Nios, lesser gods, and gilded images. All these deities are certified to have come from the Nara or Mount Hiyeizan temples, which are the miraculous sources of supply of everything sacerdotal in this part of Japan. One fortunate tourist, who bought a Buddha of Hari Shin, found that the jewel in the forehead was a diamond instead of a crystal, which, when cut in facets, proved to be worth several hundred dollars. Of this incident the old samurai prefers not to talk, and to change the subject his agile son refills the tea-cups, unrolls more kakemonos, or displays the swords and helmets " of my father's young time."

Through Kobé the colored straw mosaics of Tajima province on the west coast find their market, as well as the basket wares of Arima, a village lying fifteen miles inland. One goes from Kobé to Arima by jinrikisha, and starting in the dew and freshness of a summer morning at six o'clock, we reached the grateful shade of the Taiko's maple in the tea-house garden soon after nine. As we rose by degrees through the suburbs of Kobé, and drew nearer its glorious green hill-wall, we had a superb view of the opaline bay, set with the black hulls of great merchant ships, the white ones of foreign men-of-war, and dotted with the square white sails of hundreds of junks and fishing-boats. A sudden turn in the road took us behind the sharp spur of a hill, and a narrow cañon lay before us with the road clinging to one side wall. All the way we followed watercourses—the road now in some wild ravine, and again running up some emerald rice valley. All the way we met primitive ox-carts carrying their loads down to Kobé, each driver bearing an equally heavy load hanging from the ends of a pole across his shoulders. The oxen's horns were bound with fantastic bits of red cloth, their feet shod with straw sandals; and the cart was braked on the slopes by the main force and strength of the driver exerted against a long tongue or pole that also served to guide it. These placid, easy-going oxen, with their hard-working drivers walking beside them, afford some of the best pictures of the old road-side scenes. Small boys trudged at their fathers' heels with bundles of baskets or firewood over their shoulders, and women carried their share of the family load.

When the bamboo groves and rice fields of Arima's neighborhood appeared, the paddy fields, lying terrace below terrace on a rounding hill-side in waving, irregular lines, easily suggested the terraced basins around the Yellowstone hot springs; the Japanese farmer unconsciously repeating, in larger outlines of vivid green, what the overflowing waters have built up in snowy deposits in the Montana Park. Arima, which lines the sides of a steep gorge through which a wild mountain-stream dashes, is as picturesque as a mountain village in Switzerland. The houses are built almost one on top of another, with narrow, winding streets, where the heavy projecting roofs almost meet. Stone steps ease the steep slopes for the villagers, and the clatter of clogs and the sight of the peasants going up and down the stair-ways, half-hidden by the loads of grass or straw on their backs, recall similar pictures in the crooked little mountain hamlets of Northern Italy. At the tea-house we wandered through an intricate garden before reaching the steps of the detached pavilion, on whose balcony were chairs and hammocks, and before which loomed a

FARM LABORERS

perpendicular green mountain-wall with its base sunk in the feathery, spray-like tops of bamboo groves. To us came peddlers and packs with samples of everything the town could offer, and the rooms were soon a bazaar of bamboo wares.

All the afternoon we roamed about Arima, climbing its steep streets and threading its narrow by-ways. In the glaring white sunlight the shops were caves of cool shadow, and we found them filled with everything that bamboo will make, from clothes-baskets to toothpicks, and all selling for a song. Their weight is almost nothing, but, with the most ingenious packing, the space they consume makes the cost of shipment to America equal that of production. Except the necessaries of life, nothing seems to be sold in Arima save bamboo baskets and straw work; and every house is a basket-factory, where father, mother, children, and almost babes, weave baskets or prepare the bamboo. Heredity asserts itself again, and these descendants of generations of basket-makers work with a dexterity equalling sleight-of-hand tricksters. Arima's industrial life is a fine study in political economy.

The hill-side is musical with the boom of Buddhist bells and echoing clang of Shinto gongs; but more strangers toil upward for a drink from the sparkling, ice-cold soda spring beside one temple, than to pray at its door-way. For centuries Arima's hot-springs have wrought their cures, and sufferers from rheumatism and skin diseases have flocked to its pools. The Government has charge of the springs, and the waters are conducted to a large bath-house in the heart of the village, where free baths in the common pool are open to every one, and where private baths may be obtained at a trifling charge.

CHAPTER XXXV

THE TEA TRADE

SINCE Commodore Perry opened Japan to the world his countrymen have been consuming more and more of its teas each year, the United States and Canada being almost her only customers, England and Russia, the great tea-drinking countries of Europe, buying hardly enough to serve as samples. Each year the United States pays over $7,000,000 for the nerve-racking green tea of Japan. Besides the price of the tea, a trifle of $11,000,000 goes to Japan for raw silk and cocoons. In return, Japan imports from America less than $2,000,000 in kerosene oil, and another $1,000,000 in clocks, watches, and leather. It is this balance of trade that disturbs United States officials in Japan, who see England selling that thrifty nation over $18,000,000 in cotton, woollen, and iron goods, and taking from it a little over $3,000,000 of manufactured silks, curios, and art goods. Meanwhile Russian petroleum arrives by ship-loads, and, handled by the largest English firm in the East, is being pushed and sold by the smallest retailers at less than the Standard Oil Company's fluid.

The tea-plant, as every one knows, is a hardy evergreen of the camellia family. It grows a thick and solidly-massed bush, and at a first glance at a field regularly dotted and bordered with the round bushes setting closely to the ground, one might easily mistake it for box. In the spring the young leaves crop out at the ends of the shoots and branches, and when the whole top of the bush is covered with pale golden-green tips, generally in May, the first picking takes place. The second picking belongs to the fire-fly season in June, and after that great festival tea comes in from the plantations in decreasing quantities until the end of August. The choicer qualities of tea are never exported, but consumed at home. Choice basket-fired tea, such as is used in the homes of the rich and well-to-do Japanese, sells for one and two dollars a pound. There are choicer, more carefully grown and prepared teas, which cost as high as from seven to ten dollars a pound; but such teas are shaded from the hot suns by matted awnings, and the picker, going down lines of these carefully tended bushes, nips off only the youngest leaves or buds at the tip of each shoot. The average tea, bought by the exporters for shipment to the United States and Canada, is of the commonest quality, and according to Japanese trade statistics, the average value is eleven cents a pound as it stands, subject to the export duty and ready for shipment abroad. There are often sales of whole cargoes of Japan tea at auction in New York for fifteen cents a pound. Families who buy this same brand from their grocers at forty or sixty cents a pound may judge to whom the greater profits accrue.

Japan tea came into market as a cheaper substitute for the green teas of China, those carefully rolled young hysons and gunpowders of our grandmothers' fancy. Europe has never received the Japan teas with favor, but the bulk of American importations is Japanese, and the taste for black tea is being cultivated very slowly in the great republic. For green tea, the leaves are dried over hot fires almost immediately after picking, leaving the theine, or active principle of the leaf, in full strength. For black tea, the leaves are allowed to wilt and ferment in heaps for from five to fourteen days, or until the leaf turns red, and the harmful properties of theine have been partly destroyed. The Oolong tea of South China is nearest to green tea, its fermentation being limited to three or five days only, while the richly-flavored black teas of North China, from the Hangkow, Ningchow, and Keemung districts, are allowed to ferment for twice that period to prepare them for the Russian and English markets. The choicest of these black teas go to Russia, a part of the crop still being carried by camel trains from the end of the Grand Canal near Pekin to the terminus of the trans-Siberian railway. It is also shipped by steamers to Odessa; and as the tea is thoroughly fired and sealed in air-tight packages, it makes no difference in the quality of the infusion afterwards whether the tea-chests were jolted by camel caravans from Tungchow to Irkutsk, or pitched about in a ship's hold—much as caravan tea is celebrated in advertisements for the American public.

The Japanese Government made experiments in the manufacture of black tea in the province of Ise, but the results were not satisfactory, and no further efforts have been made to compete in that line with China. Japan will continue to furnish the world's supply of green tea, but as the demand for such stimulants declines, a great problem will confront its tea-farmers.

Kobé and Yokohama are the great tea ports, each one draining wide districts, and their streets being fragrant with the peculiarly sweet odor of toasting tea-leaves all summer long.

At Kobé thirteen firms, of which only two are American, are engaged in the tea-trade. In Yokohama there are twenty-eight firms, thirteen being English, eleven American, two German, and two Japanese. One American firm has invented machinery for firing and coloring the tea, the leaves being tossed and turned by inanimate iron instead of by perspiring coolies. As there are no patent laws in Japan, and as the Japanese are very quick at copying, this machinery has to be very carefully watched, taken apart, and locked up every night. Several thousand men, women, and even children are busily employed during the four months of the busy season—May, June, July, and August. A steam saw-mill, set up by a speculative American, makes a business of supplying tea-chests to these firms, although some still depend on their own carpenters. The matting and the sheets of lead for covering and lining the boxes come from China. Each firm, too, has a little art and printing establishment attached, where the gaudy labels for chests and cans are block-printed. One firm often has a hundred different pictorial labels for its packages of tea, that number of names being applied to the one kind of tea shipped.

Of each consignment made, a sample can of tea is forwarded by mail, while a duplicate sample can is retained by the exporter.

The young tea-leaves picked in May and early June comprise more than half of the whole season's crop, succeeding growths of leaves being coarser and having less flavor. This tea, picked by women and children in the fields, is roughly dried in shallow baskets lined with paper over charcoal fires, and is then sold to commission dealers in the interior towns and villages. They sort it into grades, toast it once more, and ship it to the treaty ports in rough paper sacks, boxes, and baskets. Some of it comes by junks to Yokohama. Over and over the tea is tested by sample infusions and the leaves carefully inspected. All summer, at the exporting houses, the tea-tasters are busy with their rows of white cups. A certain weight of leaves is put in each cup, the boiling water is poured on and allowed to stand for five minutes. The expert notes, meanwhile, the color of the liquid and the aroma, carefully watches the unrolling of the leaves, and then tastes the brew by slow sips, meditatively, discriminatingly. The tea-taster takes care to swallow very little, as its effects are disastrous in time. Tea-tasters as a rule follow their business but a few

years, severe nerve and stomach trouble being brought
on by the constant sipping of so much powerful stimulant. Of course they command high salaries. Astonishing stories are told of the acuteness of their sense of
taste and the certainty of their judgments. Their decision sets the price, and the dickering with the Japanese
commission merchant is always settled by the tea-taster's
estimates.

In the tea-firing godowns the dried leaves are stacked
in heaps as high as a haystack, when it makes a solid,
cohesive mass, that can be cut off like hay with a patent
hay-knife. In nearly every case the firing is superin-
tended by a Chinese compradore, and his assistants are
Japanese.

The tea-firers bring their cooked rice and their own
teapots with them, and snatch refreshment whenever
there is a lull in the work. They are searched at night
when they leave, and with the sweet simplicity of children they keep on trying to secrete the leaves, always
being caught at it. Their work consists in standing over
round iron pots sunk in a brick framework for the thirteen hours of a day's work, and stirring and tossing tea-
leaves. There are charcoal fires under the iron pans,
and all day they must lean over the hot iron and brick.
The tea is given this extra firing to dry it thoroughly
before its long sea-trip, and at the same time it is "polished," or coated with indigo, Prussian blue, gypsum, and
other things which give it the gray lustre that no dried
tea-leaf ever naturally wore, but that American tea-drinkers insist on having. Before the tea-leaves are put in
the pans for the second firing men, whose arms are dyed
with indigo to the elbows, go down the lines and dust a
little of the powder into each pan. Then the tossing and
stirring of the leaves follows, and the dye is worked thoroughly into them, the work being regulated by overseers,
who determine when each lot has been fired enough. It

requires a certain training to keep the tea-leaves in constant motion, and it is steady, energetic work.

This skilled labor is paid for at rates to make the Knights of Labor groan, the wage list showing how impossible tea-culture is for the United States until protectionist tea-drinkers are ready to pay ten dollars a pound for the commonest grades. During the four busy months of the tea season the firers are paid the equivalent of eleven and four-tenths cents, United States gold, for a day's work of thirteen hours. Less expert hands, who give the second firing, or polishing, receive nine and six-tenths cents a day. Those who sort and finally pack the tea, and who work as rapidly and automatically as machines, get the immense sum of fifteen cents a day. Whole families engage in tea-firing during the season, earning enough then to support them for the rest of the year; or, rather, pinching for the rest of the year on what they earn during this brief season. In autumn little tea is fired, but the whole force of workmen can be had at the shortest notice, though the godown may have been closed for weeks. One compradore, notified at eleven o'clock at night that tea must be fired the next day to fill a cable order, had four hundred coolies on hand at daybreak, many of them summoned after midnight from their villages, distant over seven miles from the godowns. This mysterious underground telegraphy in the servants' quarters is one of the astonishing things of the East.

Tea-firing begins at six o'clock in the morning, the coolies clattering into the settlements on their wooden clogs at dawn, and going home at dusk. They wait patiently outside the compounds until the lordly Chinaman comes to summon as many workers as he wants for the day, whether two hundred, three hundred, or four hundred. All these guilds in the Orient have their established rules of precedence among themselves; each one knows his rights and his place, and desperate as may be their need of the small pittance, there is no pushing or fighting. Foreigners who live near godowns complain of the babble of the coolies before daylight, and a tea-firing godown always declares its nearness by the con-fused hum of the several hundred cheerful voices all day long. The Japanese lower classes are the most talkative people under the sun, and rows of jinrikisha coolies never sit quietly in waiting, like the red-nosed Parisian cabmen, dozing or reading feuilletons, but are always jabbering, laughing, playing games and tricks on one another. The long, hot day's work does not check the tea-firers' loquacity in the least, and at dusk they are as sociable as at dawn. One frenzied resident, whose door-steps, window-sills, and shady curb-stones were favorite resting-places for the tea-firing coolies, determined to know the subjects discussed with such earnestness and sonorous phrases. His interpreter reported on three consecutive mornings that, for three mortal hours, one group of ten coolies, sitting on patient heels, cheerfully discussed the coming rice crop.

Philanthropists see fit to drop a tear over the lives of the workers in the tea-godowns, although these victims seem as cheerful and well satisfied with their lot as hu-man beings can be. The women and young girls are rather picturesque with their blue cotton towels folded over their heads, and as the Japanese have remarkably pretty hands, the play of their fingers in the moving streams of tea-leaves is pleasant to watch. How they endure the slow, killing heat of the charcoal fires in tor-rid weather, on their diet of tea. rice, and shreds of cold fish, is a marvel to indolent, meat-eating foreigners. The pathetic sights are the women with young babies on their backs trudging home from the godowns at sunset, the babies having been danced around on the backs of older children in the godown-yard all day, or laid down in some safe corner near the mother's charcoal-pan. I asked a most humane woman once why charity did not take the form of a *crèche*, or day nursery. The answer was that it would be impossible to support such an institution in so small a community of foreigners. Each godown would need a large *crèche* of its own ; the poor women could not afford to spare a half-penny of their earnings, and the problem must solve itself.

If man cannot live by bread alone, many foreign residents live by tea alone, and live luxuriously. Great fortunes are made quickly in the tea trade no longer, as in earlier days. Romance departed with the clipper ships, and the cable and freight steamers reduced the tea trade to prosaic lines. Only the best and most experienced men now succeed in this trade, but the tea-merchant toils in his counting-room and godown only from April to October. Then he closes and locks it all behind him, and usually goes over to the United States to look after his interests and orders there. Tea has its fluctuations, like corn or cotton, although it is a crop that never fails, with the added disadvantages of the great distance from the final markets and the expensive cable communications to make it uncertain and full of speculation. As it takes fifty days for the fast tea steamers to reach New York by way of the Suez Canal, the tea-picking season is over when the exporter learns of the arrival and sale of his invoices. On account of the heavier freight charges that way, only a fraction of the crop crosses the Pacific to be shipped by rail across the continent from San Francisco, the New York steamers by way of the Suez Canal requiring but a little longer time, saving half the cost to the shipper, and adding the convenience of a single handling of the cargo.

The first of the season's crop is fired and hurried off as quickly as possible ; tea steamers racing through Suez to New York, and the overland railroads rushing cargoes across the United States in special trains, as if they were

perishable. With the exception of the four Pacific Mail
steamers running to San Francisco, English ships carry all
this tea to American markets. The tea steamers discharging cargo at New York usually load there for Liverpool,
and arrive in Japan in time for the next season, or sometimes make two trips to New York in one season. While
the tea is moving freights are high, but in the autumn
they decline. One or two sailing ships take entire cargoes of tea to Tacoma each season, and send them across
the continent by the Northern Pacific Railroad. The
greatest market for Japan teas in America is now centering at Chicago instead of New York, and prophetic tea-
merchants expect to have San Francisco become the
headquarters and great distributing point.

CHAPTER XXXVI

THE INLAND SEA AND NAGASAKI

In making six trips through the Inland Sea I have
seen its beautiful shores by daylight and moonlight and
in all seasons — clothed in the filmy green of spring,
golden with ripened grain or stubble, blurred with the
haze of midsummer heat, and clear in the keen, midwinter winds that, sweeping from the encircling mountains,
sting with an arctic touch.

My first sail on its enchanted waters was a September
holiday, the dim horizon and purple lights prophesying
of the autumn. From sunrise to dark, shadowy vistas
opened, peaceful shores slipped by, and heights and
islands rearranged themselves. The coast of south-
eastern Alaska is often compared to the Inland Sea, but
the narrow channels, wild cañons, and mountain-walls
of the Alaska passage have no counterpart in this Arca-

dian region. The landlocked Japanese water is a broad lake over two hundred miles long, filled with islands, and sheltered by uneven shores. Its jagged mountains of intensest green nowhere become wild enough to disturb the dream-like calm. Its verdant islands lie in groups, the channel is always broad and plain, and signs of human life and achievement are always in sight. Along the shores stretch chains of villages, with stone sea-walls, castles, and temples soaring above the clustered roofs or peeping from wooded slopes, and the terraced fields of rice and grains ridging every hill to its summit and covering every lower level. Stone lanterns and torii mark the way to temple groves, and cemeteries with ancient Buddhas of granite and bronze attest that these little communities are centuries old. Junks and sampans lie anchored in fleets, or creep idly across the water, and small coasting steamers thread their way in and out among the islands. Only one port of the Inland Sea between Kobé and Nagasaki is open to the foreigner, and except by authority of his passport he cannot set foot on these tantalizing shores save at Hiroshima, where the Government naval station is.

At Shimonoseki the Inland Sea ends, and ships pass out by the narrowest of its channels—a channel that boils with tide-rips and across which a chain once held all craft at bay. New forts replace the old ones bombarded by the combined English, Dutch, French, and American fleets in September, 1868. The "Shimonoseki Affair" is conspicuous in the annals of the scandalous diplomacy and international bullying that has constituted the policy of Christian nations in their relations with Japan. The United States did, indeed, make a late and lame apology for its disgraceful share in the plundering of a weaker people, by restoring its portion of the indemnity, thus tardily acknowledging the injustice of its conduct.

Ships following down the coast pass by the island of Ikeshima, the scene of an outrage even less creditable to the United States than the Shimonoseki iniquity. In 1887 the U. S. S. *Omaha* chose this inhabited island as the scene of target practice, terrifying the inhabitants by throwing their shells quite across the island, and maiming and killing many villagers, who, after the mimic bombardment was over, ventured down, in the pursuit of their labors, among the unexploded shells. Our Government did, indeed, offer $15,000 indemnity to the wounded survivors; but the whole affair affords one more instance of the injustice which stronger nations have always shown towards this weaker power. No British man-of-war would do its torpedo practising on the cliffs of Mount Desert; nor a Russian cruiser carelessly train its guns on the Isle of Wight; nor a German ironclad choose an inhabited island off the coast of France for a target, and expect to atone for "the unfortunate affair" with a beggarly sum of money. In view of the enormous indemnities claimed in earlier days for the death of Richardson and for the commonest brawlers of the ports, the Japanese are free to draw their own conclusions concerning the justice and good faith of Christian peoples.

As travel increases, the harbor of Nagasaki will be everywhere known as one of the most picturesque in the world. Green mountains, terraced and wooded to their very summits, have parted far enough to let an arm of the sea cleave its way inland, and chains of islands with precipitous shores guard the entrance of the tortuous reach. The town seems to have run down from the ravines and spread itself out at the end of the inlet, and temples, tea-houses, and the villas of foreign residents cling to the hill-side and dot the groves on the heights.

But Nagasaki has seen its great days, having lost its importance when the opening of the port of Kobé took the tea trade to the upper end of the Inland Sea, around which lie the great tea districts of Japan. Its coal mines and its million-dollar dry-dock make it a harbor that no ships pass by, more vessels entering annually than at Yokohama. All the naval fleets coal here, and buy the greater part of their supplies in this cheap market, and fleets of foreign men-of-war are always at anchor. Russian convict ships on their way to Vladivostock touch at Nagasaki, but only the few shipping merchants who provision them are allowed on board during the few days which precede the departure of the gloomy hulks for Siberia.

By losing its tea trade and becoming chiefly a station for coal and supplies, Nagasaki remains less affected by foreign influences than any other open port in Japan. Its people are more conservative than those of the northern island, and cling to inherited customs and costume tenaciously. The old festivals are kept up with as much spirit as ever, and boat-loads of farmers praying for rain often make Nagasaki's harbor ring with their shouts and drum - beating. Twenty of these rustics, sitting by the gunwales in one long boat, and paddling like so many Indians in a war-canoe, go up and down the narrow fiord waving banners and tasselled emblems.

While the inhabitants kept it, Nagasaki's observance of the *Bon*, the festival of the dead, was even more picturesque than the Daimonji of Kioto. On the night when Nagasaki's spirits were doomed to return to the place of the departed, lights twinkled in all the graveyards, and the mourners carried down to the water's edge tiny straw boats set with food offerings. These they lighted and started off; and the tide, bearing the frail flotilla here and there, finally swept it out to sea — a fleet of fire, a maze of floating constellations. Many junks and bridges were burned on these festival nights, and the authorities have forbidden the observance.

While Nagasaki was the first port opened to foreigners, it now has fewer foreign residents than any other. There are large mission establishments, but, outside of their community, the society open to the consuls and merchants is very limited when the harbor is empty of men-of-war. Their villas on the heights are most luxurious, and the views these command down the narrow fiord and out to the ocean entrancing. Life and movement fill the harbor below. Ships, junks, and sampans come and go; bells strike in chorus around the anchorage-ground; whistles echo, bands play, saluting and signalling flags slip up and down the masts, and the bang and long-rolling echo of the ships' guns make mimic war. At night the harbor lights are dazzling, and the shores twinkle to the very hill-tops. The crowded masts of native junks are as trees hanging full of golden, glowing spheres, and electric flash-lights from the men-of-war illuminate sections of hill and town and harbor niches.

The Nagasaki winter is delightful—clear, bright, sunny days continually succeeding each other; but in summer-time the climate leaves much to be desired. The air is heavy with moisture, and when the thermometer registers 90° there is a steamy, green-house temperature that encourages the growth of the hundred varieties of ferns that amateur botanists collect on these hills. This damp heat is exhausting and wearing, trying to temper and patience, and annihilating to starch and artificial crimps. Man's energy fails with his collar, and although all the sights of the empire were just over the hill, the tourist would miss them rather than go to see them. Everything mildews then; boots taken off at night are covered with green mould in the morning, gloves spot and solidify, and fungi gather on any clothing packed away. Every morning, on balconies and clothes-lines, is aired and sunned the clothing that nevertheless mildews. Only a strong sense of reverence for a hero's memory can then lead one up the terraces of the public gardens near the O Suwo temple to see the tree that General Grant set out. When he came to Nagasaki, both the General and Mrs. Grant planted trees to commemorate the visit, and his autograph certificate recording the event was cut in fac-simile on the face of the large, irregular stone between the two saplings. Though the trees have been most carefully tended, one died and had to be replaced, but both now promise to spread into a generous shade. At the tea-house where the great Japanese dinner was given by the local governor, with maiko and geisha and jugglers performing between the courses, they still preserve the floor-cushion on which their illustrious guest was seated, and bring it out to show to favored Americans. To the Japanese, General Grant and Commodore Perry mean America; nor could we have sent them better types than the great sailor who peaceably opened Japan to the world, and the greater soldier who made use of war only to insure enduring peace.

The Portuguese and Dutch have left records of their occupancy here in the sixteenth and seventeenth centuries. Francis Xavier and the Jesuit fathers who succeeded him converted thousands of Japanese to Christianity, and though it had been supposed that the persecutions and tortures under Iyeyasu had destroyed the Christians, the opening of the country after the Restoration discovered whole communities of them near Nagasaki, who retained their belief, wore the peculiar dress prescribed for them by the Jesuits, knew the prayers and forms, and made the sign of the cross. Nothing in the *Book of Martyrs* exceeds the tortures and suffering of these Christians, who would not deny their religion, nor tread upon the paper picture of Christ, as they were bidden to do. The tradition goes that at Pappenberg, the precipitous little island at the mouth of the harbor, thousands of converts were forced by spearpoints into the sea, but the best scholars and authorities now discredit this wholesale horror, of which no trustworthy record exists.

From 1641 the Dutch lived as prisoners on the little island of Deshima, where the porcelain bazaar now stands, suffering incredible restrictions and humiliations for the sake of monopolizing the trade of the country. Nagasaki's children and beggars still follow strangers with the shout, "*Hollander san! Hollander san!*" as a remembrance of those first foreign residents, and in curio-shops queer clocks and ornaments show the adaptation and imitation of many Dutch articles by the Japanese.

The fact of Nagasaki's being only a port of call makes its curio market fluctuate in proportion to the number of merchantmen and men-of-war in port. When the harbor is full, no resident visits the curio-shops, whose prices always soar at such times. Tortoise-shell carving is a great industry of the place, but porcelain is still the specialty of this southern province, where the art was first introduced. Those wares of South Japan known anciently as Nabeshima and Hirado are the finest of Japanese porcelains, their blue and white beauty being simply perfect. The potters who brought the art from Korea and China settled in Satsuma and Hizen, and the kilns of Arita and Kagoshima are still firing. The Dutch carried the Arita ware to Europe under the name of Hizen. This porcelain is now more commonly termed Imari, while Deshima is another general name for the modern product, and Nabeshima and Hirado are the words used by connoisseurs in classifying the older wares. This confusion of names misleads the traveller, who cannot at once discern that Hizen is the name of the province, Arita of the town where the potters live and the kilns are at work, Imari of the port from which it is shipped, Nabeshima the family name of that daimio of Hizen who brought the potters from Korea, and Hirado of the town on the island of that name which produced the priceless pieces sent as gifts to Shogun or fellow-daimios. Modern Imari ware is much too fascinating and tempting to the slender purse, but when one acquires a fondness for the exquisite porcelains the old Nabeshima made for themselves, learns the comb-like lines and the geometrical and floral marks on the underside that characterize them, and is aroused to the perception of the incomparable " seven boy " Hirado, his peace of mind is gone. Genuine old Hirado vases or plates, with the seven boys at play, or even five boys or three boys, are hardly to be bought to-day, and the countless commercial imitations of the old designs do not deceive even the amateur connoisseur. Old Satsuma is even rarer, and a purchaser needs to be more suspicious of it in Japan than in London. It is true that the air is full of tales of impoverished noblemen finally selling their treasures ; of forgotten godowns being rediscovered ; and of rich uncles leaving stores of Hirado and Satsuma to poor relations, whose very rice-box is empty. But the wise heed not the voice of the charmer. The credulity of the stranger and the tourist is not greater than the ignorance of residents who have been in the country for years without learning to beware of almost everything on which the Emperor's chrysanthemum crest, the Tokugawa trefoil, or the Satsuma square and circle stand conspicuous.

The fine modern Satsuma, all small pieces decorated in microscopically fine work, is painted chiefly by a few artists in Kioto and Osaka, and their work and signatures are easily recognized. The commoner Satsuma — large urns, koros, vases, and plates — is made in the province of Satsuma and in the Awata district of Kioto, but it is decorated anywhere—Kobé, Kioto, Yokohama, and Tokio all coating it with the blaze of cheap gilding that catches and delights the foreign eye. Once upon a time ship-loads of porcelains, bronzes, and lacquer were sold for a song; fine bells going for ship ballast, and ships' cooks using veritable old Satsuma jars to put their drippings in. But that time is not now. A collection of old Satsuma lately gathered up in Europe by a Japanese buyer brought five times its cost when disposed of in Japan. Some notion of the wealth of art works, and of the great stores the country contained in the old days, may be conveyed by the drain of these twenty years, since Japanese art began to revolutionize the art world. The Restoration, the Satsuma rebellion, the adoption of foreign dress for the army and the court, each sent a flood of rare things into the curio market, and hard times still bring forth treasures. The great collectors and connoisseurs are now so generally known that sacrifices of choice curios are made directly to them by private sale, and not in the open market. Government has begun to realize the irrecoverable loss of the country, and the necessity of retaining what still remains, and lists and photographs are being made of all art treasures stored in the Government and temple go-downs throughout the empire. Much has been destroyed by fire, of course, and it is said that the priests themselves have put the torch to their temples at the approach of the official commission that would have discovered what priceless temple treasures they had sold in times of need. All the Buddhist establishments suffered loss of revenues after the Restoration, and only by secretly disposing of the sacred objects in the go-downs were many priests kept from starvation.

While the Dutch were there, Nagasaki had a large trade with China, and still does a great business with that country in the exportation of dried fish. It smells to heaven all along the Bund, and in the court-yards of the large warehouses men and women turn in the sun and pack into bags oblong brown things that might be either the billets of wood used in cricket, or old boot-soles. These hard blocks are the dried bonito which, shaved on a plane, stewed, and eaten with rice, are a staple of food in both countries, and not unpalatable, as we found while storm-bound on Fuji.

Almost all the coal used in China and Japan, and by the Asiatic fleets of the different nations, comes from the mines on the island of Takashima, at the entrance of Nagasaki's fiord-like harbor. Cargoes of it have been sent even to San Francisco with profit, although this soft and very dirty fuel is much inferior to the Australian coal. The Takashima mines and the dry-dock at Nagasaki are owned by the Mitsu Bishi company, which retained those properties when it sold its steamship line to the Government, and the coal-mine brings in two million yen a year to its owners. Its deepest shaft is only one hundred and fifty feet down, and barges carry the coal from the mouth of the shafts to the waiting ships in harbor.

In 1885, the year of the great cholera epidemic, the village of mining employés was almost depopulated. The harbor was nearly deserted, the American and English mission stations were closed, and the missionaries and their families fled to Mount Hiyeizan. Only the Catholic fathers and the nuns remained, much to the concern of the governor and officials, who begged them to go. On our way to China we touched at Nagasaki while the epidemic was at its height, but no passenger was allowed to go ashore, and all day we kept to the decks that were saturated with carbolic acid. It took six hours to coal the ship, and from noon to sundown we beheld a water carnival. As the first coal-barge drew near, a man in the airy summer costume of the harbor country—which consisted of a rope around his waist—jumped over the side and swam to the stern of our steamer. He was like a big, brown frog kicking about in the water, and when he came dripping up the gang-way the faithful steerage steward gave him a carbolic spraying with his bucket and brush. The barge was hauled up alongside and made fast, and our consignment of coal was passed on board in half-bushel baskets from hand to hand along a line of chanting men and women. Nothing more primitive could be imagined, for, with block, tackle, windlass, steam, and a donkey engine on board, it took a hundred pairs of hands to do their work. At the end of each hour there was a breathing spell. Many of the women were young and pretty, and some of them had brought their children, who, throwing back the empty baskets and helping to pass them along the line, thus began their lives of toil and earned a few pennies. The passengers threw to the grimy children all the small Japanese coins they possessed, and when the ship swung loose and started away their cheerful little sayonaras long rang after us.

CHAPTER XXXVII

IN THE END

AND after a foreigner has spent months or years in the midst of these charming people, what has he discovered them to be? What does the future hold for them? To what end did Commodore Perry precipitate upon them the struggle and ferment of the nineteenth century? The present generation ceasing to be what their forefathers were, what do they expect of their descendants? Is our world thoroughly to occidentalize them, or will they slowly orientalize us? Which civilization is to hold, and which is the better? These are the unsolvable problems that continually confront the thoughtful observer.

The Japanese are the enigma of this century ; the most inscrutable, the most paradoxical of races. They and their outward surroundings are so picturesque, theatrical, and artistic that at moments they appear a nation of *poseurs*—all their world a stage, and all their men and women merely players ; a trifling, superficial, fantastic people, bent on nothing but pleasing effects. Again, the Occidental is as a babe before the deep mysteries, the innate wisdom, the philosophies, the art, the thought, the subtle refinements of this finest branch of the yellow race. To generalize, to epitomize is impossible ; for they are so opposite and contradictory, so unlike all other Asiatic peoples, that analogy fails. They are at once the most sensitive, artistic, and mercurial of human beings, and the most impassible, conventional, and stolid ; at once the most logical, profound, and conscientious, and the most irrational, superficial, and indifferent ; at once the most stately, solemn, and taciturn, and the most playful, whimsical, and loquacious. While history declares them aggressive, cruel, and revengeful, experience proves them yielding, merciful, and gentle. The same centuries in which was devised the elaborate refinement of cha no yu saw tortures, persecutions, and battle-field butcheries unparalleled. The same men who spent half their lives in lofty meditation, in indicting poems, and fostering art, devoted the other half to gross pleasures, to hacking their enemies in pieces, and watching a hara kiri with delight. Dreaming, procrastinating, and referring all things to that mythical *mionichi* (to-morrow), they can yet amaze one with a wizard-like rapidity of action and accomplishment. The same spirit which built the Shinagawa forts during the three months of Commodore Perry's absence at times animates the most dilatory tradesmen and coolies.

There is no end to the surprises of Japanese character, and the longer the foreigner lives among them the less

does he understand the people, and the less do his facts
contribute to any explanation. Their very origin is mysterious, their Ainos the rock on which ethnologists founder. Their physical types present so many widely differ-
ing peculiarities that one cannot believe in any common
source, or in the preservation of the race from outside
influences for so many centuries. Some coolie possesses
the finely-cut features, perfectly-modelled surfaces, and
proudly-set head of a Roman emperor. Some peer exhibits the features, the stolidity, and the slow, guttural
articulation of a Sioux Indian, and it is common to see
coolies identical in figure and countenance with the native races of the north-west coast of America. One group
of children might come from an Alaskan village, and in
another group frolic the counterparts of Richter's fisher
boys of Italy. At times the soft, musical speech flows
like Italian ; at other times it is rough and harsh, and
rumbles with consonants.

Their very simplicity, their childlike naivete, deceives
one into a conviction of their openness, while a mysterious, invisible, unconquerable barrier rises forever between us and them. The divergence of life and thought
began in Western Asia too many ages since for the races
that followed the setting sun to find, at this late day, the
clew to the race that sought the source of the sun's rising.
China, which once gave the Japanese their precepts and
models and teachers, shows now more differences than
resemblances. Far as the pupils have departed from
the traditions of the instructor, there yet remains a celestial conservatism, a worship of dry formality, and a respect for the conventional which the new order overcomes but slowly. The missionaries in China, who have
to contend against the apathy or open hostility and the
horrible surroundings of the native population, greatly
admire the Japanese, and envy their colleagues who live
in so beautiful a country, among so clean, courteous, and

friendly a people, so eager to learn and so quick to acquire. It is true that foreign merchants and officials in China laud the superior qualities of the Celestial, and infer a superficiality and want of seriousness in the Japanese; but the alien who has dwelt in Japan experiences a new homesickness when he exchanges a Japanese port for one across the Yellow Sea, with "Nanking" instead of "Nippon" servitors about him. The Japanese make an unconscious appeal to a sentiment deeper than mere admiration, but the secret of the fascination they exercise defies analysis.

Politically and socially, the Japanese copy the examples of the western world ; and the Restoration, with its consequences, furnishes the most astonishing political problem of the century. The sudden abandonment of the old order, the upspringing of a whole nation armed *cap-a-pie* in modern panoply of peace, has been too amazing to be at once accepted, at least among Europeans, as a real and permanent condition of things. If Europe cannot take the United States seriously after a whole century of steadfastness, much less can it comprehend an alien nation like Japan in a brief score of years.

A constitution and a parliament have been voluntarily given to a people who had hardly chafed under autocratic forms, or even demanded a representation. Its military and naval establishments, its police organization, and its civil service are modelled upon the best of many foreign models. Its educational system is complete, an admirable union of the best of American, English, and German methods. Its postal establishment, its light-houses, telegraphs, railways, hospitals equal those of the West. And all this was accomplished, not by slow growth and gradual development, the fruit of long need, but almost overnight, voluntarily, and at a wave of the imperial magician's wand.

This new birth, this sudden change from feudalism

and the Middle Ages to a constitutional Government
and the nineteenth century of Europe and America, is a
unique spectacle. This spectacle — this unparalleled
effort of a people to lay aside what they were born to
reverence and follow, because alien customs seemed to
promise a greater good to a greater number—this spectacle, which should have challenged the admiration, the
sympathy, and the generous aid of western nations—
has been met almost by their opposition. A weaker
people groping towards the light, learning by the saddest
experiences, has been hampered, bound, and forced from
its chosen way by the Christian nations, who have taken
every shameful advantage of superior strength and as-
tuteness. Unjust treaties were forced upon the Japanese at a time when they could not protest, and when
they could neither understand nor foresee the workings
of them. Backed by a display of naval strength, these
treaties were pressed upon the little nation, and by the
bully's one argument a revision of these unjust agree-
ments has been denied them for these thirty years ; although the Japan of to-day, its conditions and institutions are, in no one particular, what they were at the
time of the first negotiations. Pathetic have been the
struggles of citizens and statesmen, while the most high-
spirited of races has been forced to submit to political
outrages or face the consequences of war—the imposi-
tion of yet harder terms by their oppressors. Limited
in its revenues by these very treaties, Japan can the less
consider war with unscrupulous western powers. The
Government, in its efforts to secure foreign training for
its people, has been fleeced, imposed upon, and hood-
winked, through its ignorance of foreign ways. Reluc-
tantly admitting the perfidy of one people, the Japanese
have turned to another. In consequence, they are be-
rated for their fickleness and love of change, and taunt-
ed with the fact that American, English, and German

influences, successively, have been uppermost at court, and their languages and customs successively fashionable. The Germans, to our shame be it said, have dealt with them more honorably than any other people, and the present triumph of German interests has been well deserved.

The ambition, the courage, and persistency of this small nation, in the face of such hindrances, is wonderful; and their struggles with strange tongues, strange customs, and strange dress, all at once, were heroic. Indifferent critics ascribe this peaceful revolution to a love of novelty and an idle craze for foreign fashions. They claim that it is but a phase, a fleeting fancy, a bit of masquerading, to be abandoned when the people weary of it, or attain their ends. But fickleness is not the characteristic of thousands of persons of one race, pursuing the same objects for thirty years; nor could a nation of such taste and intelligence adopt and adhere to strange customs for the mere sake of novelty. Prophecies of retrogression discredit themselves, now that a whole generation has grown up to whom the new is the established order. Japanese youths, educated and trained abroad, have returned home to fill the places of foreign instructors and managers. Each year fewer and fewer foreigners are needed in Government departments and institutions. "Japan for the Japanese" is a familiar cry. The desire for enlightenment and the impulse towards progress were the result of forces already acting from within, long before Commodore Perry's black ships came to anchor in Mississippi Bay, and still potent as then.

In this day the way to distinction and power is open to the humblest. There is a baton in every knapsack, an imperial councillor's star in every school-room. The merchant has been ennobled, the samurai have sat at the Emperor's table, the eta walks free, the equal of other citizens, and the humblest peasant has inviolable civil rights.

Women have come out of their guarded seclusion, and enjoy a social existence and importance and a legal equality, and their educational opportunities are ever enlarging. Marriage laws, divorce laws, and property laws secure to them rights greater than some European women hold. The family life and authority remain unchanged, and the privacy of the home is jealously guarded, no foreigner penetrating to that sacred centre. The family ceremonies and festivals are observed as punctiliously as ever. The nobility and the official class lead the social life of Europeans, but the conservatism of the middle or merchant class still clings to the old order, which another century may find almost unchanged.

The art of Japan has already revolutionized the western world, leaving its impress everywhere. The quick appropriation of Japanese ideas and expressions marks an era in the Occident as distinct as that of the Renaissance. For all her giving with full hands, we can return nothing to this most art-loving of nations. Western examples and teachings, and the ignorant demands of western trade, have wrought artistic havoc in the Island Empire. Wherever foreign orders have been received, the simplest work has so deteriorated. has been so vulgarized and cheapened, that recognized efforts are now making to arrest this degradation of the national art. Cultivated Japanese, appalled at this result of western teachings, encourage artists and artisans in the study of national masterpieces and the practice of the old methods, and the labors of these public-spirited citizens are ably seconded by the Government. The foreign professor of drawing, with his hard pencils and his plaster casts, is a functionary of the past. To-day the youth of Japan holds to his own writing-brush, and begins, as aforetime, with the one stroke, two stroke, and three stroke sketches that lie at the root of the old masters' matchless art. Strangely enough, all perception of the beauty and relation of color seems to leave the Japanese when they use foreign materials. The people who have all their lives wrought and used and worn the most harmonious combinations of color in their garments and household goods, will execute monstrosities in Berlin wools in place of the rich old fukusa, and combine the crudest and most hostile hues with unconcern. The very use of foreign furnishings or utensils seems to abate the national rage for cleanliness, and in any tea-house that aspires to be conducted in foreign fashion, one discovers a dust, disorder, shabbiness, and want of care that is wholly un-Japanese.

Nor in other ways has contact with foreigners wrought good to these people. Conservative families have been mortified and humiliated by what seems to them the roughness and vulgarity of the manners of their sons and daughters who had been educated abroad. Many gentlemen even, in Tokio, long refused their daughters a foreign education for this reason. The mission-schools for girls found it necessary to engage masters of cha no yu and of native deportment and etiquette, to instruct the pupils in their charge. Among the lower classes the decay of courtesy, under foreign influences, was rapid. The bold, impertinent, ill-mannered coolies and nesans of the treaty ports are as unlike as possible to the same people in interior or remoter towns.

If the people are to lose their art, the fine finish of their manners, the simplicity of living, all the exquisite charm of their homes, Commodore Perry should be rated as their worst enemy. If they refine and make better what they now receive from the Occident, as they did with what China gave them long ago, is it not possible that Japan will surpass the world in the next century? Already the art workshop of the globe, has it no greater mission, as travel brings all countries nearer together, than to become the play-ground and holiday country of all nations, occupying the same relation to both hemispheres that Switzerland does to Europe?

Surely some better lot than that awaits this charming people, who so quickly win the admiration, sympathy, and affection of the stranger that is within their gates.

INDEX

THE END

SOME BOOKS OF TRAVEL.

JINRIKISHA DAYS IN JAPAN. By ELIZA R. SCID-
MORE. Illustrated. Post 8vo, Cloth, Ornamental.
$2 00.

A FLYING TRIP AROUND THE WORLD. By
ELIZABETH BISLAND. With Portrait. 16mo, Cloth,
Ornamental, $1 25.

OUR ITALY. An Exposition of the Climate and Re-
sources of Southern California. By CHARLES DUDLEY
WARNER. Illustrated. 8vo, Cloth, Ornamental, Uncut Edges and Gilt Top, $2 50.

TWO YEARS IN THE FRENCH WEST INDIES.
By LAFCADIO HEARN. Illustrated. Post 8vo, Cloth,
Ornamental, $2 00.

SUMMER HOLIDAYS. Travelling Notes in Europe.
By THEODORE CHILD. Post 8vo, Cloth, Ornamental,
$1 25.

THE STORIED SEA. (The Mediterranean.) By
SUSAN E. WALLACE. 16mo, Cloth, Ornamental, $1 00.

WINTERS IN ALGERIA. Written and Illustrated
by FREDERICK ARTHUR BRIDGMAN. Square 8vo,
Cloth, Ornamental, $2 50.

PENINSULAR CALIFORNIA. Some Account of
the Climate, Soil, Productions, and Present Condition
chiefly of the Northern Half of Lower California. By
CHARLES NORDHOFF. Maps and Illustrations. Sq.
8vo, Cloth, $1 00; Paper, 75 cents.

SHOSHONE, and Other Western Wonders. By ED-
WARDS ROBERTS. With a Preface by CHARLES FRAN-
CIS ADAMS. Illustrated. Post 8vo, Cloth, $1 00;
Paper, 75 cents.

KNOCKING 'ROUND THE ROCKIES. By ERNEST
INGERSOLL, Author of "Friends Worth Knowing,"
"Country Cousins," etc. Illustrated. Square 8vo,
Cloth, Ornamental, $2 00.

OUR JOURNEY TO THE HEBRIDES. By JOSEPH
PENNELL and ELIZABETH ROBINS PENNELL. Illustrated. Post 8vo, Cloth, Ornamental, $1 75.

THE LAND BEYOND THE FOREST. Facts, Figures, and Fancies from Transylvania. By E. GERARD.
With Map and Illustrations. 8vo, Cloth, $1 50.

A TRAMP TRIP. How to See Europe on Fifty Cents
a Day. By LEE MERIWETHER. With Portrait. 12mo,
Cloth, Ornamental, $1 25.

THE TRAMP AT HOME. By LEE MERIWETHER,
Special Agent of the U. S. Department of Labor. Illustrated. 12mo, Cloth, Ornamental, $1 25.

MEXICO, CALIFORNIA, AND ARIZONA. Being
a New and Revised Edition of "Old Mexico and Her
Lost Provinces." By WILLIAM HENRY BISHOP. With
Numerous Illustrations. 12mo, Cloth, $2 00.

Published by HARPER & BROTHERS, New York.

*Any of the above works will be sent by mail, postage prepaid, to any
part of the United States, Canada, or Mexico, on receipt of price.*

www.ingramcontent.com/pod-product-compliance
Lightning Source LLC
Chambersburg PA
CBHW032139110726
47902CB00003B/628